TEACHING CHILDREN PHYSICAL EDUCATION

Becoming a Master Teacher

George Graham, PhD
Virginia Tech
Blacksburg, Virginia

Human Kinetics Books
Champaign, Illinois

Library of Congress Cataloging-in-Publication Data

Graham, George, 1943-
    Teaching children physical education : becoming a master teacher /
George Graham.
        p.   cm.
    Includes bibliographical references and index.
    ISBN 0-87322-340-3
    1. Physical education teachers--Training of--United States.
2. Physical education for children--Study and teaching--United
States.   I. Title.
    GV363.G68   1992
    372.86'044--dc20   91-25520
                                                         CIP
ISBN: 0-87322-340-3

Copyright © 1992 by George Graham

Acquisitions Editor: Linda Anne Bump, PhD; **Developmental Editor:** Judy Patterson Wright, PhD; **Assistant Editors:** Valerie Hall, Dawn Levy, and Kari Nelson; **Copyeditors:** Carol Hoke and Dawn Levy; **Proofreader:** Karin Leszczynski; **Indexer:** Sheila Ary; **Production Director:** Ernie Noa, **Typesetter:** Sandra Meier; **Text Design:** Keith Blomberg; **Text Layout:** Kimberlie E. Henris; **Cover Design:** Jack Davis; **Cover and Author Photo:** Bob Veltri; **Cover Models:** Raj Casper, Jessica Culver, Chuckie Hoover, and Ivy Williams; **Cartoons:** Dick Flood; **Tables and Figures:** Kathy Boudreau-Fuoss; **Printer:** United Graphics

Printed in the United States of America   10 9 8 7 6 5 4

Human Kinetics Books
A Division of Human Kinetics
P.O. Box 5076, Champaign, IL 61825-5076
1-800-747-4457

Canada: Human Kinetics, Box 24040, Windsor, ON N8Y 4Y9
1-800-465-7301 (in Canada only)

Europe: Human Kinetics, P.O. Box IW14, Leeds LS16 6TR, England
(44) 532 781708

Australia: Human Kinetics, 2 Ingrid Street, Clapham 5062, South Australia
(08) 371 3755

New Zealand: Human Kinetics, P.O. Box 105-231, Auckland 1
(09) 309 2259

For Nick and Tommy

Contents

Preface

Each spring I teach physical education at Margaret Beeks Elementary School in Blacksburg, Virginia. I refer to it as "my spring teaching." I don't have to. I'm a professor at a university, and, unfortunately, there's no incentive for me to teach at an elementary school. Why then do I do it?

There are several reasons. The first is that I genuinely enjoy teaching children's physical education. There's a feeling of satisfaction and warmth that one just doesn't get from university students. Rarely, for example, do university students express genuine joy when I enter the room. "Hooray, Dr. Graham is here!" is a greeting that I have yet to receive from university students. It *is* one I receive from the children at Margaret Beeks—along with an occasional hug around the leg.

Another reason I spring teach is that it gives me a chance to try out new ideas—ones that I have read about in the research literature, observed at other elementary schools, or heard described at conferences.

Finally, my spring teaching keeps me in touch with children—and teaching. It's easy to sit in a university office and dream up ideas that may or may not succeed with children. When I test them out each spring, however, I begin to sense which have potential and which are simply unrealistic.

In writing this book, I have tried to express the perspective of a teacher as opposed to that of a university professor. Much of the information is based on research completed in the last 20 years or so. I have applied it to teaching children's physical education so that it will be of value to undergraduates preparing to teach and to those already teaching in the schools.

This book is unique in that it focuses totally on the teaching process—the skills and techniques that successful teachers use to make their classes more interesting and appropriate for children. Future teachers will find the book helpful because it describes and analyzes many of the teaching skills and techniques that experienced teachers use. Topics such as discipline, motivation, and effective ways to plan will be of particular interest to the novice.

The experienced teacher, in contrast, will discover that some of the techniques they already use are named and described in the book. I hope that the veteran teacher will also be challenged to consider some new techniques for structuring classes, developing lessons, and adjusting tasks for individual children—ideas that will benefit them and the children they teach. We have learned a lot about teaching in the past 20 years, and the veteran teacher will find much of this information both useful and informative.

Because this book is intended for both experienced and beginning teachers, I have included many practical examples in the form of teaching scenarios and vignettes throughout the text. It is obvious that the teaching process (that is, what the teacher actually does) cannot be separated from the content to be taught. For this reason, many of the analyses and descriptions of the various teaching skills include examples of the content (activities or tasks) typically found in children's physical education classes.

FEATURES OF THE BOOK

Teaching cannot be reduced to a simple formula. There are always decisions to be made—quickly and often. Learning to make these decisions can only be done "on one's feet." We can read about what teachers do, but until we ourselves are actually in the "eye of the hurricane," it is difficult to grasp the complexity of choices confronting a teacher. In writing this book, I have attempted to explain the decision-making process by separating it into various chapters. Realistically, parts of every chapter in the book will be used in virtually every lesson that is taught. To help you integrate, I have included several features to encourage the type of thinking that we as teachers do during a lesson.

Chapter Introductions

Each chapter begins with a brief introduction designed to "set the stage." This is helpful for connecting one chapter with another and also for understanding the teaching skills and techniques that will be discussed in that chapter.

Chapter Objectives

Each chapter introduction includes a series of objectives that highlight the key points in that chapter. Some books use the word *student* instead of *teacher*. I have used *teacher* instead of *student* because those who are interested in this book are, or will become, teachers.

Insights

Throughout the book I have included informal insights or asides. These are based on experiences, my own or those of others, from teaching children in physical education settings. They are designed to provide the types of practical, interesting insights that are often not included in a book—but that help to personalize the book and make it "come alive." A sample "insight" section follows:

MENTORING

I am often struck by the fact that teaching is neither terribly difficult nor mysterious when it is one with one (e.g., a mother and daughter, an older and a younger brother, grandparent and grandchild) tutoring. The tasks can easily be changed and accommodated to suit the needs and interests of that child. The problem in schools, however, is that teachers are responsible for many children, have limited resources, and work in confined spaces—an awesome task that, viewed in perspective, is done remarkably well.

Videotape Analysis

In recent years videotaping lessons of teachers has provided both researchers and practitioners with opportunites to carefully study and analyze the process of teaching. You are encouraged to videotape several lessons of your own, if possible, before beginning to read the book. Throughout the book, sections entitled "Videotape Analysis" will provide suggested ways you can analyze and reflect on your own teaching. These sections are marked with the following icon:

If this book is used as a text for a college course, the professor is urged to have the students in the class teach a 10- or 15-minute mini-lesson to their peers (or children if possible) before beginning to read the book. An analysis of various parts of these videotaped lessons will provide interesting and valuable insights to the students as they reflect on how they were taught and are challenged to compare those teaching approaches with ones described in the book.

For those who are unable to videotape their own teaching, a companion videotape is available with this book. This videotape includes four consolidated lessons of children's physical education that will be helpful for making the book more practical.

Reflection Questions

Each chapter in the book concludes with a series of "Questions for Reflection." Because teaching cannot be reduced to a precise formula, these questions are designed to help you think about the teaching process and the reasons why we teach the way we do. I hope that they will also lead you to question some of the ways physical education has been taught in the past—finding the good points and remodeling those practices that may be counterproductive for children.

One of the things we know about good teachers is that they have a sense of wonder about their teaching. They ponder such questions as "Did that work? How could it have been better? What would happen if . . . ? Why is that way better than another way? Are there other ways to do that in less time? How can I gain the interest of more children in what I am teaching?" I hope that the reflection questions at the end of each chapter will increase and deepen your sense of wonder about teaching.

Chapter Summary and References

Each chapter concludes with a summary or parting thought and a list of the references cited in that chapter.

OVERVIEW OF CHAPTERS

One of the challenges of writing a book on the process of teaching is figuring out how to describe a process that is intertwined, complex, and nonlinear. When we "break out" various teaching skills, we tend to oversimplify their use as they are removed from the dynamic context of a lesson. Realistically, however, one has no choice in a book. I hope that the Videotape Analyses and Questions for Reflection will restore a sense of context and complexity to the variety of skills that teachers use to create lessons both stimulating and beneficial to children. Furthermore, I have tried to arrange the chapters (after the introductory chapter) in chronological order, based on the points at which various teaching skills and techniques might be used in a lesson.

The introductory chapter places the book within the settings in which children's physical education is actually taught. Discussions of the purpose, challenges, and rewards of children's physical education are described in realistic settings. The chapter concludes by describing the type of knowledge possessed by successful teachers of children's physical education and how it looks when translated into practice. The important message of the first chapter is that this book is about how to teach (the process); it is not a description of activities and games that teachers might use in teaching children.

Planning, the next chapter, is probably not a favorite subject—but it is a necessary one. It is placed at the beginning for obvious reasons. Ideas for planning and sequencing lessons and also for developing yearly plans that are sequential and developmentally appropriate are featured.

Discipline and off-task behavior are often primary concerns of teachers, so this chapter has also been placed early in the book. Chapter 3 describes how teachers minimize discipline problems by developing management routines (protocols) designed to prevent off-task behavior from the very first day of the school year.

Despite all of a good teacher's intentions and preparations, some children will manage to be off-task. Chapter 4 describes how successful teachers deal with these problems.

A successful beginning to a lesson is often the prelude to a worthwhile class. Chapter 5 discusses this important aspect of teaching. Chapter 6 analyzes the ways teachers provide instruction and use demonstrations to help children better understand and retain important concepts.

A worthwhile topic for discussion among any group of teachers is "motivating children." Chapter 7 suggests ways to do this and emphasizes intrinsic, rather than extrinsic, motivation techniques.

One of the premises of this book is that good teachers recognize the differences in children—that one class of third graders is different from the next, and that within any third-grade class, there is a wide range of abilities and interests. This child-centered approach to teaching requires that a teacher be able to accurately observe and interpret the movement of children and then adapt the lessons accordingly. Chapter 8 presents techniques of observing and analyzing children as they move.

Questions such as "What is the best way to organize the content? When should I change from one task to another? and What do you do when the children need to continue working on a task, but they want to do something else?" are addressed in chapter 9.

Chapter 10 relates when and how teachers can provide useful feedback that is consistent with the focus of the lesson. Chapter 11 examines the teaching skills of asking questions and setting problems for children to solve, emphasizing the importance of cognitive understanding.

Chapter 12 focuses on the affective domain and suggests way teachers can help children feel good about themselves and about physical activity. The final chapter on teaching skills (chapter 13) provides a realistic perspective on assessing (testing) children in schools.

The book concludes with a chapter (chapter 14) on the importance of teachers' continuing to learn and develop professionally to avoid becoming stagnant and "out of touch."

ACKNOWLEDGMENTS

The book is finished! Now I have the pleasure of acknowledging the people who have contributed, knowingly or unknowingly, to it. It's 8:00 a.m. and, as I have every morning throughout this project, I am sitting at the desk in my study. As I wait for the word processor to sort through its various files and drives, I watch the chickadees and cardinals hover around the feeder in the big lilac tree outside. I am also enjoying reflecting on all of the people and events that have influenced both what I've said in this book and the way I've said it. Where to begin?

I am grateful to David Belka and Cam Kerst for their thorough and helpful review of the entire manuscript. I also appreciate Judy Rink's review of the content development chapter. And Marilyn Bray, John Pomeroy, and Ron Speck provided valuable insights and encouragement in the book's early development.

I especially want to thank the people who worked on the technical aspects of this book. Judy Patterson Wright, the book's developmental editor, was everything a "DE" should be—thorough, a good and critical listener, patient yet firm, careful yet willing to tolerate the whims of a writer. Linda Bump was vital to the conception of the project, even at early morning breakfasts at national meetings when we both were exhausted. The encouragement and support of Scott Wikgren, Rick Frey, and Rainer Martens have been immensely helpful—and have made the book that much more enjoyable to work on. I also want to thank the cartoonist, Dick Flood, and the cover photographer, Bob Veltri, for their highly professional work. Special thanks go to my cover models, Raj Casper, Jessica Culver, Chuckie Hoover, and Ivy Williams.

Since arriving in Blacksburg, Virginia, I have been fortunate to work at the nearby Margaret Beeks Elementary School. The teachers, the administration, and the staff have always been incredibly helpful and cooperative. When I have needed to be with children, to find a setting for my university students to practice teaching, or just to explore an idea, they have never failed to make it happen. They have made my job much easier—and have, I am certain, helped make me a better teacher and writer. Over the years I have learned a great deal from the children at Margaret Beeks, even though on many days I was supposed to be the teacher. Second grade teacher Linda Smith has been overwhelmingly supportive. And I am indebted to physical education teacher Casey Jones for his support and also for his inspiration as a dedicated and successful teacher who truly cares about every child in his program.

It is also important to acknowledge the many teachers in many places who have allowed me to visit their classes, ask questions, teach their children, and generally poke around as I attempted to understand, and explain, this complicated process called teaching. I am also indebted to the students and colleagues who have challenged my thinking over the years, causing me to clarify both my ideas and the ways I explained them.

Finally, I want to acknowledge the contributions of my wife, Judy. When asked, she played the role of critic and reviewer with aplomb and intelligence. More importantly, however, her enthusiasm for this project and her belief in me as a writer and as a person have made it immensely easier to switch on the word processor at 8 o'clock every morning.

To all of those I have named, and to those I haven't, thank you. I hope you are pleased with this work.

AN INVITATION TO SHARE YOUR IDEAS

Throughout the book I have attempted to use practical examples to illustrate the teaching skills and techniques that I have described. As I conclude the preface, I would like to invite you to share with me some of the ways you teach children so that I might include your methods in future editions of the book. As you read the book, please jot down examples of techniques that you use in your classes that might help illustrate a teaching skill or clarify an example. Please send your ideas to me at the following address: Division of Health and Physical Education, Virginia Tech, Blacksburg, VA 24061. Needless to say, I will be grateful, and so will the teachers who read future editions of the book.

George Graham

Before You Start to Read . . .

Throughout this book you will be asked to observe and analyze teachers of children's physical education. Obviously the teacher you are most interested in is yourself. You will benefit most from this book if you make several videotapes of your lessons prior to beginning the text but certainly before you begin reading chapter 3. If possible, I suggest you videotape several lessons—one with the youngest children you teach and another with an upper-grade class. I would also recommend that you videotape one of your favorite classes and one that you find more challenging to work with. The following guidelines will be helpful to you as you make the videotape:

1. Choose lessons to videotape in which you are actively teaching a new concept or skill as opposed to a lesson that depicts an activity that the children have already learned.
2. Set the videocamera in one corner of your teaching area so that you can see as many children as possible at all times. If someone else is "working" the camera, ask that person to move the camera so that you are always in view but to keep the lens on a wide angle. Some teachers just set the camera in a corner and allow it to run for the entire lesson on a wide angle setting.
3. If possible, use a cordless microphone (not the one on the camera). This will allow you to clearly hear your individual interactions with the children.
4. Select content that is different for each lesson—not only game skills, or dance, for example.
5. If the camera has a date and time setting that can be included as part of the videotape, activate these features. This will allow you to locate various parts of the videotapes much more easily for future reference.

In the event that you are unable to videotape some of your own lessons, I have produced a videotape of several lessons for use in conjunction with this text. It is available from Human Kinetics Publishers and can be ordered by telephoning 1-800-747-4457.

Chapter 1

Successful Teaching

"Those who can, do. Those who can't, teach. Those who can't teach, teach physical education."

—WOODY ALLEN

Woody Allen is right! We do have teachers in our profession (obviously some of them taught Woody Allen) who can't (or don't) teach. As an unfortunate result, a number of adults in the United States recall physical education (P.E.) classes as painful, humiliating, and virtually worthless experiences.

Fortunately this is changing. Today we have a "new breed" of physical education teacher in the United States. They teach physical education in ways that cause the Woody Allens of the world to look forward to physical education with enthusiasm. These teachers care as much about the low-skilled, sensitive, unconfident child as they do about the aggressive, athletic child. And they have found ways to make their classes both pleasant and worthwhile for all children—the low- and the high-skilled, and all those in between.

The purpose of this book is to describe and analyze the techniques, behaviors, and approaches used by these successful teachers to develop and teach lessons that are developmentally appropriate—and that result in enjoyable and beneficial learning experiences for children.

After reading and understanding this chapter, the teacher will be able to

- explain why teaching children's physical education is characterized as a dynamic, constantly changing process;
- analyze both the obstacles and benefits of teaching children's physical education;
- explain the concept of *orchestration* as it relates to the selection and use of teaching skills;

- describe the distinction between content (what is taught) and the process of teaching (pedagogy); and
- delineate the major components of successful children's physical education teaching.

THE TEACHER, NOT ONLY THE CONTENT

When I think back on all of the teachers who taught me throughout my school years, several come immediately to mind—the good ones and the not so good. One of the teachers that pops into memory is my high school trigonometry teacher. I decided in elementary school that math was not one of my academic strengths. I struggled through required math courses from year to year—until I took a "trig" course in my senior year. I vividly remember the first day. The teacher informed us that our text would be a college-level trigonometry book. I thought, "I am in big trouble in this course."

Surprisingly, this wasn't so. My trig teacher, even though the topic and the textbook were difficult for me, made the material very interesting, and I actually did quite well. I almost enjoyed it despite my negative attitude at the beginning of the class.

Obviously it wasn't the subject—trigonometry—that encouraged me to do better than I had expected. It was the teacher—the way he explained concepts, took time with us, never made us feel foolish, structured the content, answered questions with understandable examples, arranged for us to succeed in small steps, and did a plethora of other "small things" that, when totaled, were the earmarks of a highly effective teacher of trigonometry.

Fortunately, this book isn't about trigonometry. It's about teachers and the kinds of things they do (or don't do) that make learning attainable and enjoyable for students. Trigonometry, reading, or physical education can all be taught in ways that are exciting and educational. However, they can also be taught in ways that are boring, confusing, and distasteful. We are not just concerned with the content to be taught. We are also concerned with the teacher and all of the things she*

does that make our attempts to learn the material productive and stimulating—so that we learn and enjoy the process.

This may sound as if I am suggesting that the content—and a teacher's knowledge of the content—is unimportant. This simply isn't true. Good teachers know the subject thoroughly; this enables them to develop it in ways that are engaging and productive for children. My high school trigonometry teacher understood the subject well; that enabled him to develop lessons that were interesting, enjoyable, and productive.

The distinction between knowing <u>what</u> to teach (the content or curriculum) and knowing <u>how</u> to teach (the process or the performance of the teacher) is an artificial one. Content and process cannot be separated. They are interwoven. In studying and understanding teaching, nevertheless, this artificial distinction is a helpful one. The chapters that follow describe many of these teaching skills and techniques and provide practical examples of how successful teachers use them to create effective lessons and programs for children.

Because physical education is a unique subject in the schools, teachers use orchestrations of skills that are somewhat different from those that their colleagues in the classroom use. This book will delineate many of the teaching skills employed by successful children's physical education teachers and the ways they are used effectively in realistic teaching situations.

HOW IS CHILDREN'S PHYSICAL EDUCATION DIFFERENT?

Teaching any subject to a class of children is challenging. Teaching children's physical education is probably the most challenging job in an elementary school. There are a number of reasons why this is so.

---

*The English language offers no truly convenient way to refer to the third person singular without excluding one gender or the other. The contortion "he/she" is both awkward and hard to read. Since both men and women teach children's physical education, the decision was made to use female and male pronouns in alternate examples.

The children are moving rather than anchored in desks; a teacher may work with 5-year-olds one lesson and with 11-year-olds a few minutes later; the range of content to be taught covers the entire spectrum of physical activity; facilities and equipment are often less than ideal. No doubt you can add to this list.

In addition to these factors, there is also a frenetic pace—30 or more children involved simultaneously in activity. Larry Locke (1975), in his now classic description of a children's physical education lesson, captured the complexity and pace of teaching with a vibrance and accuracy that is hard to find in written descriptions. Because this book is about teaching children's physical education "in the real world," it seems appropriate to begin by setting the stage with his description of a 2-minute observation of a class of 34 fourth-grade children during a gymnastics unit:

> Teacher is working one-on-one with a student who has an obvious neurological deficit. She wants him to sit on a beam and lift his feet from the floor. Her verbal behaviors fall into categories of reinforcement, instruction, feedback, and encouragement. She gives hands-on manual assistance. Nearby two boys perched on the uneven bars are keeping a group of girls off. Teacher visually monitors the situation but continues work on the beam. At the far end of the gym a large mat propped up so that students can roll down it from a table top, is slowly slipping nearer to the edge. Teacher visually monitors this but continues work on the beam. Teacher answers three individual inquiries addressed by passing students but continues as before. She glances at a group now playing follow-the-leader over the horse (this is off-task behavior) but as she does a student enters and indicates he left his milk money the previous period. Teacher nods him to the nearby office to retrieve the money and leaves the beam to stand near the uneven bars. The boys climb down at once. Teacher calls to a student to secure the slipping mat. Notes that the intruder, milk money now in hand, has paused to interact with two girls in the class and, monitoring him, moves quickly to the horse to begin a series of provocative questions designed to reestablish task focus.

This 2-minute vignette suggests how complex teaching is—but that's only 120 seconds out of 17,000 the teacher spent that day actually working with children.

ANALOGIES OF TEACHING

Teaching is complex. Sometimes it seems as if you are "in the eye of a hurricane." Balls, children, and ideas are whirling everywhere with no apparent order—but all demand immediate attention.

Teaching has also been likened to a three-ring circus. The teacher is in the center ring—the circusmaster. From this central position the teacher simultaneously directs all three rings and attempts to maintain a

ARE THEY GETTING TIRED? SHOULD I CHANGE THE TASK? IS MARIAN OFF TASK? WHAT'S WRONG WITH HAL?

pace and variety that hold the interest of the audience.

A third teaching analogy is not related to a hurricane or a circus—it's that of a composer and conductor of a symphony. There are many ways to arrange and blend the different instruments in an orchestra: the strings, the brass, the woodwinds, the percussion instruments. Some extraordinary works of music are dominated by violins, violas, and cellos. Oboes, bassoons, and flutes may be featured in another piece. Marches and military music are dominated by brass and percussion instruments. The fascinating part of listening to and watching a symphony orchestra is observing the myriad ways the various pieces of the orchestra blend in harmony to form enjoyable, often memorable, works of music.

This is how I see successful children's physical education teachers. They are artists, able to orchestrate teaching skills and develop lessons that are both absorbing and beneficial to children of all ages and abilities.

As is true of music, there is no single way to organize and teach a lesson.

CHANGING AND DYNAMIC

There is no predetermined formula that one can follow precisely to become a successful teacher. Teaching is too unpredictable. One third-grade class is not identical to another. Children are different on Monday morning from the way they are on Friday afternoon. So are teachers! Our understanding of teaching has increased over the years, but knowing what skills, strategies, and tactics to use when and with whom is still an artistic decision that varies from class to class and from teacher to teacher.

True teaching, as distinguished from "rolling out the ball," is not like working on an assembly line—it's constantly changing and dynamic. Schon (1990) uses the phrase *indeterminate zone of practice* to describe the uncertainty and ambiguities faced by teachers. Some professions appear to be driven by rules: When this happens, do this; when that happens, do that. Although one may try to reduce teaching to a precise science or formula, there is always a substantial degree of artistry and judgment involved in every lesson we teach.

One isn't simply born an artist—or teacher. There are techniques to learn and concepts to understand. A painter, for example, might learn painting techniques for use with watercolors, oils, and pastels. And there are concepts that need to be understood and expressed through the chosen medium: harmony of color and light, shading, combining colors to create various hues and tones, perspective, form, unity, and abstraction. The artist selects from among these skills to express desired meanings on a canvas.

Good teachers follow an approach similar to that of good artists. They acquire a range of skills and techniques, not necessarily at a university, which then allows them to develop and teach lessons that are meaningful and worthwhile for children. Whereas some of the skills are learned consciously, others seem to be acquired subconsciously. Regardless of how the skills are acquired, successful teachers possess a repertoire of abilities from which they select to consistently and intentionally provide children with developmentally appropriate experiences in physical activity.

Our scientific understanding of the skills and techniques used by expert teachers continues to grow (Brophy & Good, 1986; Rink, 1985; Siedentop, 1991; Silverman, 1991). We are learning more about what good teachers do (and don't do) with children. As with virtually any profession, however, knowing when and how to use this information requires an artistic decision.

DIFFICULT TO CAPTURE IN WORDS

Try to tell someone how to juggle—without demonstrating. It's hard to find the right words and phrases. We may be excellent jugglers ourselves, but words are often inadequate tools for helping someone else learn the skill. As with juggling, teaching children's physical education is a process that is easier to observe than to describe. Good teachers are artists with children—but they have a hard time relating what they do. We can recognize a good teacher when we see one, but it's much harder to tell why that teacher is so much better than another teacher.

One of the techniques used by good teachers is one that I am going to use in this book. I am going to break the complex teaching process into small parts with the hope of providing a more penetrating analysis and deeper understanding. This is possible on paper—but not with 30 children on the playground or in the gym. Writing (and reading) about teaching is a luxury because it allows the reader to pause and reflect on the various aspects of teaching: how they're used, why they're used, and how they might be used differently in various settings. When we're teaching, we don't have the opportunity to say to a class every few seconds, "Freeze. I want to spend 3 minutes thinking about what I am going to do next as a teacher." In writing, however, the challenges of teaching—and how they are met by successful teachers—can be described and discussed at a more leisurely pace than the frenetic, urgent one described by Locke (1975).

THE CHALLENGE OF TEACHING CHILDREN'S PHYSICAL EDUCATION

Teaching any subject in American schools today is a challenge—even when viewed from the perspective of the written word that can be frozen in time. There are obstacles that all teachers face; there is also satisfaction when the job is done well.

The Obstacles

In a single day an elementary school physical education teacher typically works with 7 to 12 classes of children. The ages may range from 5 to 11, the physical abilities from poor to excellent, the needs and interests varying from children interested in sports and physical fitness to those who have already decided that physical activity is not for them. In addition, many teachers have jump rope programs before school, juggling clubs at lunch, and gymnastics programs after school. Some also coach. When an elementary school physical education teacher ends her day, she has typically interacted with several hundred children, several classroom teachers and parents, and one or more principals, secretaries, custodians, and cooks—and she wonders why she is so tired. That's a challenging day.

Needless to say, few teachers complete their days under ideal circumstances. During cold and rainy weather, some teachers' gyms become lunchrooms from 11:15 a.m. to 1:15 p.m., so P.E. is taught in halls, lobbies, classrooms, and on stages. Some classroom teachers insist on bringing their classes to P.E.

early and arriving late to pick them up; others view P.E. as a time to help individual children "catch up" on math or reading, often the children who enjoy physical education the most. Schedules are always a complex conundrum in elementary schools. The result is that a class of fifth graders may be followed by kindergarteners, followed by second graders, and then another fifth-grade class. Field trips and visiting speakers often present surprises to the physical education teacher—especially when the principal and classroom teacher forget to notify the P.E. teacher, who discovers that his next class has just left on a bus to visit the entomology museum. Equipment budgets of $200 for the year represent yet another challenge to the physical educator, who quickly learns the value of collecting soup labels and attending PTA meetings at budget time.

NO WONDER I'M TIRED

Interview a teacher (or keep a log if you are already teaching) and list all of the people interacted with during one typical teaching day. Try to calculate the number of minutes the teacher spent not interacting with anyone else during the day—the time that the teacher was alone—and had time to think or relax.

As virtually any elementary school physical education teacher will attest, these are real challenges. They weren't simply invented to catch the reader's attention. Obviously, however, there are also rewards. If there weren't, we wouldn't be able to find many teachers spending more than one or two years teaching in elementary schools.

The Benefits

Clearly the primary benefit of teaching is not the pay. I have yet to meet a physical education teacher with an expense account or company car. And summers, which appear on paper as two and a half months of "rest and recuperation," are often spent taking courses required for continued certification—or working a second job. What then are the benefits?

One of the most obvious benefits is simply the joy of being with children—the contagious giggles, the naive curiosity, the honesty that makes you sometimes wish you hadn't asked,

the exuberance and willingness to try, the hugs around the knees, the barely legible notes that mean "thanks for paying attention to me," the fact that the bad things that happened today will be forgotten by tomorrow, the refreshing "unsophisticatedness," the true need of so many of today's children to be with adults who can be trusted for their predictability and caring, the fun that children associate with physical activity and the brief respite from the classroom routine, the touch on the arm that says "I appreciate your caring," and the opportunity to introduce children to the pleasures that derive from the various forms of moving.

These minirewards occur frequently. In fact, as long as we remain sensitive to the children, there are few other jobs that are so gratifying.

A benefit that occurs less frequently is the satisfaction of seeing children grow and develop. It's a sobering thought when a teacher who remains at the same school for five or six years observes his classes in May and realizes that much of what the 10- and 11-year-olds know, or don't know, is a direct result of the physical education program provided by that teacher.

There's a strong sense of expectation held by successful teachers. They share a common belief that, under the right circumstances, they can make a difference. In physical education they make this difference by introducing children to various forms of physical activity and beginning to build the movement foundation that eventually leads to enjoyment, satisfaction, and the benefits of participation in a physical activity throughout a lifetime. Many educators are convinced that the foundation is built or destroyed by the time a child leaves elementary school—in physical education, in math, in art, in reading.

In many ways a physical educator with a good program does her part to make the world a better place for children to grow up in. When we help children lead their lives in a productive direction, we can feel good about our work. Clearly this is a benefit of teaching children.

Some will label my comments thus far as those of an optimist. Good—I am an optimist. In fact, to me the terms pessimism and teaching are antonyms. If we don't believe we can make a difference as teachers, then I don't know how we can accept the responsibility of working with children.

My experience tells me that good children's physical education teachers are optimists who believe fervently in the value of their work. They are also realists, however, recognizing the challenges and difficulties of the job. This book is written for those teachers, whether they're just beginning their student teaching or are in their 30th year, who believe in the importance of physical education for children and are willing to dedicate themselves professionally to providing high-quality programs of physical education to children.

HUGS, GIGGLES, AND TOUCHES FOR THE TEACHER

Pick one of your favorite classes or observe a teacher with a favorite class. During the class, try to be keenly sensitive to all of the ways the children find to say they like the teacher and the program. Be sensitive to the smiles, the touches, the nods, the way they move close to the teacher, all of the ways they find to say, "Watch me!" When the class is over, or as soon as you can, take a few minutes to bask in all of the warm feelings the children have shared.

THE TEACHER MAKES THE DIFFERENCE

Physical education teachers are really no different from teachers of any subject. We want our students to learn. We also want them to enjoy our classes.

Some physical education teachers emphasize learning motor skills and playing games. Others emphasize the development of physical fitness. Still others place their major emphasis on the development of positive student attitudes towards themselves and physical activity. And, of course, many teachers would list a blend of these purposes for their programs.

It's relatively easy to list goals for a program. It's difficult to accomplish these goals, especially when classes are large and the number of meetings is limited to two or three days a week.

A few years ago we began to understand that teachers who were successful weren't necessarily so because of *what* they taught. Ten teachers could teach the same unit. Two or three might be highly successful (i.e., the successful teachers' students would report that they had enjoyed the unit, and a posttest would demonstrate that, in fact, they had learned much of what had been taught in the unit). The posttest of students of two or three other teachers might reveal that they hadn't learned anything from the teacher, and they would tell you they had disliked the unit. The students of the other four to six teachers might reveal mixed outcomes, with no apparent trend as a result of participating in the unit.

In the past 20 years or so, we have increased our understanding of how those two or three successful teachers worked with their students, so that the students learned from and enjoyed the unit. This book describes and analyzes many of the teaching approaches, behaviors, skills, and techniques (the *pedagogical knowledge base*) that successful teachers select from to create effective lessons.

We don't understand fully the orchestrations of skills and attributes that combine to make teachers successful or effective. We know more than we did 25 years ago, however. We also know that the use of teaching skills is situation specific and will vary according to the content taught as well as the grade level.

WORKING DEFINITION OF "SUCCESSFUL"

The purpose of this book is to define and describe the process of teaching used by successful children's physical educators. The emphasis on successful is an important one. This book is about more than simply keeping children "busy, happy, and good" two or three days a week so that classroom teachers can have a planning period. Successful implies that children learn and develop positive attitudes, that teachers derive satisfaction from their jobs, and that physical education programs are consistent with the overall focus of a school (Figure 1.1).

The Children's Goals

The first component of successful teaching, obviously, is the children. If a physical education teacher and program are successful, the foundation is built for a child to become a physically educated person. Recently a committee of the National Association for Sport and Physical Education (NASPE) (the Outcomes Committee) spent several years developing a definition of a physically educated person (Franck et al., 1991). Figure 1.2 con-

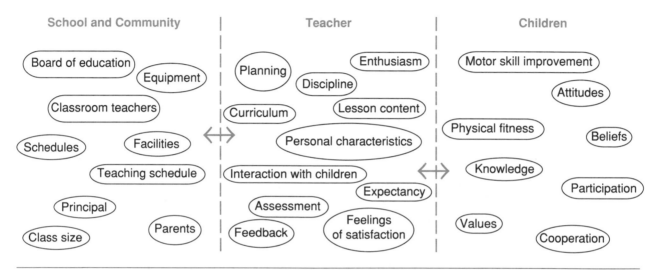

Figure 1.1 School and community, teacher, and children: influential factors related to successful programs of physical education.

A PHYSICALLY EDUCATED PERSON:

- **HAS learned skills necessary to perform a variety of physical activities**

    1. . . .moves using concepts of body awareness, space awareness, effort and relationships.
    2. . . .demonstrates competence in a variety of manipulative, locomotor and non-locomotor skills.
    3. . . .demonstrates competence in combinations of manipulative, locomotor and non-locomotor skills performed individually and with others.
    4. . . .demonstrates competence in many different forms of physical activity.
    5. . . .demonstrates proficiency in a few forms of physical activity.
    6. . . .has learned how to learn new skills.

- **IS physically fit**

    7 . . .assesses, achieves and maintains physical fitness.
    8. . . .designs safe, personal fitness programs in accordance with principles of training and conditioning.

- **DOES participate regularly in physical activity**

    9. . . .participates in health enhancing physical activity at least three times a week.
    10. . . .selects and regularly participates in lifetime physical activities.

- **KNOWS the implications of and the benefits from involvement in physical activities**

    11. . . .identifies the benefits, costs and obligations associated with regular participation in physical activity.

Figure 1.2 Characteristics of a physically educated person. (Reprinted by permission from Franck et al., 1991.)

12. . . .recognizes the risk and safety factors associated with regular participation in physical activity.
13. . . .applies concepts and principles to the development of motor skills.
14. . . .understands that wellness involves more than being physically fit.
15. . . .knows the rules, strategies and appropriate behaviors for selected physical activities.
16. . . .recognizes that participation in physical activity can lead to multi-cultural and international understanding.
17. . . .understands that physical activity provides the opportunity for enjoyment, self-expression and communication.

- **VALUES physical activity and its contributions to a healthful lifestyle**

18. . . .appreciates the relationships with others that result from participation in physical activity.
19. . . .respects the role that regular physical activity plays in the pursuit of life-long health and well-being.
20. . . .cherishes the feelings that result from regular participation in physical activity.

Figure 1.2 (Continued)

tains this definition, which was reviewed by more than 500 professional physical educators during its development.

The Teacher's Goals

In addition to the benefits accrued by the children, for any program to be successful, the individuals responsible need to feel a certain sense of satisfaction and accomplishment. For teachers this often means that acts of support and nurture are communicated by administrators and parents. As with any profession, when we don't feel successful, it is too easy to give up and go through the motions. In physical education jargon we call it "rolling out the ball."

Teachers who continue to plan, develop innovative curricula, teach actively and enthusiastically, and evaluate and assess simply must experience a sense of satisfaction if they are going to continue this type of teaching throughout a career (chapter 14). Interestingly, this doesn't mean that the only way a teacher can be happy is to have ideal conditions. In fact, it seems that part of the job description for any children's physical education teacher must be to battle continually for improved working conditions and an increased understanding of the importance of physical education for children. For example, many teachers seem to be constantly working toward one or more of the following:

- Convincing other teachers and administrators of the value of physical education for children so that classes are not considered "breaks" that can be cancelled for field trip, plays, and special events
- Obtaining more and better equipment for classes
- Attaining realistic teaching loads (e.g., a maximum of seven or eight classes a day)

- Arranging teaching schedules that provide reasonable transitions between grades (e.g., not a fifth grade followed by a first followed by a third grade)
- Lobbying for daily physical education for every child, with class sizes of 30 or fewer students
- Securing facilities that are truly designed for physical education

These teachers, who are constantly struggling to improve their programs, often feel effective, however. They have developed the understanding that successful physical education involves more than simply teaching children well—it entails other responsibilities, too.

The School's Goal

An important responsibility of any teacher is finding ways to contribute to the overall goals of the school. The goals of good physical education programs (Franck et al., 1991) are compatible with the overall goals of good schools—helping children to learn and feel positive about themselves and school and working cooperatively with others toward common purposes. Only when a physical education program is compatible with an overall school program can it be considered successful.

SUMMARY

"What is it that successful children's physical education teachers actually do when they teach children?" is the question this book attempts to answer. The focus will be on the skills and techniques used by good teachers, not on the content of their lessons.

In recent years we have increasingly come to understand that there is no such thing as the perfect lesson that will succeed for every teacher. A good teacher is able to take virtually any content area and weave it into an interesting and worthwhile experience for children. Unfortunately, an ineffective teacher can take virtually any content, no matter how appealing it may seem to children, and "teach" it in such a way that the children not only fail to learn anything but also fail to enjoy the experience.

This book describes and analyzes the pedagogy of children's physical education—the orchestration of techniques and skills teachers use to involve children in physical activities that are interesting and worthwhile. It is designed for the teacher, or future teacher, whose goal is to help children develop the skills, knowledge, and attitudes to eventually become a physically educated person—and enjoy the benefits of physical activity for a lifetime.

QUESTIONS FOR REFLECTION

1. When you think about children's physical education, what do you see as the biggest challenges? How do you think you will meet them as a teacher?
2. Chapter 1 describes a number of benefits of teaching children's physical education. Which of the benefits do you see as the most motivating to you?
3. If we talked with the children you teach (or plan to teach), what would you like them to say about you as a teacher? What kinds of things might you do to encourage children to feel the way you would like them to feel about you and your program?
4. Why does the book make a distinction between the teaching process (pedagogy) and the content (what is taught)?
5. For 5 minutes watch another teacher (or a videotape of yourself) teaching a lesson to children. Write down all of the questions that you think may be going through that teacher's mind.
6. Figure 1.1 depicts the influential factors related to successful teaching. How would you revise it to better reflect your views?

REFERENCES

Brophy, J., & Good, T.L. (1986). Teacher behavior and student achievement. In C.M. Wittrock (Ed.), *Handbook of research on teaching* (3rd ed.) (pp. 328-375). New York: Macmillan.

Franck, M., Graham, G., Lawson, H., Loughrey, T., Ritson, R., Sanborn, M., & Seefeldt, V. (1991). *Physical education outcomes: A project of the National Association for Sport & Physical Education.* Reston, VA: National Association for Sport and Physical Education.

Locke, L.F. (1975, Spring). *The ecology of the gymnasium: What the tourist never sees.* Paper presented at the meeting of the Southern Association for Physical Education for College Women, Gatlinburg, TN. TN.

Rink, J. (1985). *Teaching physical education for learning.* St. Louis: Times Mirror/Mosby.

Schon, D.A. (1990). *Educating the reflective practitioner.* San Francisco: Jossey-Bass.

Siedentop, D. (1991). *Developing teaching skills in physical education* (3rd ed.) Palo Alto, CA: Mayfield.

Silverman, S. (1991). Research on teaching in physical education. *Research Quarterly for Exercise and Sport,* **62**, 352-367.

Chapter 2

Planning to Maximize Learning

In the first chapter, teaching was described as an orchestration of teaching skills. Effective planning is an integral part of this orchestration—the part of teaching that provides the focus for the lesson. Planning is to teaching as writing music is to a symphonic performance. It's analogous to the notes, the scales, the written plan that the musicians follow. Without the written music, a symphony orchestra would be reduced to nothing more than discordant noise with no connection or purpose.

After reading and understanding this chapter related to planning, the teacher will be able to

- analyze the important link between planning and teaching;
- describe the tendencies to avoid extensive planning and ways these tendencies can be avoided;
- explain why planning is so important to a successful program of physical education for children;
- describe the concept of and need for personalized planning;
- analyze the use of objectives as a guide for creating lessons; and
- compare and contrast the important reasons for connecting long-term and daily planning.

This chapter discusses many of the important features of planning. It begins by describing the need for planning and follows with a straightforward analysis of why there are tendencies to avoid planning in physical education. Realistic ideas about planning for busy people is the third section, and long- and short-term planning are discussed in the final part of the chapter.

I THINK I'LL SKIP THIS CHAPTER . . .

When I envision you reading this book, I wonder if you will be tempted to skip to the later chapters—"the good stuff." If you do, I hope you will return to this chapter at some point. It has been designed to provide some realistic and candid thoughts not only about the importance of planning but also about ways that planning can be done in the real world of teaching.

THE NEED FOR PLANNING

In theory, teachers spend an hour or two each day at their desks planning. In fact, teachers plan in the shower, on the drive to work, at meetings, and as they are falling asleep at night—as well as at their desks (Graham, Hopple, Manross, & Sitzman, in press; Placek, 1984).

Few would question the importance of planning (Lambert, 1989). The question, however, is how much planning is necessary. We know that in the beginning of our careers we need to spend a lot more time planning than we do after we have gained experience. This is no different from taking a trip for the first time—we need to study maps and landmarks to know exactly where to go. After the trip has been made a number of times, however, we can spend far less time reviewing maps.

We also know that the amount of planning necessary is related to the type of program a teacher decides to provide for children. Teachers who "roll out the ball" probably spend 5 to 10 minutes a week thinking about what they will do. In contrast, teachers who have truly educational programs spend considerable amounts of time poring over books and notes in order to design lessons that fulfill the needs of children. My assumption is that you are a teacher who sincerely wants to de-

velop the best program of physical education for children that you can; you therefore recognize the need to plan extensively. There are a number of reasons why planning is necessary in such programs.

Limited Actual Teaching Time

The minimal amount of time allotted for physical education in many schools is one of the major reasons planning is crucial. Thirty-minute classes that meet twice a week, for example, have approximately 32.4 hours a year of available time (Tables 2.1 and 2.2). Realistically, however, there is even less time for actual practice. In fact, Kelly (1989) estimated that the actual instructional time in a 2-day-a-week program is 16.2 hours a year.

His estimate for a 5-day-a-week program is slightly over 40 hours (Kelly, 1989). Forty hours seems like a lot, yet when we consider how long it takes to learn to hit a golf ball in a straight direction or stand on a pair of ice skates, it's obvious we don't have much time—even if we taught only two skills a year.

Table 2.1   Annual Time Available in Physical Education by Number of Days of Instruction Per Week for a 36-Week School Year

Days of instruction per week	1	2	3	4	5
Total instructional days available per year	36	72	108	144	180
Minutes per class	30	30	30	30	30
Total time scheduled per year in minutes	1080	2160	3240	4320	5400
Uncontrolled lost instructional time	108	216	324	432	540
Available instructional time per year in minutes	972	1944	2916	3888	4860
Available instructional time per year in hours	16.2	32.4	48.6	64.8	81.0
Actual learning time per year in hours assuming 50% on-task time	8.1	16.2	24.3	32.3	40.5

Table 2.2 Method for Calculating Amount of Available Instructional Time and the Number of Objectives That Can Be Addressed

A = # of weeks of school per year: 36

B = # days of instruction per week: 2

C = Length of instructional period in minutes: 30

D = Instructional time available per year: A(36) x B(2) x C(30) = 2160

E = Adjustment for lost instructional days: D(2160) x .9 = 1944

F = Estimated on-task time percentage: 50% (.5)

G = Actual instructional/learning time available: E(1944) x F(.5) = 972

H = Time converted from minutes to hours: G(972)/60 = 16.2

I = # of objectives to be taught in a given year: 25

J = Average time available to teach each objective: H(16.2)/I(25) = .65 hours or 39 minutes

Note. Reprinted by permission from Kelly, 1989.

Teaching Environment

In addition to the limited amount of time, we also need to plan carefully because of the variables that influence our lessons. Class sizes, equipment, and facilities all dictate what can be taught successfully. So too does the climate. Teachers in Florida and southern California can teach outside comfortably much of the year; in Anchorage the tennis courts used in warm weather become ice hockey rinks in cold weather.

Physical education class sizes of 50 or 60 are still common. Many teachers use cafeterias and multipurpose rooms during the winter months and on rainy days. Equipment for physical education has improved since the days when a teacher started the program with three red, rubber playground balls that wouldn't hold air past lunch and two dozen wooden bats and softballs. All of these contextual factors require teachers to plan carefully and adjust lessons based on their particular environments. Fortunately, however, these limitations don't prevent teachers from developing quality programs of physical education, but developing quality programs does require creative and thoughtful planning.

Teacher Background

Our experiences in and out of schools also influence our need to plan. When we don't know something very well (dance or rhythms, for example), we need to spend a lot more time planning and developing the expertise to teach these activities effectively.

Some teachers enrich their backgrounds through reading (chapter 14). Others attend conferences and workshops. Some ask other teachers for help. In recent years teachers have started to exchange videotapes of successful lessons. Some districts also organize monthly sharing meetings which focus on a topic of interest to the teachers in the district.

The elementary school physical education teacher is expected to be an expert in virtually every subject taught in physical education—similar to what is expected of the classroom teacher. This means that we often need to find ways to learn about new activities or ones that were neglected in our teacher preparation programs so that we can offer children a complete and well-rounded program. This is also a part of planning.

Children's Backgrounds

A fourth reason we need to plan carefully is that not all children are alike. One fifth grade is different from another. Schools are different also. Should the skills of basketball be taught in an inner city where many of the children play basketball continually at recess, after school, and on weekends? Should the skills of soccer be taught in a suburban school where most of the children have opportunities to join a soccer team when they're five years old?

Obviously the yearly plan for a teacher whose children have daily P.E. will be different from that for a teacher whose children have physical education only twice a week. If the program is effective, when the children reach fourth or fifth grade, the children with daily P.E. will have different needs from those of their twice-a-week counterparts.

PRO OR CON

Imagine that you teach in a community where basketball, soccer, or softball is very popular. Would you devote a lot of time to those skills as a teacher or would you assume that the children can learn them outside of your program? Discuss your response with a friend or colleague. You probably won't have to search far to find someone who has a viewpoint different from yours.

Follow-up by Classroom Teachers

A fifth reason physical education teachers need to plan has to do with the classroom teachers in a school (Faucette & Hillidge, 1989). Does the P.E. teacher have to write weekly plans for the classroom teachers to follow? Do the classroom teachers actually follow them?

Some P.E. specialists work with classroom teachers who organize lessons designed to follow up the lesson taught on Tuesday, for example. Other classroom teachers view physical education as a "break" for both them and the children—and physical education times are considered as recess; therefore, the children in their classes receive no instruction designed to reinforce the lessons taught by the P.E. teacher.

Obviously the school principal plays a pivotal role in the way physical education is taught by classroom teachers. When the specialist has effectively "educated" his principal, the classroom teachers are required to supplement the lessons of the specialist; when the principal neither understands nor values physical education for children, classroom teachers rarely reinforce the lessons taught by the P.E. teacher.

All of these factors (the time available, the teaching conditions, the background of the teachers and the children, and the support of the classroom teachers) suggest that, because conditions and situations are so different, the planning needs of each teacher are quite different. Planning is necessary, but it's not necessarily the most enjoyable part of teaching. As a consequence there is a natural tendency of many teachers, I suspect, to avoid planning.

TENDENCIES TO AVOID PLANNING

Because the content of physical education is so enjoyable to children, it's relatively easy to avoid a lot of planning. Every P.E. teacher has a "bag of tricks" to pick from to provide 30 minutes of enjoyment. Because of this, teachers can avoid careful planning.

Another reason to avoid planning is that there is no universally agreed-upon purpose for physical education in elementary schools. Some teachers see physical fitness as the major purpose; others emphasize motor skill learning; some focus on cognitive understanding, learning lead-up games and sports, or learning to cooperate with others as the major purpose of a physical education program for children. Consequently, there is no single recognized goal. In contrast, math or reading teachers seem to agree on a generally accepted and recognized purpose for their programs. (The recently approved document defining a physically educated person [Franck et al., 1991] should be of some help in providing a common direction for physical education teachers. It has the potential to assist physical education teachers and program coordinators to focus on the most important goals of physical education.)

In addition to the current lack of consensus about the goals of physical education, another reason that physical education teachers may tend to avoid planning has to do with the perceived value of physical education in a school. When a content area such as physical education, art, or music is undervalued, it's hard for teachers to remain convinced that their work is important. When this is the case, it's harder to put the time and energy into planning a truly educational program.

Many administrators and parents do not understand *educational* physical education. As long as the children appear happy and there are no serious injuries or complaints, they are delighted with the program. Therefore, little accountability is placed on the physical education teachers. This is in marked contrast to reading, for example, in which children are tested throughout the year and expected to improve their reading abilities.

PERSONALIZED PLANNING

If all teaching situations were identical, there wouldn't be a need to plan individually. Teachers in a district could design a single plan and use it throughout the district. Because situations are different, however, planning should be personalized to match the needs and interests of the children at your school. It's easy to create "ideal" plans; it's much harder to develop plans given the equipment, facilities, and scheduling and background limitations that are typical of children's physical education programs. Above all, planning must be realistic. If it is going to be of any value, it needs to be designed with a specific school in mind. We want to do so much for the children, but typically there isn't time to accomplish as much as we hope to.

Let me illustrate with an example. One state guide, since revised (Table 2.3), suggested 25 objectives to be accomplished in third grade (Kelly, 1989). Based on Kelly's analysis, that means that children would have approximately 40 minutes to learn each objective (Table 2.2). Children in a program of daily physical education would have about 100 minutes to learn each objective. While 100 minutes per objective is certainly better than 40 minutes, one wonders how realistic it is to think that children can learn to kick a ball efficiently or do a forward roll in that amount of time. Is there enough time for children to develop a functional understanding of the skill so that it can be used successfully in a game or routine?

Table 2.3 Number of Objectives Targeted for Instruction by Grade and Goal Area in the State of Virginia Standards of Learning for Physical Education

Grade	Fit	M/E	R/D	S/T/G	G/S	I/S	T/S	Total
K	3	8	3	5	4			23
1	3	7	3	4	6			23
2	4	3	4	7	6			24
3	4	3	3	9	6			25
4	5		6	8	10			29
5	5		5	5	9			24
6	4		6	4	9			23
7	4		4	5	9			22
8	2		4	5		5	9	25
9	3		3	2		7	4	19
10	3		3	3		9	2	20
11-12	3		1	1		4	2	11
Totals:	43	21	45	58	59	25	17	270

Fit = Physical fitness; M/E = Movement education; R/D = Rhythm and dance; S/T/G = Stunts, tumbling, and gymnastics; G/S = Games and sports; I/S = Individual sports; T/S = Team sports.

Note. Reprinted by permission from Kelly, 1989.

HOW CAN I DO IT ALL?

Make a list of the motor skills you believe children should learn by the time they leave elementary school. How many are in your list? My list totals 18. In a 2-day-a-week program that means, using the figures from Tables 2.1 and 2.2, I would have approximately 55 minutes to devote to each of the 18 skills. Of course, there are many other areas I want to include as part of the program. Realistically, then, I have substantially less than 55 minutes to spend on each of the motor skills. As a teacher, should I be satisfied with simply exposing children to these skills? Or should I eliminate some of the skills? If so, which ones?

As specialists we have two ways to solve this perplexing problem. One way—perhaps the easier—is simply to expose children to the various motor skills, concepts, and experiences that compose physical education. The second alternative—to me the harder one—is to teach only skills that can truly be learned in the short amount of time provided, which means difficult decisions about what to exclude.

Beginning teachers are faced with the dilemma of not knowing how long it takes children to learn a particular concept or skill. Experienced teachers typically have a much better understanding of this, although there is hardly a consensus. This is one of the reasons that experienced teachers and beginning teachers typically use different formats for planning.

HOW LONG WILL IT TAKE TO LEARN?

Here is a list of skills and concepts we might typically see taught in an elementary school program of physical education. Estimate how many lessons (or minutes if you prefer) you think it will take for children to learn the skill described. Compare your notes with other teachers; expect to find differences based on both the estimates of time and also your expectations for when a skill or concept has been learned (i.e., your operational definition of when children have truly acquired a skill or concept). If you are a beginning teacher, try to compare notes with an experienced teacher. How many lessons (minutes) do

- second graders need to show the difference between symmetrical and asymmetrical balances;
- third graders need to be able to catch a gently thrown yarn or a rag ball from a distance of 50 feet; and
- fifth graders need to be able to cooperate, without arguing or fighting, when they work in groups of six?

PLANNING FORMATS AND COMPONENTS

Now that I have described the need for planning and explained why one plan doesn't suit all teachers in all schools, I want to focus on formats for planning. If I had written this book ten years ago, I would have suggested a single format for planning. Today I realize that teachers have many ways of planning. There simply isn't a single approach to planning that can be expected to be successful for every teacher. Both research (Graham, Hopple, Manross, & Sitzman, in press; Housner & Griffey, 1985; Placek, 1984) and my own experience tell me that we plan differently as we gain in experience. In this section a discussion of ideas and thoughts about planning is divided

into three sections: program (the entire 5 or 6 years), yearly, and daily planning.

Program (Exit) Goals

What do you want your first graders to know (be able to do) in five years when they move on to middle school? This is a hard question to answer. I know of few teachers who have these exit goals written out, although many of them are able to describe the goals in general terms. Increasingly I have come to realize that this is a valuable exercise even though it may change for a variety of good reasons. Figure 2.1 provides one example of how a district defined its goals for a program (Kelly, 1988).

EXIT GOALS

List the five or six most important goals that you think students should have reached when they leave a program. Have all of the current fifth or sixth graders in a program accomplished them? Will your current first graders be able to do so? Are the goals realistic? Probably the most important time to measure a program's success is when children leave a program after 5 or 6 years. What can they do? How do they feel about physical activity? What do they know?

If we're not careful, our exit goals become lists of what we will cover in the program; they will not be statements of what we want children actually to learn. The definition of a physically educated person (chapter 1) serves as a good resource for beginning to think about exit goals that can be accomplished by the time children leave your program.

Ideally, the long-term goals for a program are consistent with the goals of the middle (junior high) school and also the high school. This assumes that the teachers representing K-12 meet from time to time and discuss the goals for the various grade levels. Unfortunately, this is rare in education. The elementary school program may or may not dovetail with the middle school program. This explains, at least in part, why middle and high school teachers often wonder aloud, "What do they teach in the elementary school?" An exchange day, when teachers move up or down to a different school for a day, has a way of quickly answering this question. "I didn't realize . . ." and "No wonder . . ." preface many of the comments teachers make after an exchange day.

			K-5 program plan					
			K	1	2	3	4	5
Locomotor patterns	1.1	Run	XX					
	1.2	Gallop	XX					
	1.3	Horizontal jump			XX			
	1.4	Vertical jump			XX			
	1.5	Hop (right-left)		XX				
	1.6	Slide		XX				
	1.7	Skip				XX		
	1.8	Leap					XX	
Object control	2.1	Underhand roll	XX					
	2.2	Bounce/dribble			XX			
	2.3	Underhand throw		XX				
	2.4	Overhand throw					XX	
	2.5	Kick				XX		
	2.6	Punt						XX
	2.7	Two-hand side arm strike (baseball)				XX		
	2.8	Catch/fielding						XX
	2.9	Underhand strike (volleyball serve)				XX		
	2.10	Chest pass (basketball)			XX			
	2.11	Bounce pass (basketball)				XX		
Physical fitness	3.1	Knowledge						XX
	3.2	Training concepts						XX
	3.3	Terminology					XX	
	3.4	Leg strength			XX			
	3.5	Flexibility			XX			
	3.6	Abdominal strength				XX		
	3.7	Endurance					XX	
	3.8	Arm & shoulder strength						XX
	3.9	Agility					XX	
	3.10	Speed						XX
Social	4.1	Self-discipline (control)		XX				
	4.2	Cooperation		XX				
	4.3	Good sportsmanship				XX		
	4.4	Handling winning & losing			XX			
	4.5	Respect equipment & property	XX					
Body management	5.1	Nonlocomotor	XX					
	5.2	Body awareness	XX					
	5.3	Spatial awareness	XX					
	5.4	Use of space			XX			
	5.5	Quality of movement			XX			
	5.6	Relationship of body to other objects				XX		
	5.7	Basic dance patterns					XX	
	5.8	Forward roll						XX
	5.9	Rope jumping				XX		
Game & sport skills	6.1	Follow directions	XX					
	6.2	Knowledge of safety & rules		XX				
	6.3	Member of team					XX	
	6.4	Participates in games and sports						XX

XX indicates when the objective is to be mastered. This does not mean that the objective is only worked on during this year. Many objectives will be worked on during all the years preceding mastery and even after mastery has been achieved for retention.

Figure 2.1   Sample kindergarten through fifth-grade program plan. (Reprinted by permission from Kelly, 1988.)

"I THINK THE SKILLS USED IN BASKETBALL SHOULD BE TAUGHT IN ELEMENTARY SCHOOL... THE RULES TAUGHT IN MIDDLE SCHOOL, ALONG WITH OFFICIAL GAME..."

WHEN SHOULD _____ BE TAUGHT?

With several other physical educators (ideally, elementary through secondary teachers), discuss these questions:

- At what level (elementary, middle, or high school) should the rules for team sports be taught?
- What basic motor skills can children be expected to have learned by the time they leave elementary school?
- At what level should a major emphasis be placed on learning the important concepts of physical fitness?
- Should folk and square dance be taught at the elementary, middle, or high school level? Should the same dances be taught? Or different ones?
- Basketball dribbling lessons, at all levels, often begin with the basic information about using the finger pads, not looking at the ball, and so forth. By what grade should children have learned these refinements so it is no longer necessary to start with those concepts?

Obviously, as the discussion progresses, you will think of many more questions that will be helpful in establishing exit goals for all levels of physical education programs.

Because the content of physical education is somewhat less understood than many of the other content areas taught in the schools, this communication between grade levels is especially important. It makes little sense, for example, for an elementary specialist to teach the rules for playing various sports when the students will spend several days learning them again in sixth or seventh grade. It also doesn't make much sense for students to be taught how to grip a bat or throw a ball in 10th grade when they have learned to do so in fourth grade.

Planning for the Year

It's hard to know what can be accomplished in 5 or 6 years. It's somewhat easier to figure out what can be achieved in a single year. Some teachers accomplish this task using a calendar. They list the days and weeks of the school year and then write in the topic(s) for various days. Some teachers believe that children learn best when lessons are massed together in a series of lessons on the same topic (units) (e.g., gymnastics or ball-handling units). Others believe that topics should be reviewed throughout the year and organize their year around various themes (e.g., balancing, kicking, striking).

In either case, successful teachers make realistic assessments of what the children are going to learn that year. These types of plans also serve as a guide for the year's lessons. When this isn't done, there seems to be a tendency for teachers to plan the year more by "how they feel on a given day" than by a systematic plan that leads in a desired direction.

The physical education teacher who doesn't stick to a plan for the year is no different from the history teacher who announces one day in April that "we need to cover the second half of the book in the final 6 weeks of the year.'' Time spent on unrelated topics or unfocused discussions in the beginning of the year detract from the overall direction.

What I have written up to this point may suggest that effective teachers stick to a plan regardless of the progress made by the children. I don't think so. If the children aren't grasping a concept, teachers spend more time on it than allotted on the yearly calendar. They remain sensitive to the overall plan for the year, however, and attempt to stay on schedule if possible. In fact, some teachers even post the calendar for the year with the various units and themes listed so that the children have an idea of what they will be learning and when. This has an added benefit. It avoids the ever-present question asked by children of virtually every teacher, ''What are we going to do today?''

Obviously there is no single right answer to the question of how to sequence content for the year. However, we know that it makes sense to distribute lessons on various topics throughout the year rather than massing them together in relatively long units (Schmidt, 1991). This allows a teacher to review important ideas to promote retention and understanding. When this isn't done, children seem to forget from one year to the next key concepts that were emphasized 10 or 11 months earlier. For example, when children are reminded three or four times a year, several months apart, to turn their side to-

ward the target when striking with a racket, the potential for remembering that important cue is far higher than if they heard it for one week in October and then not again until the next fall.

HOW MANY DAYS IN A ROW?

Refer to Table 2.3 in this chapter. Look at the fourth-grade objectives in games and sports (G/S). As you might assume, the 10 objectives include skills such as throwing, catching, and volleying. Assume that you have a daily program of physical education and have approximately 81 hours for the year (Table 2.1). These 10 objectives represent roughly 35 percent of the objectives for the year, about 28 hours (or roughly 56 lessons). Use a calendar and decide how you will organize the G/S objectives for the year.

- Will you spend 56 lessons in a row (roughly 11 weeks) on these objectives?
- Will you spread them out in eight consecutive lessons at seven different times during the year, separated, for example, by sequences focused on fitness and dance?
- Or do you think it might be more effective to teach four lessons in a row focused on the games/sport skill objectives at 14 different times during the year?

In concluding this section, it is important, as with the 5- or 6-year goals, that the yearly

plan be realistic if it is going to be of any value. For example, I have seen lists of motor skills that children were going to *learn* (not simply *do*) in a 2-day-a-week program. My hunch is that these lists must have been written to appease a superintendent or coordinator or state department because they were virtually impossible to accomplish—even for "superteacher." There was just not enough time in the year for the teacher to do anything but expose children to these skills because there were so many. In that sense the yearly plan is similar to a budget or a diet plan—easy to write but quite hard to stick with when it's unrealistic.

Daily Planning

As with yearly planning, there is no single, correct way to plan individual lessons. Some beginning teachers, for example, spend countless hours writing out detailed plans. They consult notes and various texts and reflect on their own experiences to develop interesting lessons. Because elementary school physical education specialists typically teach 7 to 11 classes a day, they often group the classes (e.g., first and second; third and fourth). Some plan for each grade level; others use different clusters.

Experienced teachers who have developed a schema for the content (Graham, Hopple, Manross, & Sitzman, in press; Livingston & Borko, 1989; Shulman, 1987) typically write less on paper than does the beginning teacher because their planning takes the form of mental processing. Nevertheless, because of their years of experience and insights, effective teachers seem to have an acute and obvious sense of the purpose of the lesson and its place within the overall plan for the year. It is also clear to the children and to the occasional observer that the lesson has a specific purpose.

Figure 2.2 and Figure 2.3 are the lesson plans of a student teacher and an experienced teacher. The plans were written for a dribbling lesson taught to the same class of children. It's easy to see that the plan of the beginning teacher was far more detailed than that of the experienced teacher. At the beginning of his career, the experienced teacher also wrote extensive and detailed plans (Graham, Hopple, Manross & Sitzman, in press). With experience, however, it was no longer necessary to outline the lessons in such detail.

WHERE'S THE PERFECT REFERENCE

I remember how I planned my lessons during my first years of teaching. I would get to school early, start the coffee, and then go to my desk. I always wanted to find the "perfect" plans for the day in a single book. Before long, however, I had six or seven books spread over my desk as I tried to discover the best way to accomplish my objective(s) for that day. Interestingly, I still plan many of my lessons that way. No single book seems to have all the ideas I want for a single lesson—even ones I coauthored!

Lesson: Dribbling

I   Student Objective:
    1) Control in g.s. while moving and dribbling a ball.

II Teacher Objective:
    1) Use student names (6)

III Equipment: Jump ropes, red rubber playground balls

IV Warm-up: Jump rope (blue handle)

Intro: Today we are going to dribble while moving in general space.

Q→ Can you dribble beside your body?
Q→ What part of your fingers do you use?
Q→ Can you dribble with the other hand?
Q→ Can you dribble around one leg?
Q→ Can you dribble around the other leg?
Q→ Can you dribble in and out around both legs?
Q→ Can you move down to the ground and back up, keeping the ball going?
Q→ How many times can you go up and down without losing control of the ball?
Q→ Can you dribble beside your body and travel forward?
Q→ Can you dribble backwards?
Q→ Can you dribble to the right?
Q→ Can you dribble to the left?
Q→ Can you dribble 5 x with one hand and switch to the other hand while moving forward?
Q→ Can you walk forward 5 steps, stop your feet, but keep the ball going for 5 bounces, then walk 5 more steps?
Q→ Can you do the same thing again (walk 5 steps, dribble 5 x) but after you dribble 5 x, switch hands?
Q→ What can you do with your legs to help control the ball while you move?
Q→ Can you walk forward and dribble 5 times with one hand and then 5 x with the other hand?
Q→ Can you walk backwards, 5 x with one hand then switch to the other hand?
Q→ Can you move to the right and dribble 5 times and then dribble 5 x to the left?
Q→ Can you dribble right and left again, but not go in a straight line?

V   Closure:
    — What skill did you work on today?
    — What part of your hand do you use?

Figure 2.2 Example of a lesson plan written by a beginning teacher focusing on teaching children to maintain control of a ball while dribbling and traveling.

> Monday and Tuesday – Dribble: The kids are to warm-up jumping rope. Ask them to work on changing direction. The lesson will focus on dribbling and traveling. The refinement is to be in control of the ball while moving. I will begin with the children in p.s. and move into g.s. if possible.

Figure 2.3 Example of a lesson plan written by an experienced teacher focusing on teaching children to maintain control of a ball while dribbling and traveling.

As with the program planning and the yearly planning, one of the challenges for a teacher is to determine what is realistic for a given amount of time. In my work with beginning teachers, for example, I find that they will list the purpose of a lesson for third graders as "learning to strike a ball repeatedly with a paddle." When I ask them if that is possible in 25 minutes, they quickly realize it's not. As we work through the process, however, I help them realize that learning to stand with one's side towards the target is an objective that can be accomplished in a single lesson.

Learnable Pieces

Interestingly, my experience suggests that when we designate an achievable objective for a 20- or 30-minute lesson as a *learnable piece* ("side to the target"), we teach differently than when the objective is simply unrealistic for a particular lesson. We seem to improvise more to develop experiences that really help the children learn to stand with their side toward the target. When our objective is unrealistic, our lessons seem to consist of simply presenting a series of activities for children without modification or adaptation.

When—if—we write objectives (realistically define a learnable piece for that time period), it is helpful to be as specific as possible. Otherwise our objectives are general and therefore hard to evaluate. For example, the statement "The children will learn to volley a ball" is not only general but unrealistic for 30-minute lessons. "The children will learn to bend their knees as they receive and volley a ball" provides a specific guideline for observation. The second statement provides a specific direction or focus for the teacher and, as we will see in subsequent chapters, becomes the focus of the entire lesson. While some advocate using behavioral objectives as a guide for planning, my experience indicates that the exact format recommended in behavioral objectives may be unnecessary. Specificity is important, however. Helpful questions to ask about the way you write your objectives are as follows:

- Is this truly a learnable piece for the 30 minutes I teach the children?
- Can I actually see if I have accomplished these goals when I observe my children?
- Could someone else see if I have accomplished these goals?
- Are my objectives helpful in letting me know how successful my program has been?
- Am I thinking about my objectives when I am actually teaching, or are the objectives just statements on paper?

Additional Lesson Components

In addition to one or two objectives for the lesson, most plans include the following components.

A format for indicating the topic of the lesson, the grade level, the date, and other information that will be helpful for keeping track of which class has been taught which lesson. This is especially important for those who teach 20 or more different classes of children in the same week—especially when they are at different schools.

An introduction to the lesson that is quickly organized and stimulating to the children. This may or may not be related to the remainder of the lesson (chapter 5).

A brief introduction to the purpose of the lesson to provoke interest in the lesson. This is often referred to as *set induction* or *anticipatory set.* Often this portion of the lesson relates to other lessons that have already been taught (chapters 3 and 11 provide additional information about this component).

A brief description (in many instances a list) of the tasks or activities that will be developed in that lesson (also see Figure 9.1). This progression clearly relates to the objectives of the teacher. It is not simply a list of things to keep the children busy; rather, there is a clear progression of tasks that logically lead to the desired outcomes for the lesson.

One of the reasons that beginning teachers especially list a number of tasks (Figure 2.2) is so that they can make a lesson flow smoothly from one task to the next in a logical and orderly progression. When this isn't done, there is a tendency in the beginning to skip all over and lose sight of the focus.

I REMEMBER

I remember watching a student teacher whose lesson was focused on jumping and landing. She decided to use hoops as a prop for the children to jump over. About halfway through the lesson, some of the children began picking up their hoops and tried to "hula" with them. Other children soon began doing the same thing. The lesson ended with the teacher trying to show the children how to hula hoop—hardly the focus she had started with 20 minutes before.

Teachers often write down the cues, prompts, refinements, or questions they will emphasize during the lesson. These are the secrets or shortcuts that help children learn more quickly and efficiently. Chapters 6, 8, 9, 10, and 11 include discussions of these segments of the lesson.

Many teachers use sketches or diagrams to outline the formations and arrangements they will use in the lesson. This is especially helpful early in the teaching career because it virtually forces the teacher to visualize how the transition from one activity to another will be made.

Finally, a closure is often included as a way of slowing down the end of the lesson and reminding children of the important features of the lesson (Marks, 1988) (chapter 13). Often this is a question or two related to the objective(s) of the lesson. Some teachers also use this time to assign "P.E. homework."

These are some of the segments of a daily lesson plan typically used by P.E. teachers. Some teachers write this information in planning books; others use three-ring binders, and some use 5 x 8 cards. In time teachers typically write less as they develop the schemata of various sequences of lessons. This economy comes from teaching 10 or 20 classes a week on the same topic. This isn't meant to suggest, however, that experienced teachers don't plan. They do. The format they use is different, however.

SUMMARY

The interesting problem faced by physical education teachers is that there just isn't enough time to do all that we would like to do for children. In fact, many teachers who see their children only once or twice a week face a real dilemma—"What can I effectively teach in such a small amount of time?" This assumes, of course, that a teacher is truly focusing on children actually learning important concepts and skills.

If a teacher's program consists of simply teaching some fun games, neat stunts, and dances that children enjoy, then planning is far less difficult. In that case it is simply a matter of choosing activities with little thought to progression and sequencing. In fact, planning for this type of teaching can be done relatively quickly at the beginning of the year.

When a teacher is truly focusing on what and whether the children are learning, however, planning is more involved. Lessons are carefully designed and sequenced to be certain they provide maximum opportunities for children to learn. Each lesson is based on the teacher's observations and reflections from previous lessons. What does this class need? Have they learned to change directions quickly yet? Are they placing their hands in the appropriate position? Do they understand the difference between symmetrical and asymmetrical shapes? How is Mr. Olinger's third-grade class different from Mrs. King's third-grade class?

When teachers are truly focusing on helping children to learn, planning is crucial. Without it, lessons become haphazard and random. The children have fun, but they don't learn as a result of a sequential progression that the teacher designs to help them learn. Without effective planning, a program can easily become simply a fun time for children, unfortunately, with little long-term benefit to the children.

QUESTIONS FOR REFLECTION

1. What are the consequences of teachers not planning? Can you think of any specific examples from your past that may have been a consequence of either limited or superior planning?
2. Why do you think teachers tend to avoid planning? Do you think it has any connection to the universal distaste for homework?
3. In this chapter I used two analogies to planning: consulting maps before taking a trip and the music (notes) followed by a symphony orchestra. Create your own analogy to express the relationship between planning and teaching.
4. Think about your elementary school. What contextual factors would a teacher have to consider in planning at that school? (For example, I recall that my elementary school had no grass, only blacktop.)
5. All teachers, beginning through advanced, have a tendency to describe their goals and objectives in general terms. Why do you think this is true?
6. The objectives for each lesson are theoretically tied to a yearly plan, which is based on a number of exit goals. Describe one exit goal you think is important for children to have accomplished by the time they leave elementary school. How would this goal be reflected differently in each yearly plan? In actual lesson plans?
7. The final section in the chapter describes features that many teachers incorporate into their lesson plans. Why do you think I didn't provide a single guide for you to follow? Figures 2.2 and 2.3 will provide some interesting insights into your reflection.
8. If you are a beginning teacher, reflect on the features typically contained in lesson plans and develop a format that you think will be helpful. If you are an experienced teacher, consider the way you plan now. Which features do you typically include and exclude? Why?

REFERENCES

Faucette, N., & Hillidge, S.B. (1989). Research findings—PE specialists and classroom teachers. *Journal of Physical Education, Recreation and Dance*, **60**(7), 51-54.

Franck, M., Graham, G., Lawson, H., Loughrey, T., Ritson, R., Sanborn, M., & Seefeldt, V. (1991). *Physical education outcomes: A project of the National Association for Sport and Physical Education*. Reston, VA: National Association for Sport and Physical Education.

Graham, G., Hopple, C., Manross, M., & Sitzman, T. (in press). Novice and expert children's physical education teachers: Insights into their situational decision-making. *Journal of Teaching in Physical Education*.

Housner, L., & Griffey, D. (1985). Teacher cognition: Differences in planning and interactive decision making between experienced and inexperienced teachers. *Research Quarterly for Exercise and Sport*, **56**, 45-53.

Kelly, L.E. (1988). Curriculum design model. *Journal of Physical Education, Recreation and Dance*, **59**(6), 26-32.

Kelly, L.E. (1989). Instructional time: The overlooked factor in PE curriculum development. *Journal of Physical Education, Recreation and Dance*, **60**(6), 29-32.

Lambert, L.T. (1989). Making the strange familiar: Theory and practice in physical education. *Journal of Physical Education, Recreation and Dance*, **60**(2), 51-55.

Livingston, C., & Borko, H. (1989). Expert-novice differences in teaching: A cognitive analysis and implications for teacher education. *Journal of Teacher Education*, **40**(4), 36-42.

Marks, M. (1988). A ticket out the door. *Strategies*, **2**(2), 17, 27.

Placek, J. (1984). A multicase study of teacher planning in physical education. *Journal of Teaching in Physical Education*, **4**, 39-49.

Schmidt, R.A. (1991). *Motor learning and performance*. Champaign, IL: Human Kinctics.

Shulman, L.S. (1987). Knowledge and teaching: Foundations of the new reform. *Harvard Educational Review*, **57**, 1-22.

Chapter 3

Creating an Atmosphere for Learning

How do you prefer to teach? Are you loud and excitable? Or do you prefer an atmosphere that is relatively quiet and calm? Do you stop the children by blowing a whistle, hollering, giving a hand signal, or beating on a drum? Are you loud when you talk to the children, or do you talk in a conversational tone? What are the characteristics of a pleasant physical education atmosphere that also encourages children to become involved in activity?

Obviously there is no single definition of a "pleasant atmosphere." We all have our preferred approaches to working with children in a physical education setting. The significance of these questions, however, is that they are decisions made by the teacher, not the children. As teachers we decide the characteristics of the environment for which we have control—and then we teach the children to function within that environment.

The atmosphere we create is an important one. After all, this is our job! We spend many hours in schools, and it makes sense to make the atmosphere as pleasant as we possibly can—given the obvious limitations. An elementary school gymnasium or multi-purpose room is not a luxury hotel. There are a number of things teachers do, however, to build a pleasant atmosphere. The purpose of this chapter is to describe ways that teachers go about creating the environment for lessons that both the physical education teacher and the children enjoy.

After reading and understanding this chapter, the teacher will be able to

- analyze the concept of teacher expectancy and its importance in creating a pleasant atmosphere in physical education;
- describe the various management protocols that teachers develop with the children;

- relate the important difference between explaining and teaching management protocols; and
- describe the characteristics of teachers who create pleasant environments in physical education.

Why place the chapter on creating the learning environment so early in the book? Most books that devote a chapter or section to this topic place it at the end or near the middle but not at the beginning. Actually, I did this for two reasons.

The first reason is that, especially for beginning teachers, the question "Will I be able to 'control' the children?" is very important. It's a genuine concern that deserves some attention. There's an honest fear that the children may run wild and never stop and listen—hardly a pleasant atmosphere in which to work every day. So why put off a discussion of how to achieve order in physical education classes when it is uppermost in the minds of many novice teachers?

The second reason is that teachers who design and implement effective learning environments are successful because they begin to develop an environment for learning at the beginning of school. In fact, they start the process on the first day of the school year (Carter & Doyle, 1989; Fink & Siedentop, 1989). Recognizing this fact, it seemed logical, albeit unorthodox, to place this chapter near the start of the book—partly because it deals with frequently asked questions whose solutions require early and carefully planned and implemented strategies.

TEACHER EXPECTANCY

The teacher designs and then builds the atmosphere for his classes. Teachers, sometimes in conjunction with the children, decide how they want their classes to operate. Beginning teachers often find this attitude, known as *teacher expectancy*, difficult to develop (Martinek, 1983). There is a feeling that children "are a certain way" and that we have to adjust to the children. Not true. Children can learn to stop, for example, when they see the teacher raise her hand or when they hear a hand clap. The type of signal doesn't really matter (as long as it can be heard or seen); what matters is that the children learn to understand and follow the directions of the teacher. The teacher expects certain things of

the children—for example, not to push and shove—and then insists that children follow that rule in physical education class. Interestingly, the difficult part for many teachers is to learn to actually *expect* children to operate within the framework that the teacher wants to establish for the gymnasium or playground. Perhaps an example will help illustrate this point.

In church we expect people to behave a certain way. There are times when it's unacceptable to speak out loud. Many churches also have dress codes. We teach our children these "protocols" for operating in church as soon as we can. Gradually they learn to function in concert with the protocols of the church we attend. It doesn't happen simply because we tell them not to talk in church, for example. We have to work at it together—often over a period of weeks or even months.

In many ways the same is true in physical education classes. The protocols are obviously different, but the process of learning them also takes time and practice. And just as parents insist that their children learn how to behave in church, the effective physical education teacher insists that his children behave in physical education. The challenge for the physical education teacher, however, is to simultaneously teach 25 or 30 children the protocols of behavior.

For most teachers, I suspect, this is one of the least enjoyable parts of teaching. There's not much satisfaction in teaching children how to put away equipment or choose a partner. Consequently, there is a temptation to devote less time to these protocols than may be necessary. Nevertheless, it's important, if we are going to be satisfied in our teaching, that the children learn the customs of our gymnasium or playground. And when they do, our teaching lives are far more enjoyable.

DETERMINING THE MANAGEMENT PROTOCOLS FOR YOUR CLASSES

Technically, the word *protocol* refers to established forms or courtesies that have been predetermined and used, for example, in official dealing among heads of state. Most children's physical education classes that I see and teach are far from ceremonial or official, however. Nevertheless, there are predetermined ways we want the children to function in our classes. There are also courtesies we want the children to extend to us and to one another. These are really protocols or routines that we expect our children to be guided by in our classes. The summary of these protocols is expressed in the rules we post on the gym wall. Typically we have protocols for the following aspects of our classes: entering and leaving the playground or gym; starting and stopping at a signal from the teacher; gathering up equipment when the stop signal is given; getting out and putting away equipment; and selecting partners, teams, and groups.

Entering and Leaving the Playground or Gym

Whenever possible it's preferable to have the classroom teacher bring the children to physical education. This allows the P.E. teacher to teach longer classes—when we have only a few minutes, every one is important (chapter 2). In the beginning of the year, however, many teachers prefer to go to the room and talk with the children about the protocols for entering and leaving the gym as well as the signals for stopping and starting. (I prefer the classroom teacher to be present when I do this so that she understands the routine.)

Most principals insist that the children walk to and from physical education in quiet,

orderly formations—typically in lines. If the classroom teacher brings the children, this is his responsibility. In those schools in which it is the P.E. teacher's responsibility to bring the children from the classroom, it is important to practice the protocol for walking to and from physical education. Because children are often excited about our classes, this can be somewhat problematic because they are in a hurry to get to us and eager to begin.

What seems to work best is to have children actually practice moving from the classroom to the playground—quietly and orderly. In fact, this is an important part of the first day's lesson. Once children get to the playground, they are expected to do one of several things. For example, some teachers have the children line up in squads; some have them sit quietly on a circle or line; some write directions on a chalkboard or posterboard that tell the children what to do that day. Regardless of the way we begin the class, that routine needs to be practiced. In a few cases this means that the children will have to return to their classroom—because they ran noisily through the hallways—so that they can practice the routine again. The important point for the children to realize is that this is a protocol; it's the routine used at that school for getting to and from the gym. It's not just a nice idea; it's a routine to be learned (even if it means returning to the room several times) and then followed.

Typically the same routine is to be followed when the children leave the playground to return to the classroom. This, too, needs to be

FIND A ROPE AND BEGIN JUMPING

practiced. When it isn't, the classroom teacher spends 10 or 15 minutes trying to calm things down before the children are ready to function productively.

HOW CHILDREN DEFINE WALKING

Children have interesting definitions of "walking." For many it means that as long as you don't bend your knees it's acceptable to travel as fast as you can and have it still be considered walking. We can see those children—stiff upper bodies, head erect, wildly swinging arms, rushing to be first—who, when reprimanded, reply in unison, "We were walking!" Perhaps we shouldn't define the mode of traveling, but rather the speed. If you get to the gym in 45 seconds or less, you will be given a speeding ticket. The penalty is to return to the classroom and try again.

Starting and Stopping Signals

Once the children have entered the gym according to our protocol, we need to have a stopping and starting signal. The type of signal we use doesn't really matter as long as the children can hear or see it. Most teachers use their voices inside. Some use a hand clap or a beat on the drum. A few teachers use a whistle, but, especially inside, many teachers prefer to create more of a pleasant, business-like atmosphere as opposed to a loud and rowdy recess environment. For this reason the voice or hand clap seems to be preferred because it is less harsh and piercing than a whistle, and the children need to keep their talking to a level that permits the teacher to be heard.

As with entering and leaving the gym, this, too, needs to be practiced. It's reasonable to expect all of the children to be stopped 2 or 3 seconds after the signal is given. And the signal is given once, not four or five times.

The starting signal most teachers use is "Go." This is important because children typically don't want to stop and listen for long; once they think they understand the teacher's directions, they want to begin immediately. Often, however, the teacher has another item or two to add; thus, it's important that the children learn to wait until the teacher is finished talking before they start. As with the stop signal, this needs to be practiced. When the children start before the

signal, they are called back and reminded to wait for the "go" signal. To keep the children's attention, some teachers vary the word that means "go" to encourage the children to listen carefully (e.g., "hopscotch," "Friday," "Nintendo").

TEACHING STOPPING AND STARTING

There are a number of activities that are excellent for helping children learn to listen while they move. "Numbers" is one example. The children are asked to walk, hop, or skip in a defined area. When the teacher calls out a number, the children quickly form groups totaling that number. For example, four children group up when the teacher says "four." The key is for the teacher to say, rather than shout, the number so that the children have to listen carefully. A variation of this game is "Colors." The teacher calls out different colors that are on the floor or pavement. As quickly as they can, the children hop or skip to that color. Another version is "Body Parts." When the teacher calls out various body parts, the children touch those parts to the ground or floor (e.g., hands and feet, seat, back, elbows and knees).

Typically, the words *stop* or *freeze* signal the class to stop moving and be silent. Sometimes a drum is necessary, for example, when the children are dribbling balls and it is hard to hear the teacher over the noise made by the balls hitting the floor. Some teachers also use a whistle when they're outside.

Once the stop signal has been given, most teachers insist that the children listen, without talking, to the teacher and to other children that may be responding to a question by the teacher, for example. This should be practiced. Probably the most frequently used approach to practicing listening is for the teacher to start over if she thinks the children are inattentive and to repeat the comments. Another tactic that helps the children listen more effectively is for the teacher to practice talking as briefly as possible without repeating comments. This takes time to learn, but it does help the children listen more intently. When a teacher falls into the trap of repeating comments two or three times, it's no wonder the children don't bother to listen to every word. My experience suggests that teachers probably talk far more than is necessary for the children to understand directions, especially when a demonstration accompanies the instructions.

WHAT DO CHILDREN HEAR?

In recent years an increasing number of children are in our schools who do not speak English as their native language. As an observer I am always fascinated to see how quickly they are able to follow the teacher's directions even though they were unable to understand what the teacher said. I also see this with children who talk the entire time the teacher is talking, yet are able to begin a task quickly. Obviously these children have learned to rely on observing their peers and not on listening to the teacher talk.

Equipment

Often the instructions are related to the equipment that is to be used in the lesson. There are typically three protocols to be established in relation to the equipment: how to get it out, what to do with it when the teacher is talking, and how to put it away.

Getting the Equipment

As always, the children can't wait to get started, so all 25 want to rush up and get their equipment so they can begin. Teachers typically use two approaches to distribute equipment quickly and efficiently. One—the quicker way—is to spread equipment throughout the area in small piles. This prevents the overcrowding that results when everyone in the class tries to get a ball from the same basket at the same time.

Another approach is to call on a few of the children at a time to get their equipment. Some teachers will tap children on the shoulder as a signal to get their equipment. Sometimes teachers will call out birth months; color of shirts, hair, or eyes; or type of shoes to signal different groups to get their equipment.

Once the children get the equipment, they need to know what to do with it. Some teachers ask the children to get equipment and then hold on to it. Many teachers find it more effective to provide a task for the children to begin working on once they get their equipment (e.g., "After you get your hoop, find a self-space and warm up by jumping over your hoop."). I find it seems particularly difficult for children to stand still and hold a ball; it's as if they were given a chocolate ice cream cone and asked to hold on to it without taking even a single lick until everyone in the class has a cone.

I WANT THE BLUE ONE . . .

Distributing equipment is easier when types and colors of equipment are either identical or very different. When all of the balls but two are yellow, some children will always compete to get one of the two different colored balls. The same is true for ropes, hoops, and so on. For this reason many teachers try to purchase equipment of either the same color or a variety of colors. To an adult this seems like a trivial matter, but it's not to children.

Holding on to Equipment

The difficulty of holding a ball without playing with it is one of the reasons that many teachers have a protocol as to what needs to be done with equipment after the stop signal is given. Some teachers require the children to place the ball immediately on the ground. Others require them to hold the ball next to their belly button. When teachers fail to teach this protocol to children, it is inevitable that the teachers will constantly be saying, "Remember not to play with the ball when I'm talking."

KEEPING THE AIR IN BALLS

I've always thought that it would make sense for children to sit on their ball when the teacher is talking. Sitting on the ball is comfortable and it keeps the ball out of the way. Early on, however, I was taught that sitting on a ball causes it to lose air quickly. Consequently, I have always taught my classes not to sit on a ball. I wonder, however, whether balls really lose air more quickly when they are sat on. I wonder, too, if it is excessively harmful for volleyballs to be dribbled or kicked.

I have learned that pulling a patch from a ball is fascinating to children; unfortunately, patch pulling results in flat balls. So, too, does plucking foam balls. These are two more good reasons for requiring children to put a ball down or hold it a certain way when instructions are given—and for making the instructions as brief as possible.

Putting Equipment Away

Children can't wait to get the equipment, and once they get it, they don't want to put it away. This, too, needs to be practiced.

Some teachers use the same technique as for getting equipment—it's done in groups or individually. Others prefer to have the children simultaneously replace the equipment where they got it. One of the greatest temptations, of course, is to throw a ball from 30 feet away and try to land it in the cart. This is why the technique of placing, not throwing, equipment is taught. One technique that some teachers use is to ask one or two children to show the remainder of the class how the equipment is to be placed, not thrown, when putting it away. As with the other protocols discussed in this section, this protocol is taught—and practiced until learned—at the beginning of the school year.

Selecting Partners, Teams, and Groups

Throughout the year we are constantly asking children to work with a partner or in a group. This is an especially important time to be careful not to damage a child's self-concept. In the old days we used to assign captains to pick teams. Today there are far too many adults who suffered through the emotional pain of being picked last class after class and who continue to be anti-physical education, largely as a result of the embarrassment of repeatedly being chosen last.

Fortunately we know better today. One of the techniques that many teachers use is simply to ask children to find a partner or form a group of five, for example. The advantage of this approach is that it is relatively quick, and the children tend to select partners or groups of about the same ability level. The game of "Numbers" can also be used a a quick way to form groups. There are times when the teacher will want to form the groups or teams himself to accomplish a specific purpose.

BOYS DO THIS, GIRLS DO THAT

Some teachers use gender as a way to group children—"the boys here, the girls there." This tends to perpetuate the boy-girl stereotype emphasizing differences rather than similarities. It also seems to discourage the idea of boys and girls cooperating and working together, especially in the upper grades. For this reason many teachers discourage grouping children by gender. It has always struck me as interesting that fifth-grade boys and girls, for example, will work together on a project in the classroom but somehow expect not to work together on the playground. I hope that, in a few years, grouping by gender will be as rare as captains picking teams.

There are myriad ways to organize children into groups. The protocol that the children need to practice is how to do this quickly and without hurting the feelings of others. Many teachers emphasize that it's not OK to say "no" to classmates when they ask you to be their partner or in their group. As with every protocol, however, there are exceptions. I am reminded of the few children we teach who, for whatever reason, are very difficult to work with as partners or in a group. For these children, exceptions need to be made because it is unfair for them to continually ask the same child to be their partner. This is the art of teaching: How do we take care of the children's feelings and still remain fair to all children involved?

Other Protocols

These are some of the protocols that children's physical education teachers regularly use in their programs. It goes without saying that there are others that I haven't discussed—as well as variations in the way teachers use the ones I have described. What to do during fire drills, what to do if a child is hurt, how to carry gymnastic mats, and how to put away the parachute are examples of other protocols that the effective teacher will explain and teach to the children. In this sense the behavior protocols are no different from so many other aspects of the teaching process; they depend on the teacher and the school situation.

SHUFFLING THE DECK

Lambdin (1989) has developed a variety of ways to organize and group children by using a deck of playing cards. As they enter the gym, the children are each given a card and asked to memorize it. Then, to form partners, she asks them to find a partner who

- has the same color and number;
- has the same number;
- has the same color;
- has the same suit;
- has the same suit and pairs 1 and 2, 3 and 4, 5 and 6; or
- has an even number if their number is even, odd if their number is odd.

In addition, she has devised ways to organize a class into two or four groups based on the cards the students were given at the beginning of class.

Four groups:	Two groups:
Clubs, spades, diamonds, hearts	Reds and blacks
Even black, odd black, even red, odd red	Odd and even numbers
Black 1-3, red 1-3, black 4-6, red 4-6	Clubs & hearts and diamonds & spades
	Ace to 3 and 4 to 6

Note. Reprinted by permission from Lambdin, 1989.

VIDEOTAPE ANALYSIS

Watch one of the taped lessons you made before starting this book (or one from the companion videotape you purchased along with the book). Pay special attention to the protocols the children have learned. Focus on

- how they enter the gym or playground;
- how quickly they stop on the teacher's signal;
- whether they wait to begin activity until the teacher gives a start signal; and
- how efficiently they get out the equipment and put it away.

After viewing the videotape, make some judgments about the management protocols the children have learned—those that were efficient and those that needed improving to make the atmosphere even more pleasant and functional.

Decision to Practice Protocols

One of the most important decisions a teacher makes, once the protocols have been thought through, is to actually spend time practicing them. This is especially difficult in children's physical education because the time is so limited, yet this is exactly why the protocols need to be rehearsed—to save time. When protocols aren't learned, an inordinate amount of time is wasted over the course of a year.

The research on teaching physical education is very clear on this topic; unfortunately, children in physical education classes spend more time listening, managing, and waiting than they do in purposeful physical activity. In fact, it's common for children to spend less than one third of a class moving. When children learn the behavior protocols at the beginning, more time can be devoted to the content of physical education the rest of the year.

TEACHING THE BEHAVIOR PROTOCOLS

Deciding on the management protocols to use in one's classes is a relatively easy task. The challenging part is to teach these protocols to the children.

As with any teaching process, there is no single approach that works for all teachers. There are certain attributes that teachers who create pleasant atmospheres seem to display as they work on building the environment for the children. Teachers who effectively teach the behavior protocols often display two characteristics. They are firm but warm while displaying a high degree of "critical demandingness." They also post their rules for children to see and often discuss the rules with the children so that the children feel a certain degree of "ownership."

Firm But Warm

At one time we thought successful teachers threatened children, that is, that they scared them into being good. Today we know better (Doyle, 1986; Fernandez-Balboa, 1990; Kounin, 1970). Successful teachers exhibit a certain degree of firmness; they mean what they say. At the same time, however, they are warm and caring toward the children. They don't want to frighten the children, but they want the children to know they mean business. Children quickly learn to distinguish when a teacher means what he says and when he doesn't. Successful teachers mean what they say, and they exhibit it by not allowing the children to get away with not following the protocols. They don't get excited or hysterical or threaten children, however. In calm, reassuring, firm ways they simply communicate the message that things are going to be done a certain way and that not much else is going to happen until the protocols are learned. This is one of those skills used by effective teachers that is difficult to put into words, yet if we watched 10 teachers we would quickly be able to identify those teachers who were firm but warm.

Critical Demandingness

We would also be able to quickly recognize critical demandingness when we saw it. In many ways these two teaching skills overlap, yet they are different. The significant aspect of this skill is that the teachers have a built-in knowledge of how they expect the children to follow the protocols, and they insist that the protocols be followed. In other words, they know how they want the children to enter the gym. When the children enter that way, the lesson proceeds as planned. When the children don't follow the protocol for entering the gym, the teacher doesn't accept their behavior. She insists (demands) that they go back and enter the gym according to the way they had practiced earlier.

This is especially difficult because, typically, we, as teachers, want to get on with the lesson we have planned. It's hard for us to spend the time having the children reenter the gym. In the long run, however, teachers who are critically demanding spend less time on these distracting events than do those who don't spend the time at the beginning of the year. One of the advantages for the children who have a critically demanding teacher is that they know exactly what to expect. The teacher is consistent, day after day.

Rules—Clear, Positive, Posted

Posted rules also help with consistency. Rules are essentially brief reminders of the behavior protocols. Most teachers list five or six rules, state them in positive ways, and post them prominently. Simply writing and posting them, however, is no guarantee they will be followed. They must be practiced.

One reason for posting the rules, in addition to serving as reminders, is their benefit for children new to the school. This allows the teacher to briefly review the behavior protocols with these children. In recent years, with the easy availability of videotapes, some

teachers are beginning to videotape classes of children following the various behavior protocols which demonstrate the rules. This videotape can then be made available to new students for viewing so that they can understand exactly what is expected of them in physical education class.

In certain parts of the United States, where teachers are continually threatened by malpractice lawsuits, it is suggested that teachers make a practice of making a videotape illustrating the behavior protocols. They should then ensure that every new child views the videotape before participating in physical education. In extreme instances teachers may actually quiz children (written or oral) or ask them to sign a copy of the rules indicating that they have viewed the videotape.

While these suggestions may seem extreme to some, others who have been involved in malpractice lawsuits will quickly recognize the potential benefit to be derived from this procedure. This is especially important for those who teach in schools that have high rates of student turnover. And, in fact, this is an effective approach for teaching new children the protocols of behavior that will save time in the long run.

Developing Ownership

We know that the rules (behavior protocols) will be followed more closely when the children understand why they are necessary and

when the children develop a certain sense of ownership for them. For this reason many teachers, as part of actually practicing the rules, include discussions with the children to help them understand the importance of rules. It's interesting to make a videotape of children who are intentionally *not* following the protocols in order to illustrate what happens when the rules are not followed. (You will have no problem recruiting a class who would be thrilled to help you make a videotape demonstrating all of the ways to not behave in the gym!) The videotape then becomes an excellent resource for involving children in discussions about why it's important to have and follow selected management protocols.

In addition to sharing the rules with the children, it's a good practice also to provide the principal and classroom teachers with a copy of the rules. This is especially true in schools that do not have a unified discipline plan (e.g., assertive discipline [chapter 4]). In some schools it may also be worthwhile to share the rules with parents, especially when the teacher plans on sending notes to the parents of children who do not follow the established behavior protocols. This will depend, however, on such factors as the philosophy of the school and the policies of the principal and the board of education.

SUMMARY

Essentially, teachers who develop orderly learning environments with a minimum of disruptions to the system of work perform three different functions (Carter & Doyle, 1989):

1. They *design* the system in advance by thinking about how they want the children to function in physical education; at the same time they envision the various management procedures that will be necessary to develop and maintain a smooth, flowing program of action.
2. They *communicate* to the children the various protocols that combine to form a management system. They do this as they would teach any topic in physical education, that is, they explain it, furnish examples, set up tasks for the children to practice the protocols, and provide feedback about how well the children are progressing. They begin this process on the first day of school.
3. They *monitor* the children to be certain that they are following the protocols within reasonable limits. This reduces the need for frequent reprimands because, by noticing the early signs of potential disruption, crises can be avoided.

QUESTIONS FOR REFLECTION

1. Think of yourself teaching children. What are the characteristics of a pleasant teaching environment that are important to you? Can you explain why?
2. Why is teacher expectancy such an important aspect of establishing a pleasant learning environment?
3. Why do you think the phrase *management protocols* was used rather than a term such as *rules* or *procedures*?
4. When you think of yourself teaching, which of the protocols is the easiest for you to develop? The hardest? Do you know why?
5. Why is the distinction made between "explaining" the management protocols and "teaching" them?
6. Reflect on teachers you have had in the past. Can you remember teachers who were firm but warm or who were critically demanding? Do you think these are natural attributes, or can they be gradually learned?

REFERENCES

Carter, K., & Doyle, W. (1989). Classroom research as a resource for the graduate preparation of teachers. In E. Woolfolk (Ed.), *Research perspectives on the graduate preparation of teachers* (pp. 51-68). Englewood Cliffs, NJ: Prentice Hall.

Doyle, W. (1986). Classroom organization and management. In M.C. Wittrock (Ed.), *Handbook of research on teaching* (3rd ed.) (pp. 392-431). New York: Macmillan.

Fernandez-Balboa, J.-M. (1990). Helping novice teachers handle discipline problems. *Journal of Physical Education, Recreation and Dance*, **67**(2), 50-54.

Fink, J., & Siedentop, D. (1989). The development of routines, rules, and expectations at the start of the school year. The Effective Elementary Specialist Study [Monograph]. *Journal of Teaching in Physical Education*, **8**(3), 198-212.

Kounin, J.S. (1970). *Discipline and group management in classrooms*. New York: Holt, Rinehart & Winston.

Lambdin, D. (1989). Shuffling the deck: A flexible system of classroom organization. *Journal of Physical Education, Recreation and Dance*, **60**(3), 25-28.

Martinek, T. (1983). Creating Golem and Goleta effects during physical education instruction: A social psychological perspective. In T. Templin & J. Olson (Eds.), *Teaching in physical education* (pp. 59-70). Champaign, IL: Human Kinetics.

Chapter 4

Minimizing Off-Task Behavior and Discipline Problems

Wouldn't it be great if we could just teach? No children misbehaving, no children off-task, every child eager to listen and learn. It would be, but that's a dream. Even teachers who develop the management protocols described in the previous chapter still have children who misbehave. The reality of teaching is that there are always going to be a few children who, for whatever reason, are going to march to the beat of a different drummer. The purpose of this chapter is to describe and analyze some of the ways teachers prevent off-task behavior.

As part of the introduction to this chapter, I want to emphasize that the techniques described here are typically necessary for only a few children in a class. Most children try to please the teacher, follow the rules, and work hard at the tasks. This assumes, of course, that the tasks are appropriate for the skill level of the children and are modified at appropriate times in the lesson. Activities or tasks that are too easy, too hard, or too protracted invite off-task behavior by the children.

My experience suggests that, when a class or child that is typically well behaved is off-task, it is often my teaching, not the class or child, that needs to be modified. There are a few children, however, who have a difficult time staying on-task. As we well know, the tendency of these children toward misbehavior is often rooted in situations outside the school; nevertheless, we have the responsibility and the challenge of working with them in our classes.

After reading and understanding this chapter, the teacher will be able to

- describe strategies that teachers use to minimize off-task behavior;
- describe the general concepts of two popular discipline systems used in schools today: Canter's Assertive Discipline and Hellison's Levels of Affective Development;
- analyze the role of parents, principals, and classroom teachers in the effective use of a discipline system; and
- describe the feelings and strategies of teachers during discipline confrontations.

STRATEGIES FOR MINIMIZING OFF-TASK BEHAVIOR

Even those teachers who effectively teach the behavior protocols described in chapter 3 are still going to have incidences of off-task behavior. Therefore, a teacher needs strategies that can minimize the misbehavior of children. Unfortunately, they are just strategies, not guarantees. Some of them succeed with some children some of the time. I wish I knew foolproof strategies that would be successful for all teachers all of the time, but I don't; no one does. Good teachers seem to have a repertoire of strategies which they use, sometimes consciously and sometimes without really thinking about them. They include back-to-the-wall, proximity control, with-it-ness, selective ignoring, overlapping, learning names, and positive pinpointing.

Back-to-the-Wall

One of the simplest strategies is referred to as "back-to-the-wall." By standing on the outside of the boundaries (the wall in the gym or the edge of the playground), a teacher can better see what is going on in a class. When a teacher stands in the middle of a class, automatically about 50 percent of the children will be out of his sight; this means that he may not be able to see the off-task behavior until it has gone on for some time.

The ability to detect off-task behavior as soon as it begins appears to be a characteristic of successful teachers. Immediate detection seems to prevent it from escalating. When it persists for several minutes, however, there is the potential for several children to become involved. Consequently, a relatively minor incident can escalate into a major incident, for example, as one child tries to wrestle a ball away from another child. This is known as the "ripple effect" (Kounin, 1970). When a teacher sees the beginning of such an incident, he can quickly prevent it from escalating because his *targeting* and *timing* are appropriate. He identifies the children correctly and quickly, thus preventing the behavior from developing into a crisis.

Proximity Control

One of the techniques the teacher may have used to prevent the ball-taking episode from escalating is *proximity control*—simply walking in the direction of the off-task child to let him know that she sees him and, by "the look," to let the child know he's off-task.

Veteran teachers know what I mean by "the look." It's a certain way a teacher looks at a child to say, "You're off-task; now get back to work." Obviously, however, a teacher needs to be close enough to the child so that he can see the teacher's expressions.

Sometimes the look isn't even necessary. Simply standing by a group of children on the verge of becoming off-task is often enough to let them know you see them and expect them to remain focused.

Proximity control implies that a teacher is moving around the gym. Early in our careers we have a tendency to stand in one place. Although standing in one place may be more comfortable for the teacher, it's not as effective. Virtually without exception, good teachers move about the classroom, the gym, and the playground.

With-It-Ness

The strategies of back-to-the-wall and proximity control provide the impression to the children that a teacher has *with-it-ness*—"having eyes in the back of your head" (Kounin,

1970). When he began his series of research studies on discipline, Kounin hypothesized that teachers who had classes that were well-behaved and consistently on-task would be those who threatened children and, in fact, scared them into behaving. He discovered, however, that this wasn't true. The teachers who had the fewest discipline problems communicated to their classes in a calm and reassuring way that they knew what was going on in their classes; they knew the tricks, and the students shouldn't even bother to try them. By keeping their backs to the walls and quickly targeting and timing children tending towards off-task behavior, they were effective in convincing the children that indeed they were "with it."

WITH IT AND WITHOUT IT

Remembering my days in elementary school, I can recall a sixth-grade teacher in particular who was "with it." She was friendly and warm, yet from the first day we could tell that she wasn't about to let us get away with anything. It was uncanny how she could identify children who were "off-task types" and, with looks and proximity control, keep them from misbehaving much that year. The next year, however, we had a teacher who was "without it"; the same class of children quickly escalated into a rather rowdy group who were continually yelled at and threatened, but without much success. I am sure we were difficult to teach that year. We were essentially the same children, but, among other things, the teachers possessed different degrees of with-it-ness.

Selective Ignoring

Yesterday I watched a first-grade lesson focused on round, narrow, wide, and twisted shapes. At times the children were making shapes in their own space; at other times they were traveling around the gym in their shapes. Whenever the opportunity was given to travel, one of the children, Bryan, ran. My reaction and that of my college students who were also observing was to immediately want to stop Bryan from running. The teacher ignored him, however. As we watched I realized that Bryan really wasn't bothering other children. In fact, they ignored him also. Another teacher may have considered it off-task; Bryan's teacher didn't. And, after watching the entire lesson, I think she was right. Bryan was one of those "high-energy" children—some would label him "hyperactive." He was doing what the teacher asked but at a fast speed. The teacher obviously saw him but chose to *selectively ignore* him. It was an effective strategy in that lesson.

Selective ignoring works with many classes because the children in the class have been helped to understand why a child looks or acts a certain way. The ability to understand children who behave in ways outside the "normal" pattern of behavior has been one of the major advantages of mainstreaming in schools. As I observe children work with children who have special needs, I am always warmed by their ability to understand the situation and their genuine willingness to help. This understanding doesn't happen automatically, however. Good teachers intentionally teach their classes to understand and work with these special children.

Overlapping

Overlapping is more of a teacher skill that is learned with practice than it is a strategy that can be easily learned such as back-to-the-wall. It's the ability to focus on several things that are happening simultaneously and still maintain an intended direction.

Teachers are continually required to deal simultaneously with several children or situations. For example, the teacher nods his head "yes" at the child who has to go to the bathroom; smiles at the child who says "watch me"; puts his hand on the shoulder of the child who wants to talk to the teacher, signaling "wait a second"; and continues to observe the whole class as he determines whether to change the task or continue with it for several more minutes. Locke's vignette in chapter 1 is another illustration of how teachers need to develop the ability to overlap.

Overlapping is a pedagogical skill learned through experience. It's a critical skill, however, because when we work with 30 or so children, there are times when we need to overlap unless we want the lesson to come to a complete stop. Obviously, by establishing routines and protocols we try to minimize the need for overlapping, yet there are times when it is needed.

Learning Names

Overlapping is a difficult technique to acquire; learning the names of the children is also difficult, but it is possible even for those teachers who have 600 or so children. One of the frustrating aspects of teaching is attempting to get the attention of a child whose name we don't know. As we try to find out, we often halt the flow of the lesson as several children volunteer her name and then stop moving to watch what we have to say to her. When we know a youngster's name, we can often speak it across the gym to let the child know that we see her and offer praise or remind her to get on-task.

Some teachers learn names with relative ease. For others it's a struggle. We have all heard of name-learning techniques (e.g., alliteration, using the name several times in conversation, having the children tell you their names when they enter and leave the gym, and taking photos of the children). Increasingly, classroom teachers are making name tags for the younger children who then wear them to P.E. until the teacher has time to learn their names. Learning names is even more challenging for those teachers who work in schools that have transient populations. Half of the children they teach in September will be gone in May and replaced with a new group of children. I wish I could suggest a magical, instant solution to this challenge of learning several hundred names, but I can't. I do know, however, that it really helps to know the children's names when we are trying to prevent off-task behavior.

Positive Pinpointing

When teachers identify one or more children and point them out to the rest of the class as modeling the desired behavior or skill, we call it *pinpointing*. This is a commonly employed strategy in elementary schools. "I like how Ron and Jan are standing quietly" is one example of positive pinpointing. My experience suggests that this technique is more effective with younger children who want to please the teacher. It can be overused, however. Some children seem to ignore it because the teacher is constantly talking about how well someone is doing something. As with any of these strategies, it can be effective depending upon the type of children, the way the strategy is used, and the frequency of use. Chapter 6 explains how pinpointing is used when teaching motor skills.

Many of these strategies or techniques seem to be innate characteristics of successful

teachers. They are never taught or even discussed, yet they're effectively used by many teachers. But not all teachers use them—especially in the beginning of their careers. It's common, for example, to see a beginning teacher anchored in the same location for a lesson or fail to see a child misbehave because the teacher's back is turned to the child. As with so many of the skills discussed in this book, it's easy to write about them—far more challenging to actually use them when teaching. I hope, however, that both beginning and experienced teachers will reflect on the subtle orchestration of teaching skills and strategies and their value for minimizing off-task behavior. No matter how well we use these strategies, however, some children will simply refuse to do what we ask. When that happens they're not off-task; they are a discipline problem.

DISCIPLINE PROBLEMS

All teachers have students with discipline problems. Some of us minimize the problems, however. What strategies do successful teachers use to minimize discipline problems?

To begin with, they spend the first few days of the school year establishing the routines and teaching the management protocols described in chapter 3; they insist that the children learn these routines. They also use many of the strategies previously mentioned for minimizing off-task behavior.

DISCIPLINE SYSTEMS

In recent years systems designed to minimize misbehavior have become popular. Canter's Assertive Discipline and Hellison's Levels of Affective Development represent two of these systems. These systems are based on the assumption that some children will misbehave and that teachers need ways to deal effectively with misbehavior for the sake of the children who are misbehaving and also the other children in the class.

These systems are designed to be taught to the children from the beginning of the year and used as needed. This is in contrast to the teacher who hopes she doesn't have a child misbehave and, when she does, tries to invent a solution on the spot. As any teacher will attest, individuals who can continually invent ways to successfully deter off-task behavior amidst all the goings-on in a class can be found only in the movies and on television. The advantage of having a discipline system in place is that it provides teachers with a structure for making decisions related to discipline—rather than placing them in the unenviable situation of asking, "How can I get this child to stop doing that when I have 29 others who need my attention?"

Assertive Discipline

One of the most helpful trends in elementary schools across the United States has been the inception of schoolwide discipline plans.

Assertive discipline is one example of a popular, albeit controversial, schoolwide discipline plan (Canter, 1976; Hill, 1990; Sander, 1989). Art, music, and physical education teachers find plans such as this one especially helpful because these instructors teach so many classes in a day and for relatively short periods of time. When there is a schoolwide program in place, these teachers have a general idea of the expectations and understanding that the children have been taught regarding behavior in a class. When a school is able to agree on the rules for behavior and the consequences of misbehavior, it makes the atmosphere more consistent for the children and somewhat easier for the specialist teachers because, at least in theory, they will need to spend less time teaching the children their own discipline systems. The major concepts of Canter's Assertive Discipline Model are outlined in Figure 4.1.

1. All students can behave responsibly.
2. Firm control (not passive or hostile) is fair.
3. Reasonable expectations (rules, appropriate behavior, etc.) should be clearly communicated.
4. Teachers should expect appropriate behavior from students and receive administrative and parental support to stimulate it.
5. Appropriate behavior should be reinforced while inappropriate behavior should be met with logical consequences.
6. Logical consequences for not meeting expectations should be clearly communicated.
7. Consequences should be consistently reinforced without bias.
8. All verbal and nonverbal communication to students should be firm with definite teacher-student eye contact.
9. Teachers should mentally practice expectations and consequences for consistent use with students.

Figure 4.1 Canter's Assertive Discipline Model: major concepts. (Reprinted by permission from Sander, 1989.)

I realize that simply adopting a schoolwide discipline plan doesn't necessarily mean that it will be uniformly enforced. Critical demandingness and teacher expectancy (chapter 3) vary from one teacher to another as do the children in a class. The concept of schoolwide discipline heightens the chances that teachers in a school will be more consistent with their rules and consequences, thereby providing a more secure environment for the children because they know what to expect from different teachers.

In addition to agreeing on how the children are expected to function throughout the school, there is also agreement on the consequences for misbehavior. Figure 4.2 provides an example of the consequences that are part of an assertive discipline system (Hill, 1990).

1st time a child breaks a rule—child is warned
2nd time a child breaks a rule—5-minute time-out
3rd time a child breaks a rule—10-minute time-out
4th time a child breaks a rule—teacher calls parents
5th time a child breaks a rule—child is sent to principal

Good behavior all week earns, for example, 10 minutes of "free choice" time or a tangible reward (e.g., smiley-face sticker).

Figure 4.2   Consequences for misbehavior.

In some schools the P.E. teacher will implement his own system of discipline. In other schools, where a schoolwide discipline system is in place, the P.E. teacher will provide a record of checks for misbehavior to the classroom teacher who then adds them to her checks for the week. The use of bonus or free time on Friday is widespread, although some teachers, particularly with classes that tend toward misbehavior, use a daily plan rather than a weekly plan, allowing the children a few minutes at the end of a class to choose among several activities. Children who earned checks are not provided with the choice and are required to work on an activity chosen by the teacher.

Time-Out

Obviously not every teacher and every school uses a formalized discipline system. There are a number of other strategies teachers use to prevent misbehavior that may or may not be a part of an overall plan. *Time-out*, part of the assertive discipline system, is probably one of the most commonly used techniques in physical education outside of an actual discipline system. It is especially effective because of our subject matter: Some children may see time away from math or science as a bonus, but they enjoy physical activity, so time-out can be a rather potent technique.

Most teachers provide children with a warning first. (For example, "If you talk again when I am talking, you will be in time-out.") If it happens again, the child is told to take a time-out. Borrowing from the assertive discipline approach, time-out is most effective when a teacher assumes that some children will be in time-out at various times during the year. They "teach" time-out at the beginning of the year, almost as one of the management protocols so that the children clearly understand the process. Some teachers place time-out numbers on the walls. The misbehaving child is then told to take a time-out at Number 4, for example. This prevents several children from getting together to chat as often happens when there is no designated time-out location and two or more children are timed out at the same time.

Some teachers use a clock for a time-out. For example, the children are taught that they can return to the lesson after 2 minutes. Others provide paper and pencil on a clipboard and ask the children to write the reason they were placed in time-out (e.g., the rule they violated) before returning to the class. Some teachers require the children to come to them and verbally explain why they were timed out before returning to class.

If a child receives a second time-out in the same lesson, many teachers simply require them to remain out of the lesson for the rest of the class. While this may seem harsh, the fact is that often these are children who are so disruptive and demanding that the other children in the class, who are on-task and trying hard, are often shortchanged.

Desirable Rewards and Undesirable Consequences

When teachers choose to use a discipline system (such as assertive discipline) based on extrinsic rewards, it is important that the rewards be desirable for the children and the consequences, undesirable. Let me illustrate with several examples. Popcorn parties, in some instances, are desirable. I have been in schools, however, where the air is permeated with the smell of popping popcorn on Friday afternoons. My guess is that popcorn every Friday is not a very desirable reward—beyond perhaps the first few Fridays. It is almost taken for granted after a few weeks.

I have also observed teachers who use free time on Friday as a reward. While this is motivating for some children, it seems to be more of a reward for the teacher than for the children. The children are frequently threatened with a loss of free time, but somehow part of Friday's lesson is always free time. I also wonder how teachers can justify free time when time is so limited (chapter 2).

Obviously my observations tell me that popcorn and free time are not effective when they are the only rewards. Some teachers create their own awards. The "golden sneaker" award is a favorite—an old sneaker spray-painted gold and mounted on a board.

In creating an award, the key is to give it value through the presentation. Perhaps this

requires a bit of acting by the teacher, but for some it is effective. In addition to old sneakers, some teachers cleverly create awards from an old deflated ball, a rusty trophy, a whistle without its pea, a worn-out or knotted jump rope, or other equipment ready for discard. It's the idea of a reward, more than the value of the item, that is important. Some teachers use stickers as a way of saying "good job"; others use nontoxic stamp pads with messages such as "Right on" or "Super kid," which can be stamped on the back of a child's hand.

The undesirable consequence that is probably the most effective is loss of time in physical education. One of the most successful ways this is used is when children who have received misbehavior checks are not permitted to participate in an activity that the children really enjoy. Parachute activities are often used with the younger children, a group game with a cage ball for older children—with some of the children not allowed to participate in these activities because of their misbehavior during the day or week.

The important idea here is that, if a teacher is going to use a system of extrinsic rewards, the rewards must motivate the children if the system is going to succeed. If the rewards are ones that the children don't really care about, then the system will not be very successful.

Levels of Affective Development

Some teachers prefer intrinsic rewards for children (i.e., internally motivated rewards that are derived from working hard and getting along with others). The rationale for this type of system is the philosophy that children naturally want to do well and that extrinsic rewards are, over the long term, counterproductive. Teachers want children to participate in and enjoy physical activity for its own sake, not because they can earn an extrinsic reward for participating.

The most popular "intrinsic motivation" system in physical education was developed by Don Hellison (1985; Hellison & Templin, 1991; Masser, 1990). Essentially the model is designed to help children understand and practice self-responsibility. The motivating factor in his model is the innate desire of children to get along with others and take responsibility for their own behavior, rather than relying on a teacher to reward them for being good. As with other discipline plans, the model is clearly explained to the children, and they are encouraged to accept responsibility for their own behavior and to work with others. The model has five levels:

Level 0: Irresponsibility. At this level children are unable to take responsibility for their own behavior and typically interfere with others by belittling, intimidating, or verbally or physically abusing their classmates.

Level 1: Self-Control. This is a level of minimal involvement. Children will do what the teacher asks without interfering with others. This is done with minimal prompting from the teacher, although in most instances children at this level appear to be simply "going through the motions."

Level 2: Involvement. Children at this level become actively involved in the lessons. They try hard, avoid disturbing others, and genuinely take an interest in learning and improving.

Level 3: Self-Responsibility. This level is the point at which children are encouraged to begin to take responsibility for their own learning. This implies that they need not work under direct supervision from the teacher and that they are able to make decisions independently about what they need to learn and how they might go about learning it. At this level children are often asked to design their own games, sequences, or dances in small groups. When children are not at this level, however, the challenge of working in groups to create their own versions of an activity is typically doomed to failure as they spend more time arguing than moving.

Level 4: Caring. Children at this level go beyond simply working with others—they genuinely want to support and help others in the class. Children at this level are the ones who will volunteer to be a partner for a day with a child in the class who is unpopular, without being asked to do so by the teacher.

Figure 4.3 provides examples of the various levels (Masser, 1990). The different levels are exemplified at home, on the playground, in the classroom, and in physical education class.

Needless to say, this model requires more than simply explaining it to a class of children and then expecting that they will all want to work at Level 4. As with the assertive discipline system, the different levels are ex-

What's your level?

Level 0: Irresponsibility

Home: Blaming brothers or sisters for problems

Playground: Calling other students names

Classroom: Talking to friends when teacher is giving instructions

Physical education: Pushing and shoving others when selecting equipment

Level 1: Self-control

Home: Keeping self from hitting brother even though really mad at him

Playground: Standing and watching others play

Classroom: Waiting until appropriate time to talk with friends

Physical education: Practicing but not all the time

Level 2: Involvement

Home: Helping to clean up supper dishes

Playground: Playing with others

Classroom: Listening and doing class work

Physical education: Trying new things without complaining and saying I can't

Level 3: Self-responsibility

Home: Cleaning room without being asked

Playground: Returning equipment during recess

Classroom: Doing a science project not a part of any assignment

Physical education: Undertaking to learn a new skill
 through resources outside the physical education class

Level 4: Caring

Home: Helping take care of a pet or younger child

Playground: Asking others (not just friends) to join them in play

Classroom: Helping another student with a math problem

Physical education: Willingly working with anyone in the class

Figure 4.3   What's your level? (Reprinted by permission from Masser, 1990.)

plained to children at the beginning of the year and then used throughout as a way to encourage them to cooperate with the teacher and with other children. Some examples follow:

- Children are asked to select equipment. Teacher asks how Level 0 persons would get their equipment. Level 1? Level 2? Level 3? Level 4? The children are then asked to walk over and get their equipment, showing the teacher the level they think they can work at (Masser, 1990).
- When the children are learning a new skill, the teacher asks how children at the various levels might practice. They are then encouraged to work at the upper

levels and complimented for doing so as a group, or they are pinpointed (chapters 4 and 6) (Masser, 1990).

- A misbehaving student is asked to sit out for a few minutes (time-out) and is told why the misbehavior is Level 0. The child is invited to return to the class when he is able to tell the teacher what a Level 1 behavior, or higher, would be like—and assures the teacher that he can participate at that level (Masser, 1990).
- A student complains about another student. The student with the complaint is asked to identify the level the other student is functioning at and is then asked for ways to deal with others functioning at that level (Masser, 1990).

- Fourth- and fifth-grade children are asked to work in groups. Prior to beginning they discuss how children at Level 4 would work in a group setting. The focus is on how to work with children who might display Level 0 or 1 behavior (Masser, 1990).

CHARACTERISTICS OF EFFECTIVE DISCIPLINE SYSTEMS

Whether a teacher chooses to adopt or adapt a discipline system based on extrinsic motivation (assertive discipline) or intrinsic motivation (levels of affective development), it seems that there are three important characteristics that contribute to the ultimate success or failure of the discipline system: The discipline system is carefully explained to the children at the beginning of the year; the teacher consistently adheres to the criteria; and the principal, classroom teachers, and parents are supportive.

Developing a Clear Understanding

When a discipline plan works, one of the reasons it does is that the children clearly understand its operation and the reasons for its existence. Typically the system is introduced at the beginning of the year; it is explained thoroughly with examples and then practiced. At this time children are invited to ask questions and helped to understand why such a plan may be necessary. In either type of system, it helps to involve the children in the implementation of the plan so they truly understand why it is important and how it will be used.

In contrast, when a plan isn't set in place from the beginning, misbehavior is a "judgment call" for the teacher: What should I do? How severe should I make the penalty for misbehavior? Can I explain Level 0 in 30 seconds so the child will understand?

Think of the discipline system as similar to the system set up to deal with automobile parking violations. Decisions are made regarding the length of time one is permitted to park at a meter and the places where cars can and cannot be parked. Once these rules are established, consequences for noncompliance are determined.

- In the assertive discipline model, the children are helped to understand clearly the consequences for misbehaving (Figure 4.2).
- In the affective development model, the levels are explained along with examples (Figure 4.3).

When a discipline plan is set in place and explained at the beginning of the year, the children can understand exactly what to expect—the violations and the consequences are spelled out. Many believe this helps prevent misbehavior.

Consistency by the Teacher

A second characteristic of a successful discipline plan is consistency. Once the protocols and rules have been established, the teacher needs to use the same standards from one day to the next. This is easy to say, yet so hard to do. Nevertheless, it's important for the children to understand exactly what is expected.

There is a tendency in teaching toward *slippage*. We start off consistently enforcing the protocol, for example, that when the teacher says "stop," equipment is placed on the floor. After a few lessons, however, there is a tendency to slack up. One child doesn't put the ball down and we ignore it. Gradually, however, it becomes two or three, then six. Slippage has crept in. Effective teachers prevent slippage by their consistency. Pretty quickly children understand that the teacher is really going to enforce the rules as they were discussed at the beginning of the year.

Role of the Principal and Classroom Teacher

Occasionally we find children who are unwilling, perhaps even unable, to sit out for a few minutes without disrupting the others in the class. The time-out doesn't work; rewards and consequences aren't effective, either. In these instances the teacher has little choice but to actually remove the child from the class. When this happens the child's classroom teacher, the principal, or a guidance counselor can be helpful in two ways. First, they may be aware of the reason the child misbehaves and provide effective strategies. They may also be helpful in creating a location in the school where the child can be when he is unable to function in a class without disrupting others.

Clearly we prefer to have these children in physical education classes. The reality, however, is that there are days and times when they may simply be unable to work in a group setting. Thus a teacher has no choice but to remove them from the gym or playground. When this happens the cooperation of others in the school is vital.

---

65 MPH? OR IS IT REALLY 72 MPH?

As I write this section on slippage, I am reminded of the 65-mph speed limit. Drivers seem to understand that the limit isn't really 65 mph. The conventional wisdom in this part of the United States is that it's really 72 mph. So that's where we set our cruise control—until our radar detector sounds. Then we slow down to 65 mph. Children see their parents drive this way. The message is clear: There are rules, but they aren't really what they say; they can be stretched. The same is true in our classes. We establish rules and then allow them to be stretched; that is, we allow slippage. It seems that the rule we post on the wall is meant to be negotiated (Tousignant & Siedentop, 1983). As teachers we determine whether and how much our rules can be stretched.

Role of the Parents

In some schools parents can be counted on to help when their children are misbehaving. In these schools phone calls or letters home are very effective.

Some teachers make it a weekly practice to telephone the parents of several hard-working children and tell them how well their children are doing in physical education. These teachers also call the parents of misbehaving children. When possible, however, they try to call the parent again as soon as possible with "good news," that is, that the behavior in physical education has improved. This is a potent combination.

Whether a teacher decides to write letters or make telephone calls, it seems to be more effective when the teacher can be specific about the behavior of the child, citing specific protocols or rules that have been followed or broken. This is particularly true for the "bad news" phone calls.

Unfortunately, involving parents is not effective in every school setting. In certain schools the principal and teacher are forced to rely on the types of things they can do for a child during the school day because a parent cannot be counted on to work with a child in desirable ways. When parents can become involved in situations in which a child is chronically misbehaving, however, it can be very effective.

THE DISCIPLINE CONFRONTATION

The strategies discussed so far are designed to minimize and prevent discipline problems. Nevertheless, most teachers, even in ideal situations, will occasionally find themselves confronting a child who has misbehaved. At times this can be upsetting for a teacher. There are several strategies that can make the discipline confrontation less unsettling and ultimately beneficial for both the teacher and the child.

Try to remember that the child's misbehavior is not personal. Try not to be upset. In fact, at times it's wise to catch your breath, become centered, and then deal with the child.

These confrontations are often most successful when they are done in relative privacy. It's not a good idea to holler across the gym at a child. Rather walk over, call the child to the side, and then conduct a brief interaction. I prefer to give the other children a task so that they are active, rather than standing and watching the confrontation. This makes it easier on the child who is being confronted, especially when this child is older and so concerned with what his peers will think.

The most effective strategy is to calmly and quietly use the child's name, explain the rule (protocol) she violated, and then pause. At times it may be wise to ask for student input. When we do ask the child if she has anything to say, it's important to listen with respect and try to understand her view of the situation. With some children, however, it may be counterproductive to ask for their version of what happened. When to ask and when not to ask for input can be determined only as a teacher gets to know his children. In either

case, when the interaction is finished, the teacher concludes by telling the child the predetermined consequence of her behavior—a check, a time-out, a loss of free time.

ASSERTIVE COMMUNICATION

Communicating effectively is always a challenge—this is especially true when we are angry or upset. Fernandez-Balboa (1990) suggests strategies that beginning teachers can use to assist them in communicating assertively to children when they misbehave:

1. Describe the behavior in a non-judgemental way—"Jim, you are taking Mary's equipment away from her."
2. Express your feelings as a teacher—"I am annoyed because you haven't been listening."
3. Acknowledge the feelings of the child—"Are you . . . (frustrated, sad, angry)?"
4. Explain the effect the described behavior is having on you, and the rest of the class—"When you talk when I am talking it distracts me and the others in the class."
5. State your expectations for future behavior—"I expect you to listen, and not talk, when I am talking." (pp. 51-52)

It seems to be more effective when a teacher thinks through the confrontation process ahead of time. Often, when we are upset or excited, anger enters into the confrontation, which makes it ultimately less productive than it might be under calmer circumstances. I don't mean to suggest, however, that suc-

cessful teachers never get angry. They do from time to time, but calm interactions seem to be far more effective than angry ones. Even though a child has misbehaved, we still want to preserve his dignity. Once the child's feelings of hurt, anger, or frustration have somewhat dissipated, we want the child to understand that what he did was a violation of the rules, but that he is OK as a person.

SUMMARY

Teachers who minimize off-task behavior and discipline problems do so largely because they have thought through a number of strategies that are effective for preventing problems from escalating into major confrontations. As they teach, they are constantly aware of off-task behavior and attempt to minimize it by employing teaching strategies that help keep children focused and on-task. In addition, they typically have implemented a discipline system which the children understand: the teacher's expectations, the consequences of misbehavior, and the benefits of cooperating with the teacher and other children. Some discipline systems are based primarily on extrinsic motivation (e.g., Canter's Assertive Discipline System), and others are designed to emphasize the development of intrinsic motivation (e.g., Hellison's Levels of Affective Development). Regardless of the type of discipline system that a teacher chooses, it is imperative that the teacher be consistent and rigorous in the implementation of the system while also respecting the dignity and feelings of the children in the class.

QUESTIONS FOR REFLECTION

1. In this chapter, a number of teaching strategies that teachers use to minimize off-task behavior and discipline problems were described. Think about your own teaching. Which strategies are most natural to you? Which ones may be less comfortable to use? Can you explain why?

2. Two discipline systems were selected as representative examples. Which of the two is more appealing? Why?

3. Remembering teachers you had as a student or teachers you know, are you able to think of ways these teachers used aspects of either of these systems? Do you recall how effective they were?

4. Think about the use of intrinsic and extrinsic rewards for children and the reason that some teachers might favor one over the other. Create two scenarios—one featuring an extrinsic discipline system, the other an intrinsic discipline system—that might explain why the teachers in either scenario would use that system and not the other one.

5. Look at one of the lessons on your videotape. Analyze the use of the following teaching skills: back-to-the-wall, proximity control, with-it-ness, selective ignoring, overlapping, and positive pinpointing. Reflect on the use of these skills and how they might help to minimize discipline problems if used differently.

6. From time to time teachers do get angry at a child or a class. Can you understand and explain the reasons for this?

7. What are the consequences of believing that children today are harder to teach than they were in the past? How might that belief be reflected in the way we deal with children who are off-task?

REFERENCES

Canter, L. (1976). *Assertive discipline: A take-charge approach for today's educator.* Santa Monica, CA: L. Canter & Associates.

Fernandez-Balboa, J.-M. (1990). Helping novice teachers handle discipline problems. *Journal of Physical Education, Recreation and Dance,* **67**(2), 50-54.

Hellison, D.R. (1985). *Goals and strategies for teaching physical education.* Champaign, IL: Human Kinetics.

Hellison, D.R., & Templin, T.J. (1991). *A reflective approach to teaching physical education.* Champaign, IL: Human Kinetics.

Hill, D. (1990, April). Order in the classroom. *Teacher,* pp. 70-77.

Kounin, J.S. (1970). *Discipline and group management in classrooms.* New York: Holt, Rinehart & Winston.

Masser, L.S. (1990). Teaching for affective learning in elementary physical education. *Journal of Physical Education, Recreation and Dance,* **67**(2), 18-19.

Sander, A.N. (1989). Class management skills. *Strategies,* **2**(3), 14-18.

Tousignant, M., & Siedentop, D. (1983). A qualitative analysis of task structures in required secondary physical education classes. *Journal of Teaching in Physical Education,* **3**(1), 47-57.

Chapter 5

Getting the Lesson Started

The children are in their classroom. Eyes glance at the clock. It's 10:25 a.m. P.E. begins at 10:30. Then they'll have 30 minutes to move, play, and escape the confines of the classroom. Hearts beat faster as they move toward the gym. Some feel as if they are going to burst with excitement as they anticipate exploding into movement.

These feelings are characteristic of some children (we hope the majority) immediately before physical education class. The way the teacher begins the lesson will determine how the children feel in a few minutes. The purpose of this chapter is to describe successful ways of beginning physical education classes.

As a result of reading and understanding this chapter, the teacher will be able to

- describe techniques for involving children in activity as soon as they enter the gym or playground;
- analyze the pros and cons of instant activity for children;
- explain the purpose of and techniques related to set induction and lesson scaffolding; and
- analyze the roles of calisthenics and lap running as an introductory activity.

INSTANT ACTIVITY

Children come to physical education class ready to move! They want to be active, not listen to the teacher talk. Consequently, many teachers provide instant activity for the youngsters. As soon as they arrive at the gym door or the edge of the playground, the children are encouraged to begin moving. This is one of the protocols that is taught at the beginning of the year (chapter 3). Teachers use posters, bulletin boards, verbal reminders, and music as ways of involving children in activity as quickly as possible.

Posters and Bulletin Boards

Depending on the physical setting, some teachers have bulletin boards inside the gym that tell the children how to begin (e.g., get a rope and work on your jump rope routine). Others use posters on stands that sit outside the gym. Here is an example:

- If your last name begins with A-L, practice your sequence on the mats.
- If your last name begins with M-Z, find a ball and practice your dribbling routine.
- When the music stops, put the equipment away and sit on the center circle.

The written instructions work well for many teachers. One of the advantages of providing different tasks (rather than the same task for the entire class) is that it encourages the children to read the poster or bulletin board, rather than simply relying on what the first few to arrive are doing.

Verbal Reminders

Obviously many of the younger children are not yet reading. In this case some teachers tell the children how the next class will begin at the end of the present class. "Next class the scoops and the balls will be against the wall. As soon as you come in, find a scoop and a ball and start throwing and catching to yourself." Depending on the number of days between classes, some of the children will forget. There always seem to be a few who will remember, however, and they quickly remind the others. This is one of the routines that is practiced from the beginning of the year, so children gradually learn to listen carefully so that they can remember how the next class will start.

THE CONTENT
OF THE INTRODUCTORY ACTIVITY

The actual content of the introductory activity may be related to that day's lesson, or it may be a review of something done in the past. Some teachers use it to provide practice on skills or routines that are best practiced for relatively short spurts (e.g., jump rope). It can also serve as a warm-up for that day's lesson.

Music

Some teachers start their classes with music. The music is on when the children arrive, and they start traveling as instructed by the teacher (jogging, hopping, log rolling, skipping backwards, roller skating like an ele-

TODAY WE ARE GOING TO PRACTICE LANDING FROM A JUMP. I AM GOING TO SHOW YOU A SECRET — THAT WILL HELP YOU LAND AS QUIETLY AS A CAT.

phant, etc.). The advantage of using music, aside from the obvious fact that it creates a pleasant atmosphere, is that it also provides a relatively consistent guide for the length of the introductory activity. Most songs range from 2 to 3 minutes, adequate time to allow children to move before beginning the more formal part of the lesson.

PROS AND CONS OF INSTANT ACTIVITY

Some children's physical education teachers express a concern that the children will be "wild" or out of control if they don't enter the gym and sit down quietly prior to moving. As I watch teachers who begin their classes with instant activity, I rarely find this to be true. After a few minutes of vigorous activity, the children seem far more ready to listen to instruction. It's important to remember, however, that the teacher taught the children how to begin each lesson as part of the protocols that were practiced in the first few days of the school year (chapter 3).

In contrast, I have observed teachers require their children to enter the gym and sit quietly on a line before any activity can begin. It often seems that several minutes are wasted because the children are so eager to begin moving that their squirming and fidgeting leads to talking and pushing—which means they have to try to sit quietly even longer.

Another advantage of instant activity is that it allows children the opportunity to talk to the teacher without disrupting the entire class. As any elementary teacher will attest, especially with the primary grades, there is always a child or two that wants to tell you about something that happened at home since the last class: the new TV, the lost tooth, the baby sister, the puppies, the accident down the street, the game over the weekend, the friendship bracelet, etc. The few minutes of activity at the beginning of the class allow the children to share a few moments with you privately while the rest of the children continue moving.

COMMUNICATING THE PURPOSE OF THE LESSON

After a few minutes the introductory activity ends. The children then gather around the teacher and listen quietly for instruction about the day's lesson. As part of their protocol for beginning a class, some teachers have the children sit on a circle with the teacher. Some use squads. Some simply ask the children to come over and stand or sit by them. It is during this time that the teacher typically explains the purpose of that day's lesson.

Set induction and scaffolding aid the children in understanding how lessons interconnect and how they relate to the children's lives today—and in 20 years. These strategies shouldn't take much time, yet they are most helpful in answering that important question, "What is the purpose of physical education? Why are we doing this stuff?"

Set Induction

Successful teachers do more than simply tell the children what they will be doing, however. They find ways to provoke the children's interest and enthusiasm so that the children are eager to become involved in the lesson. The technical term for this teaching strategy is *set induction* (also referred to as *cognitive set* or *anticipatory set*).

The purpose of set induction is to motivate the children so that they become interested in the lesson and understand its purpose, thereby encouraging them to practice efficiently and eagerly. Set induction has the advantage of helping them to understand why they will be doing certain activities or tasks during a lesson.

The following are examples of set induction that teachers have used in an attempt to heighten the children's interest in a lesson:

- "When you jump, how quietly can you land? Can you land as quietly as a cat? A feather? Today I want to help you practice quiet landings."
- "Do you remember which test we did last week? Right. The pull-up test to assess upper-body strength. The purpose of today's lesson is to find ways we can improve our upper-body strength when we're at home watching TV."
- "When you play a basketball game, does anyone ever steal the ball from you? In today's lesson we are going to practice two 'secrets' that will help you keep others from stealing the ball."
- Teacher stands 10 feet from a wall and hits a ball to the wall with a racket 25 times without a miss. Then she says, "In

today's lesson I want to show you two cues that helped me become a good tennis player."

- "Do you ever get mad at your friends when you're playing a game? Do you ever say mean things to one another? The purpose of today's lesson is to understand why we say mean things to others and to find some ways to avoid making our friends feel bad."

All too often the teacher knows the purpose of the lesson, but the children don't. It's obvious to us, not to them. This is often demonstrated at the end of a lesson, during closure (chapter 13) when we sit and talk with the children. We then discover that they didn't really understand the purpose of the lesson and they can't recall the key points of the teacher's objectives.

FOREHAND OR BACKHAND?

Yesterday I watched one of our undergraduates teach a lesson on the tennis backhand to his peers. Because he wasn't clear, two of his students spent the entire 10-minute lesson practicing the forehand. He realized the problem later when he watched a videotape of his lesson.

Effective set induction may be harder for specialists because we teach so many classes a day—often on the same topic. After teaching four or five balancing lessons in a row, we are ready to get on with the lesson, rather than attempting to stimulate the interest of the children. It's a brand new lesson for the children, however, even though it may be the sixth lesson for the teacher.

"I WONDER WHAT'S GOING ON HERE"

Watch the first 5 minutes of a videotape or an actual lesson. Try to enter the world of the children and view the beginning of the lesson from their eyes. Would the purpose of the lesson be clear? Would you know what is going on? Would you be excited about the lesson?

Scaffolding

Have you ever been in a class and wondered, "What are we doing? I have no idea what the purpose of this lesson is and what point the teacher is trying to make." Along with set induction, *scaffolding* also is designed to communicate the purpose of that lesson and especially its relation to past and future lessons. Scaffolding links a series of lessons in a unit or skill theme or, in some instances, the year. It is often difficult for the children to realize that our lessons are designed sequentially to help them improve their understanding of motor skills (i.e., to realize that one lesson is related to another). When we relate a lesson to past experiences, we help them to understand a lesson and place it in perspective.

This is especially important for children because they live so much in the present. It's hard for children to understand that practicing striking a ball with a racket may someday lead to easier, faster progress in tennis, badminton, or racquetball. When we are able to show them the interconnectedness of these activities, however, much as a scaffold is erected outside a building at the beginning of construction, we help them develop a schema (a mental outline) of the overall purpose of the series of lessons on a particular topic. Because we have the advantage of teaching many of our children over several years, we can gradually fill in this scaffolding as we revisit lessons and units from year to year.

Post the Yearly Plan

There are several ways that teachers erect a physical education scaffolding for children. Some teachers, typically those who have taught at the same school for several years, post the yearly outline (chapter 2) on a bulletin board. This allows the children to see the entire sequence of lessons and, if guided by the teacher, how they connect over the year. It also minimizes one of the most often-asked questions of physical education teachers as they interact with children in the halls and cafeteria, "What are we going to do today in P.E.?" As the youngsters enter the gym, a quick glance at the topic for the day tells them very quickly what will be happening.

While the idea of posting a yearly schedule is logical, beginning teachers or teachers new to school find it difficult to know exactly how long they will spend in various activities throughout the year. When they develop a yearly plan (chapter 2), they often revise it frequently because the children and settings at schools are so different. After several years at the same school, however, a teacher begins to develop a reasonably accurate portrait of the time needed to develop a particular theme or unit.

Physical Education Vocabulary

Another technique that helps children understand the scaffolding for physical education is to display the program *vocabulary* on the wall of a gym or on a bulletin board designated for physical education. This permits the teacher not only to verbally tell the children about the lesson but also to show them the written terms. This is especially helpful when referring later on to terms that were studied months earlier.

Notebooks

Another technique that some teachers use is to have the upper grades keep P.E. notebooks or logs. Obviously these notebooks have a variety of uses, but one is that they can help the children link different lessons (units) together by using the same terminology and concepts over a number of lessons. Notebooks are useful for storing and referring to

- written descriptions of child-designed games, sequences, or dances that can be recalled in future lessons;
- completed worksheets on various topics studied throughout the year, for example, names of muscles and bones;
- individual skill and fitness test scores that can be used as a benchmark for measuring improvement;

- individual entries recording how children feel about themselves and physical activity at various times; and
- records of activity performed at home, for example, minutes of physical activity vs. minutes of television watching or Nintendo playing.

Obviously the notebooks can be used at various times and in various ways. Their advantage, of course, is that they help the children to better understand and link activities practiced throughout the year. Notebooks are an aid to understanding the scaffolding of the overall physical education program and, in turn, the entire curriculum.

TRADITIONAL WAYS TO START A LESSON

In concluding this chapter, it is important to comment on how we have traditionally started lessons—with calisthenics and laps—and explain why some teachers believe we have better ways to begin physical education classes for children.

Calisthenics

Research in recent years has caused many to question the value of calisthenics as they were done in the past (i.e., the same calisthenics done as a warm-up routine to every class) (Branner, 1989). We know today that there

are many different ways to warm up the body and that, ideally, calisthenics or stretches are designed to prepare the children's bodies to participate in a certain type of activity (Anderson, 1980).

We also know that some calisthenics, as done in the past, are simply bad practice—no matter when they're done. Straight-legged toe touches, straight-legged sit-ups, and sit-ups with the hands clasped behind the head are potentially harmful to children—and adults, for that matter (Anderson, 1980; Branner, 1989). Many experts today are also recommending that stretching be performed as a "cool-down" to a lesson rather than as a warm-up.

As a result of this research and also the limited amount of time available for physical education in many schools, some teachers simply skip calisthenics. Their introductory activity serves as the warm-up for the lesson. Rather than simply doing calisthenics because they have traditionally been done at the beginning of physical education lessons, many teachers use calisthenics only when they think it is necessary. They are trying to teach the children the correct way to use calisthenics as well as the reasons to use (or not use) them.

At times, before a gymnastics lesson, the teachers will have the children do gentle stretches as a warm-up. This time is also used to teach the children the recent innovations in stretching (e.g., long, slow stretches as opposed to the "bouncing" stretches that we used to do). Some teachers have the children stretch at the end of a lesson (e.g., calf and hamstring stretches after the children have done a lot of running).

Laps

Some teachers are also questioning the value of running laps as a way to start every physical education lesson. Three to five minutes of jogging (as in running laps), while perhaps beneficial as a warm-up, does not lead to improved cardiovascular fitness—that would take at least 15 or 20 minutes. Obviously, then, the purpose of running laps is not to improve cardiovascular endurance.

Consequently, some teachers use the activities described at the beginning of this chapter as an alternative to running laps. This allows the children to obtain much-needed practice while also warming up. Examples include tag games, listening games (chapter 3), running and dribbling a ball with hands or feet, jumping rope, and practicing leaping with a partner. To these teachers, simply running is not only boring to children, but it is also wasted time because the children aren't really learning anything.

When these teachers do have the children run laps, they are often trying to teach the children to "pace" themselves so that they can run or jog the entire time. As anyone who has ever tested children on a distance run will recall, the children who haven't learned about pacing will quickly run the first lap or so, only to end up walking the last half of the distance. Running laps, if the teacher focuses on pacing, is valuable for helping children to

understand the concept of running slowly at the beginning to avoid having to walk at the end.

Increasingly, elementary schools are providing opportunities for children to jog or walk vigorously at the beginning of the school day. Rather than the children arriving at school to sit for 15 or 20 minutes, the teachers have outlined a course for the children to walk or jog, and they are encouraged to do so. Programs like these allow the physical education teacher to focus on the important skills, knowledge, attitudes, and behaviors that the children need to learn. Parents, classroom teachers, and paraprofessionals are quite capable of supervising these walk-jog programs.

PHYSI-KIDS

At Margaret Beeks Elementary School in Blacksburg, Virginia, two parents, in cooperation with the physical education teacher, began the "Physi-Kids" program. It was a before-school, walk-jog program. Each day they totaled the distance the children traveled (children received an ice cream stick for each lap) and plotted it on a map of the United States which was posted on one of the school walls. The children took a walking trip across the USA. As I observed this program I was amazed at the surprisingly large number of children who participated each morning, even in cold weather. No doubt the children benefited from the exercise—they also enjoyed chatting as they walked and jogged their collective way across the United States.

SUMMARY

The first few minutes of a physical education lesson are important. When a child comes to our class and her curiosity and understanding are stimulated immediately, the odds are increased that she will not only be an eager participant but also that she will learn from our lesson. In contrast, when the child is greeted with the same old calisthenics and laps, lesson after lesson, there is a message that perhaps these classes are to be endured rather than enjoyed. The ways we involve children in our lessons, provoke their curiosity and intellect, and stimulate them to learn and practice go a long way toward setting the tone for the entire lesson—and the entire program.

Obviously the examples and discussion in this chapter represent only a sample of the ways a teacher might begin a lesson and provoke the children's interest and involvement. I do not mean to suggest, however, that there is one "right" way to begin a physical education lesson. There are myriad ways. The essence of this chapter is that the beginning of a lesson is important and that successful teachers devote time and energy to ensure that the opening relates to that day's lesson, lessons from the past, and future lessons. Teachers are able to provoke the children's eagerness for that day's lesson while also helping them to understand how it connects with what they did in past lessons and where it will lead in the future.

QUESTIONS FOR REFLECTION

1. Try to recall how you felt as a child when you had been in a classroom for several hours and it was finally time to go outside or to the gym. Describe your feelings and how you would react to instant activity as compared with having to sit and listen for the first few minutes.
2. Some teachers feel uncomfortable with having children enter a gym and begin activity immediately without first talking to them. Why do you think this is true? How would teachers who ask their children to begin activity immediately differ in their feelings?
3. Set induction is commonly found in many aspects of our lives—movies, books, lectures. Can you think of several examples that were motivating to you?
4. Think about the concept of set induction and how it might be used to stimulate children's interest in a lesson. What types of things do teachers say and do that different ages of children find interesting and exciting?
5. The strategy of providing children with a scaffold to help them understand the overall curriculum is something that effective teachers do. Can you recall teachers who were adept at providing effective scaffolds? And those who weren't? Describe and analyze the differences for you as a learner.
6. What is your view of calisthenics and laps as a way to start a physical education lesson? If possible, try to find someone with a contrasting view and discuss your reasons for beginning lessons in a certain way.

VIDEOTAPE ANALYSIS

Look at one of your videotaped lessons (or one of the companion videotaped lessons). Based on this chapter, analyze the first 5 minutes of the lesson. Were the children quickly involved in activity? Was there set induction?

Was a scaffolding provided to connect this lesson with other lessons?

REFERENCES

Anderson, B. (1980). *Stretching*. Bolinas, CA: Shelter.

Branner, T.T. (1989). *The safe exercise handbook*. Dubuque, IA: Kendall/Hunt.

Chapter 6

Instructing and Demonstrating

The lesson is 4 minutes old. As soon as the second graders arrived at the playground, they were challenged to "run and find different ways to jump over the carpet squares spread throughout the blacktop." The torrent of energy stored up after 3 hours in the classroom erupts. Bursts of running interspersed with leaps, hops, giggles, and jumps foretell the children's exuberance at being outside in a space where movement is not only allowed but encouraged. To be able to move—unrestricted, free, emancipated for a few minutes from the confines imposed by walls, tables, and chairs—creates genuine joy.

The song that has been playing on the tape player, "Jump" by Van Halen, ends. The children know that is the signal to stop and assemble around the teacher. They do so quickly, realizing that the teacher will not talk long and that they will be able to move shortly. Set induction is followed by a brief period of instruction and demonstration designed to help the children understand exactly what and how to practice. The children have no questions. On the signal "go" they quickly gather their equipment and begin the first task. This chapter focuses on two of the teaching skills used by the teacher in this vignette: instructing and demonstrating.

As a result of reading and understanding this chapter, the teacher will be able to

- explain the differences between the two types of instructing: organizational and informational;
- describe the guidelines for effective informational instruction;

- describe the characteristics of effective demonstrations by the teacher and by the children;
- analyze the way the children spend their time in a lesson;
- explain the use of pinpointing and the ways it can be used effectively;
- describe the technique of checking for understanding and its role in instructing and demonstrating;
- analyze the role of play-teach-play as part of the instruction/demonstration process; and
- explain the way videotapes and other audiovisuals can heighten the interest and understanding of children in physical education settings.

The ideas presented in the two previous chapters, when implemented effectively, allow successful teachers to arrive at the point in a lesson at which they can provide effective instruction and demonstration. As one quickly realizes, however, when a group of children doesn't listen or stop when told, the quality of the instruction is virtually irrelevant.

We need to recognize that before instruction and demonstration can be successful, no matter how adept a teacher might be at this part of the teaching process, the children must have learned to pay attention to the teacher—and they must be ready to do so. Once the groundwork has been laid, the children are then ready to benefit from the information and demonstrations provided by the teacher.

INSTRUCTING

Instructing is the process of providing information to the children primarily, but not exclusively, by talking. Over the years a number of studies have analyzed physical education lessons. These studies, both individually and collectively, present a very clear portrait: Many P.E. teachers spend a lot of time talking; many students spend a lot of time listening, waiting, and getting organized (Metzler, 1985; Siedentop, 1991). Teachers need to talk, but in physical education classes children need to move. The purpose of this chapter is to discuss ways teachers can communicate to children so that they understand and learn without subtracting a lot of time from their opportunities to move.

For purposes of discussion, I have artificially divided instruction into two categories: organizational and informational. This is an oversimplification and also a false division, as the two are often intertwined.

I hope, however, that this division will be helpful in clarifying the process teachers use to provide information to children.

Organizational Instructing

One of the challenges of teaching physical education is organizing large groups of people in undefined spaces. Classrooms have chairs and desks—obvious places to sit. In contrast, playgrounds and gyms have lines and walls; grassy fields have a few trees and perhaps a backstop. What are the boundaries in a gym or on a playground or field? Where do the children go for instruction? How do they avoid running into one another?

One type of instruction, *organizational instructing*, tells the students what to do, with whom, where, and with what equipment. This is necessary at the beginning of most lessons and typically occurs after an introductory activity. When it is done with clarity, the students understand and can proceed quickly to activity (again this assumes that the management protocols have been learned by the children) (chapter 3).

Organizational instruction doesn't tell the children anything about how to throw a ball or perform a static stretch. It does tell them how the activities can be done without interruption in a safe and enjoyable environment. Effective organizational instruction answers the following questions:

- Where will I do the activity? What are the boundaries?
- Will I do it alone or with others? How will my group be formed?
- Do I need any equipment? Where will I find it?
- When will I start? Stop? What do I do if I finish early?
- What if I have a question?

Obviously this is a lot of information for children—especially young children or ones who are new to a program. One technique that many successful teachers use to enhance the clarity of their organizational instruction is to ask one or more children (depending on the activity) to actually show the other children how the task is done. For example, after telling the children they will need to choose a partner, a ball, two cones, and a space away from others to begin their game, a teacher calls on two children and "talks them through" the actual beginning of the task:

"Jennifer, would you please show us how to begin? Right. First she picks a partner—Rachel. Now she and Rachel pick a ball from the pile, get two cones, and find a spot by themselves. Now they're ready to begin their game. Thank you for showing us how to get organized for the game. When I walk by and tap you on the shoulder, please select your partner and begin."

Asking children to "walk through" the organization may seem like a waste of time. In fact, it often saves time because the children can visualize how their activity is to be organized.

The decision as to whether to talk them through depends on the task and the particular class. If the class has done the task before and if they are good listeners, it may be unnecessary to demonstrate.

INTO THE GREAT BEYOND

One of the things we learn in our "ed. psych." classes is that young children have yet to develop adult concepts of space awareness. I am always reminded of this when I watch a teacher describe a rather poorly marked general space. Typically, after the explanation, the teacher asks the children, "Do you understand where the boundaries are?" Twenty-nine 6-year-old heads all bob "uh-huh" in unison. The teacher says "go." Ten seconds later, seven children are happily traveling beyond the boundaries without realizing that they are out-of-bounds.

In general, however, the clarity of instruction about organization is aided by demonstration. In time, the children will learn the shortcuts. The other day, for example, at the end of the lesson I was observing, the teacher said, "Now I need you in two seated lines." I wondered which of the many lines in the gym he meant. The children knew exactly. They quickly sat on two red lines by the door ready to move into the hallway.

Informational Instructing

The organizational instruction tells the children what they are going to be doing. It doesn't tell them how to do the activity successfully, however. Instruction about how to land from a jump, make a symmetrical shape, pace a distance run, and form a group, I have classified as *informational instruction*. It has also been termed *lesson presentation* (Mustain, 1990).

TEACHING IS MORE THAN INSTRUCTING

Instructing is one aspect of teaching. It is the single aspect, however, that the general public considers to be the total process of teaching. A teacher who is clever and witty is often considered to be effective. What experienced teachers know is that the real measure of success as a teacher is what the children are doing—and how they feel about what they are doing—that makes the difference. Motivating children to work hard and continue to practice requires much more than simply providing a clever set of instructions. If teaching and instructing were synonymous, then perhaps this would be a book with only one chapter!

There are four guidelines that successful teachers follow in providing skill (informational) instruction.

1. One Idea at a Time

One guideline is to keep it simple. For a novice, an explanation of how to grip a racket, how to move to the ball and prepare to swing, and then how to actually swing—in the same minilecture—is information overload, even for an adult learner. Students simply can't remember all of that information. By explaining and demonstrating one idea at a time (e.g., "move quickly to the ball"), the learners can better remember the concept and begin to incorporate it into their schema. When several concepts are explained simultaneously, it is difficult for the children to know which one they should think about as they practice. Instruction about one idea at a time is especially effective when the teacher then provides feedback to the children about the way they are (or are not) moving quickly to the ball (i.e., feedback that is congruent with the instruction) (chapter 10).

Obviously in some instances, more than one idea can be successfully explained, especially when one is a review of past lessons. Too often, however, we provide the children with far more information than they can process—even if they want to remember it all.

2. Keep it Brief

Another advantage of explaining one idea at a time is that the instruction can be brief. Children are far more willing to listen when they know an explanation will be quick and they can return to activity.

In keeping with this guideline, it is important to avoid falling into the habit of repeating the same explanation two or three times. Beginning teachers are particularly prone to this habit as they try to find words to enhance their explanation. This is because, in many instances, they haven't talked about the ideas they are attempting to teach—the content is new to them as a teacher. Consequently, some children tend to hear the first explanation and not bother to listen to the next one; conversely, some may prefer to wait until the second or third explanation because they know the idea will be explained more than once.

"UH'S . . . , UM'S . . . , OK'S, AND YOU KNOW'S"

It's common for teachers, especially early in their careers when they are unaccustomed to public speaking and are presenting information for the first time, to use certain phrases or words that are distracting to listeners. The most common are "uh . . . ," "um . . . ," "OK," and "you know," but there are others that also unknowingly creep into our vocabulary. There is a reason for using these words—they allow us to stall for time as we think about what we want to say next. It's natural. It's also distracting. One of the quickest ways to discover these habits is to audio- or videotape a lesson to determine if any of these habits have crept into our instruction. If they have, simply becoming aware of them is often enough to eliminate them from our speech. In some cases, however, a habit has become so ingrained that it won't go away. Fortunately, there is an effective technique for eliminating these habits. Select a class you work well with. Ask them to help you eliminate your habit. They will already be aware of it. Ask them to repeat the distracting phrase to you every time you say it. For example, every time you say "OK," ask them all to say "OK?" back to you. Although that lesson may not be very good, you will quickly stop using that word. It works—and the children really enjoy helping you change the habit.

3. Reminder Word or Phrase

Our explanations, of necessity, require a number of words. When we can provide the

children with a *reminder word* or phrase, it helps them recall the idea more easily (Melville, 1988). It presents them with an easily remembered "mind picture." For example, the cue often used with beginners when striking a ball with a racket is that the side is ideally facing the target when the ball is struck. Designating the word *side* as the reminder word serves as a shortcut to remembering this concept. This also makes it easier for the teacher to provide feedback because she can simply say "side" as a reminder to try to turn the side toward the target. While this may not seem important at the beginning of the day, after seven or eight classes, a shortcut like this can be very helpful (Figure 6.1).

At times these reminder words are not easy to create. Many times the children can help identify a word or phrase to serve as a reminder. For example, the refinement of bending the knees, hips, and ankles when landing from a jump was identified by children as "squashing" the landing.

4. Based on Observation

As explained previously, some classes will have needs different from those of others. Effective teachers have the ability to observe a class, reflect on the students' movement, and then select the appropriate cue from their repertoire of understanding about that skill and how it is learned, to determine the content of the instruction that will be most beneficial to children at that skill level.

In teaching dribbling with the hands, for example, the following cues (chapter 8) might be helpful:

- Use the "finger pads."
- Push, rather than slap, the ball.
- Look away from the ball.
- Dribble low.
- Keep the ball on the side away from the opponent.

If the children are beginners, the first two or three cues might be emphasized. More skillful children would benefit from the latter two cues. The decision about which cue or refinement to emphasize (chapter 9) is based on the teacher's observation (chapter 8) and then combined with his knowledge of what cues the children will find most beneficial.

THE KNUCKLE OF THE BIG TOE

In class today one of our soccer players was trying to help another student with a soccer style kick for distance. The player didn't want the other student to use his toe, but he didn't want him to use the inside of his foot either. In attempting to describe that location on the foot between the toes and the inside, middle of the foot (actually the joint of the first metatarsal), one of the students came up with the term *the knuckle of your big toe*. Perhaps not quite accurate, but easy to remember.

Motor skills	Verbal cues
Running • Elbows bent, arms close to body, not flying out to the sides • Feet straight, avoiding flat-footed landing	"Steam engines" "Heel-toe, straight we go"
Jumping • Horizontal jump using a preparatory movement that includes flexion of both knees and arms extended behind the body • Horizontal jump in which arms are forcefully extended forward and upward reaching full extension above the head	"Make a low table" "Swing for the sky"
Ball handling • Dribbling by pushing with the fingers, not slapping • Catching with eyes on the ball, arms extended in preparation, and elbows bending to absorb force • Fielding a ground ball by getting in front of the ball with hands down • Catching self-tossed balls on the finger tips (not the palms)	"Pet the kitty" "Look, reach, give" "Tunnel with bars" "Spiders playing catch"

Figure 6.1 Sample verbal cues for motor skills. (Reprinted by permission from Melville, 1988.)

The ability to observe a class and make these decisions is not a skill that comes easily. As with many of the pedagogical skills, it takes time and practice. In the beginning it is helpful to have several cues in mind and then scan the class to determine which of the refinements will benefit the class. If the majority of the students are gripping their rackets correctly, then it is of little use to explain the grip to the entire class. It can be done individually. In contrast, if the children are swinging their rackets in uneven pathways causing them to miss or mis-hit the ball, then time needs to be spent on their swing pathways. This is a decision best made through observation, however.

Watch one of your videotaped lessons (or a lesson on the companion videotape you purchased along with this text). Locate sections where the teacher is instructing the children. Answer the following questions about those segments of the tape:

- Was the instruction clear and understandable to the children?
- Were the instructions repeated? Or were they stated clearly and succinctly one time only?
- If a cue was provided, was it stated clearly? Were several cues described at the same time so that it was hard to know which cue to focus on?
- Was the task or activity clear to the children? Was it demonstrated to them? Did it need to be?

If you are with a group watching a lesson, find an instruction segment on the videotape. Play it once. Then have everyone write down the key idea (only one!) of the instruction—the idea that you would think about if you were a child in the class. When everyone in your group has finished, pass the key ideas to one another. If the instruction was clear, all will have written the same key idea. If it wasn't clear, however, there will be many different cues written on the paper.

DEMONSTRATING

Demonstrating is typically part of instruction—the part where we show the movement rather than simply talking about it. This is especially important for young children, who may have difficulty understanding some of the concepts. It is also crucial in many schools that have classes with non-English-speaking or hearing-impaired children.

Much of our teaching involves using words to describe how to perform motor skills. Words are helpful but are not as efficient as actually demonstrating the skill. The same is true for music or art. Words are helpful, but hearing a symphony or viewing a portrait is far more descriptive than trying to create a verbal explanation. Once we have the idea,

words are effective in focusing our attention on particular aspects, phases, or sequences of a movement. As with instruction, there are several components that together compose a successful demonstration (Rink & Werner, 1987).

Location for Demonstrating

The first component is simply common sense. Stand in a location in which all of the children can see you easily. If you're outside, be sure to stand so the sun isn't in the children's eyes. Be sure that you can also see all of the children. This is obvious, yet from time to time it's forgotten. There's really not much more one can write about this aspect—it's simply a matter of trying to be aware of the children and what they are seeing and hearing.

Whole/Part

Generally it seems that the first demonstration should be the entire *whole* movement. If the skill is kicking, the teacher (or a skilled student) demonstrates the actual kick. The next phase of the demonstration focuses on the *part* (e.g., showing the placement of the nonkicking foot next to the ball). This may or may not be followed by another whole demonstration. It's important that the critical component be featured in the demonstration; it's also important that the children see the entire skill demonstrated so that they can form a complete mental picture of the skill (Rink & Werner, 1987).

Normal/Slow

As with the whole/part idea, sometimes the children need to see the skill at normal speed; other times it helps to slow it down, often when the cue is demonstrated. If the demonstration isn't slowed down, many children will be unable to actually see the movement that is demonstrated. It will simply be a blur. This is especially true for the higher skilled children when a teacher is attempting to refine a complex sports skill (e.g., a certain sequencing of movements of body parts, as in swinging a golf club or racket or throwing). The focus may be on how the hips, arms, and shoulders move in relation to one another.

Verbal Focus by the Teacher

If the children are going to benefit from the demonstration, the teacher will need to tell them where to look before the demonstration: "Watch the 'plant' foot; notice that it is placed alongside the ball." This helps direct the children's attention. If this isn't done, as the ball is kicked many of the children will watch the flight of the ball, "oohing" and "aahing" as the ball sails away—forgetting to notice where the plant foot was placed.

WHAT IF I CAN'T DO THE SKILL TO BE DEMONSTRATED?

One of the questions invariably raised by beginning teachers is, "What do you do when you aren't skilled enough to demonstrate?" My answer is "don't." Most of the time you will know a child or two in the class who can demonstrate the entire (whole) skill. That child can then demonstrate the part that will be emphasized, often in slow motion.

While some may be uncomfortable with the fact that a teacher is not highly skilled in everything she teaches, I don't think the children find it especially troublesome if the teacher is honest about it. I think it's an excellent time to point out how long it takes to become proficient at a skill and how few individuals are proficient at every skill. In fact, one of the aspects of teaching I enjoy most is when the children attempt to teach me a skill that I am not very good at. The sharing, the compassion, and the support the children provide as they try to teach me to do a handstand or twirl a hoop around one leg helps create an environment that says, "It's OK not to know everything; it's fun to learn and to try; this is a place where you can feel comfortable when you try and fail—because failure is a part of learning."

VIDEOTAPE ANALYSIS

Select a videotape of one of your lessons (or a lesson on the companion videotape that accompanies this text). Focus on the teacher demonstrations to the class. Answer the following questions:

- Could all of the children see it easily?
- Was the whole skill demonstrated? The critical part (cue)?
- Was it demonstrated at normal and slow speeds?

- Did the teacher remind the children to focus on the part of the skill that was being emphasized during the demonstration?

CHECKING FOR UNDERSTANDING

At the culmination of an instruction-demonstration episode, one technique that effective teachers use is to quickly test the children to be sure they understand the instruction and the demonstration. This is called *checking for understanding*. One way to do this is to demonstrate a component incorrectly (or correctly). The children are asked to raise their hands only if the component was done correctly. For example, "Now I am going to do another balance. If my balance is symmetrical, raise your hand."

The teacher can quickly determine whether the children understand the concept by the number of hands that are raised (or aren't raised), depending on the movement that was done. Young children, especially, seem to enjoy this form of checking for understanding.

Another way to check for understanding is to ask the entire class to demonstrate the correct (or incorrect) use of a component. For example:

- "Put your elbow in middle level" (to see if they understand levels).
- "Show me where *not* to put your arms when you do a sit-up" (to check for their understanding of arm placement).
- "Show me how you look when you 'squash' your landing after a jump" (lets

the teacher observe whether the children understand the concept of bending at the hips, knees, and ankles).

Checking for understanding provides a way of evaluating the children's comprehension of the functional use of a cue. Given the number of classes typically taught by the elementary school physical education specialist and the difficulty of evaluating 300 to 600 children, this is a technique that can be helpful for assessing the progress children are making. It is relatively easy and quick to scan the children to see how many have understood the instruction and the demonstration.

STUDENTS' USE OF TIME

As I review the sections on instructing, demonstrating, and checking for understanding, I realize that it may appear that a substantial part of a lesson is devoted to these activities. I hope not. In fact, as we work with our undergraduates we encourage them to do all three (instruct-demonstrate-check for understanding) in less than 60 seconds. This is obviously an arbitrary limit, but it does reinforce the point that the entire cycle can be completed in 1 minute or less for many skills—and be easily understood by the children.

One of the ways we help our undergraduates understand how the children spend time in their classes is through a *time analysis*. This provides the undergraduates with helpful, objective insights about how long the children spend listening to them talk, for example, as compared to how long the children

actually spend in activity. The following sections explain the time analysis we use for this purpose.

Definition of Categories

The time analysis form, Students' Use of Time, is also referred to as *duration recording* (Siedentop, 1991). It is a frequently used time analysis that categorizes the time the children spend in a class into four categories (Figure 6.2):

- **Managing**—time spent getting out and putting away equipment, organizing into groups, etc.

- **Activity**—time spent moving as they do activities that are consistent with the purpose of the lesson
- **Instruction**—time spent listening to instruction, watching a demonstration, answering questions verbally, etc.
- **Waiting**—time spent waiting for a turn, waiting to get the ball in a game, or waiting for the teacher to get out the equipment or find the right song on a record

Coding the Time Children Spend in a Lesson

To record the time spent in a lesson, the observer uses a stopwatch and a reproduction

Students' use of time coding form

Teacher __Mark_____   Coder __Christine_____

Date __12/20/90___   # of students ____29____   over 50% of students ____16____

Time analysis codes: Decision is based on what 51% of the observed students are doing at the time.

M = Management: Time when *most* students (over 50%) are *not* receiving instruction or involved in lesson activity (e.g., changing activities, getting out or putting away equipment, listening to behavior rules or reminder).

A = Activity: Time when most students (over 50%) are involved in physical movement (e.g., catching a ball, throwing at a target, running).

I = Instruction: Time when most students (over 50%) are receiving information about how to move or perform a skill (e.g., how to move using all the space, watching a demonstration, listening to instructions).

W = Waiting: Time when most students (over 50%) are *not* involved in the other categories (e.g., group activity but only one or two are participating, waiting for a turn, off-task behavior, waiting for the teacher to give directions).

Percent of M time =	120	÷	1,620 X100	=	7.41	%
	TOTAL M seconds		TOTAL LESSON seconds			
Percent of A time =	1,170	÷	1,620 x 100	=	72.22	%
	TOTAL A seconds		TOTAL LESSON seconds			
Percent of I time =	285	÷	1,620 X 100	=	17.59	%
	TOTAL I seconds		TOTAL LESSON seconds			
Percent of W time =	37	÷	1,620 X 100	=	2.28	%
	TOTAL W seconds		TOTAL LESSON seconds			

Figure 6.2 Sample form for coding students' use of time.

of Figure 6.2. Start the stopwatch when the children enter the playground or gym. Each slash mark represents 15 seconds, and each number represents 1 minute. This form allows one to code a 30-minute lesson. Focus only on the children. Record what 51 percent of the children are doing at any given time by making a slash mark and then indicating what the children had spent the previous seconds doing. For example:

- If they spent the first 30 seconds of the class getting a piece of equipment, the observer would make a slash mark and then place an "M" to indicate that the children had spent that time managing (Figure 6.2).
- If the children then spent the next 180 seconds (3 minutes) in activity, the observer would place an "A" over that section (Figure 6.2).
- If the next 30 seconds were spent listening to the teacher talk, the observer would place an "I" over that section (Figure 6.2).

Obviously the times when the children change categories is not always exactly at a 15-second slash mark, so we make the best estimate of where the category changed and put our slash mark there.

Actual lessons or videotapes can be analyzed to determine how the children spend their time. If it is a videotaped lesson, the observer will have to make judgments about 51 percent of the children, based on the children that are "on the screen" at any given time.

Analyzing the Students' Use of Time

When the lesson is ended or the observation stopped, the first step is to total the number of seconds for the entire lesson. In the example provided (Figure 6.2), the lesson was 27 minutes long (1,620 seconds). All of the calculations are done in seconds, so the denominator for each of the four categories is 1,620. The number of seconds the children spent in each of the four categories is then totaled and placed on the appropriate place on the form. Divide the number of seconds for each category by the total length of the lesson (in seconds) and multiply by 100 to determine the percentage for each of the four categories. In this lesson, for example, the children spent 1,170 seconds in activity, which amounted to

72.22 percent of the lesson. Less than 3 percent of the lesson was spent in waiting.

Interpreting the Form

Obviously there are many ways to interpret the time children spend in a lesson. Some lessons require more instruction than others, for example. Therefore, the form must always be interpreted in terms of the lesson content, the class taught, the grade level, etc. Generally, however, we encourage our undergraduate students to try to design and teach their lessons so that the children are active for at least 60 percent of the lesson. We also encourage our students to aim for no waiting time at all. We assume that in virtually every lesson there will be some instruction and some management time.

PINPOINTING

Once the instruction and demonstration have been completed and the teacher has checked to be sure the children have correctly understood, the children are ready to begin the task. Typically teachers use *pinpointing* (chapter 4) after the skill has been explained and demonstrated and either some of the children are having a hard time understanding or they are focusing more on the outcome than on the cue that was taught. Coded as Instruction on the Students' Use of Time Coding Form (Figure 6.2), pinpointing should be relatively brief, ideally taking less than 60 seconds.

To pinpoint, a teacher selects two or more children who are correctly using the component currently being emphasized and asks them to demonstrate for their classmates. For example: "Stop. Now I want you to watch Bob and Lanaya. Notice how their arms are fully stretched to help them keep their balance as they walk along the beam."

Pinpointing is an effective technique because it reinforces the instruction/demonstration and also says to the children that you are more interested in how they are balancing than in whether they have to step off the beam.

It seems that it works best to ask two or more children to be pinpointed. Sometimes when we ask one child, he may be embarrassed and not want to perform solo in front of the class. This fear of embarrassment is lessened when several children are moving at the same time. It's suggested that teachers try to avoid always pinpointing the highly skilled children as even the lower skilled children, who may not have the best balance, can demonstrate how to stretch their arms to maintain their balance. This has an obvious benefit because it indirectly says to the children, "Even though you might not be highly skilled, you can learn to do this part, and I am more interested in how you do the skill than in the results." It also allows the teacher to reinforce those children who are trying hard but have yet to "put it all together."

PLAY-TEACH-PLAY

For understandable reasons, children don't want to listen to long explanations. They want to be active. This fact is compounded by children's *presentism* (i.e., they rarely see the long-term benefits of practicing a skill). It's hard for them to make the connection between practice today and proficiency several years from now. So they want to play—not practice. This means that they are often reluctant to pay attention to the instruction and demonstration provided by the teacher.

In addition to pinpointing and checking for understanding, another effective technique that is part of the instruction/demonstration process is *play-teach-play*. While this technique can be used with any age, it is typically used with upper-grade children who are interested in playing a game rather than spending time in practice—even though they may need the practice. Play-teach-play has two advantages:

1. It heightens the children's interest because the instruction/demonstration can be related to the game they have just played. It's similar to fixing a flat tire. If I decided to include a section on changing a flat tire, you might skip over it. If you had to change a flat tire, however, your interest in my instructing and demonstrating would be much greater. When they know they will be returning to a game and the teacher is describing a way to heighten their success in that game, they are more interested in listening to the idea.
2. The other advantage of play-teach-play is that the children practice tasks in the actual context in which they will be used so that the tasks become more meaningful to them.

Historically, we have structured units (lessons) so that the practice (drill) occurs first, followed by a game. The children want to play the game rather than practice because the two seem unconnected in their minds. In play-teach-play, the connections between practice and play are made clearer by initially playing the game (participating in the complete sequence or combination of skills), which then helps both the children and the teacher understand and decide on the skills or combinations of skills to practice.

In many throwing and catching games, the children have difficulty throwing a ball when they are moving. Often the receiver (their intended target) is also moving and perhaps guarded. When children are initially involved in a game which requires moving to throw and catch and when they are continually unsuccessful, then instruction in this skill (and opportunities to practice) makes much more sense to the children. The practice is related to the context of the game, not isolated and unconnected. After an opportunity to practice, the game can be resumed—the children play, practice some more, and then play again.

Obviously throwing and catching while moving isn't learned in a few minutes of practice, so the game may be stopped frequently to provide more practice. The advantage of this approach is that the children can clearly see what and why they need to practice.

This isn't always the case when practice is removed from the context of the game. Let's look at dribbling, for example. When children are practicing on their own with no opponent, they typically dribble the ball waist-high and in front of them. As soon as someone tries to steal the ball, however, they dribble lower and often to the side. When the teacher points this out to the children, the dribbling practice seems to be far more useful. This is especially true when they realize that in a few minutes they will be back in a game in which someone is going to try to steal the ball once again.

The frequency and timing of playing, practicing (instructing and demonstrating), and playing is determined by the teacher. In some instances the playing is rather brief; in others it may be longer. At times the play-teach-play cycle may be repeated several times; at other times the complete cycle may not be used because the practice is productive and interesting to the children, so there is no apparent need to return to the game. As with so much of teaching, these types of decisions will be based on the characteristics of the various classes.

Play-teach-play seems especially helpful when a teacher has a class of children who are accustomed to playing games every day as a major part of the lesson. When the game is played first, the teacher is no longer besieged by the question, "When do we get to play the game?" The children can clearly recognize that certain skills need to be practiced if the game is truly going to be a game.

SERVE-CHASE-SERVE-CHASE . . .

As I write this section I am reminded of the volleyball games I have observed in which children can neither serve nor volley successfully. How dull the game becomes when it consists of serve—chase the ball—serve—chase the ball—serve—miss a volley—chase the ball. . . ." This same pattern is often seen in tennis as played by the unskilled. The advantage of placing the children in the game context initially is that they can immediately see the need for practicing the serve and the techniques for receiving the serve.

Play-teach-play, as with so many of the ideas discussed in the book, is a helpful technique for some classes some of the time. My experience has been that as the children become accustomed to instructional physical education (emphasizing learning through practice) rather than recreational physical education (simply playing games with minimal instruction), the technique of play-teach-play is used less frequently, if at all.

VIDEOTAPES, SLIDES, MOVIES

Another technique used to heighten the children's interest in instruction and demonstration is the use of audiovisual aids: slides, movies, audio- and videotapes. Today videotape is probably the most widely used audiovisual technology in schools. Many teachers have found it quite effective, both for instructing and demonstrating and also for motivating children.

Increasingly, commercial companies are developing and marketing videotapes for use in physical activity instruction (e.g., videotapes of aerobic routines). As with any product, the range of quality is broad, and videotapes designed for adults are rarely appropriate for children.

In the future we may see the widespread use of commercially made videotapes for classroom teachers to show and for the children to follow, as a supplement to the physical education classes taught by the specialist. This will be especially effective when the videotape supports and/or expands the instruction offered by the specialist.

FOUR HEADS ARE BETTER THAN TWO

Video cassette recorders (VCRs) with four heads are preferable to ones with two heads for use in physical education. The four-head player allows individual frames to be "frozen" without distortion, thereby allowing the teacher to isolate the use of various cues. A slow motion or single-frame advance mechanism is also desirable. In the future we will see more P.E. teachers editing their own videotapes with a specially designed editor, thereby saving the time of trying to find a 30-second segment on a 60-minute tape. Many teachers who make their own videotapes find it helpful to purchase a cordless microphone because it produces a higher quality audio signal compared with that from a microphone mounted on the camera. This is especially important when there is music playing or the children are dribbling balls, for example.

Teacher-Constructed Videotapes

Now that videotape "camcorders" are available, an increasing number of P.E. teachers are making their own videotapes and using them in a variety of ways.

- Some record videotape segments of television programs and then show parts of them to their classes to demonstrate aspects of a particular skill, sequence, or game or to motivate the children to practice more diligently, as a part of the set induction (chapter 5).
- Some teachers make videotapes of older classes of children to show the younger children various movements or routines.
- Some teachers use videotapes to provide instruction when they will be absent and a substitute teacher will be responsible for the classes. This allows the "sub" to simply play the instructions of the regular teacher, thereby minimizing the "games" that children often enjoy playing as the sub tries to tell the children what they are going to do that day.
- With the increasing specter of malpractice lawsuits haunting teachers today, some teachers are videotaping their management protocols, rules, and expectations as they are explained at the beginning of the year. They also require students new to the school to view the videotape prior to participating in physical education classes.
- In a similar vein, some teachers are videotaping their explanations (routines and rules) for certain activities that tend to be classified as "high risk" (e.g., climbing ropes, adventure activities, use of equipment in gymnastics). In this way they have a permanent, visual record that can be used to document the instruction that was provided to their classes about the guidelines for participating in these activities (chapter 3).
- One of the most interesting uses of videotape is allowing the children to videotape their own creations and show them to others. This can be both instructional and motivational for the children. It also allows the teacher to select the more interesting sequences and inventions for future showings.

As with any audiovisual aid to instruction and demonstration, there is a tendency to show more than the audience can actually grasp in a single sitting. When feasible, brief episodes (5 minutes or less) are more effective than longer segments. When a teacher can place the equipment on a cart, it facilitates the use of audiovisual materials in brief segments. The cart can be easily wheeled out, and the VCR and monitor are ready to go. When substantial time has to be spent setting up and taking down equipment, it is less likely to be used.

SUMMARY

The ability to communicate clearly with children is obviously a very important teaching skill. The most common way teachers communicate with children is by talking. Demonstrations by the teacher and/or the children also help children understand what is intended. One of the techniques for communicating effectively with children is the ability to break down instructions into understandable units for the children. For this reason, teachers are encouraged to make their instructions both simple and brief. Pinpointing (asking children to demonstrate) is another technique teachers use to heighten their clarity. To determine whether the teacher is clear and the children are comprehending the instruction and demonstrations, successful teachers regularly check for understanding to ascertain what the children have understood. The technique of play-teach-play and the use of audio-visuals is also a way to heighten the children's interest in the teacher's instruction.

QUESTIONS FOR REFLECTION

1. Why do you think the distinction between organizational and informational instruction is necessary?
2. Physical activity instructors tend to tell children far more than they need to know or are able to comprehend. Why do you think this is the case? Why is it so hard to limit instruction to one cue at a time?
3. It seems that physical education teachers don't demonstrate as often as they might. Can you explain why this might be true?
4. Some lessons might require more instruction or demonstration than others. Think of examples when this might be so—consider the time of the year, the grade level, and the content of the lesson as you respond.
5. Pinpointing is another form of demonstration. Provide reasons why it can be an effective supplement to teacher demonstration.
6. Checking for understanding is a useful technique for teachers. Interestingly, it isn't employed as often as we might think—why might this be true?
7. Play-teach-play is a technique with both advantages and disadvantages. Describe each and suggest when it might be effective and when it might not.
8. Pull out your crystal ball and dream about ways that videotape might be used in classes in the future. Don't worry about costs; imagine your budget is unlimited.

REFERENCES

Melville, S. (1988). Thinking and moving. *Strategies*, **2**(1), 18-20.

Metzler, M. (1985). An overview of academic learning time research in physical education. In C. Vendien & J. Nixon (Eds.), *Physical education teacher education* (pp. 147-152). New York: Wiley.

Mustain, W. (1990). Are you the best teacher you can be? *Journal of Physical Education, Recreation and Dance*, **61**(2), 69-73.

Rink, J., & Werner, P. (1987). Student responses as a measure of teacher effectiveness. In G. Barrette, R. Feingold, C. Rees, & M. Pieron (Eds.), *Myths, models and methods in sport pedagogy* (pp. 199-206). Champaign, IL: Human Kinetics.

Siedentop, D. (1991). *Developing teaching skills in physical education* (3rd ed.). Palo Alto, CA: Mayfield.

Chapter 7

Motivating Children to Practice

Parents with only one or two children understand the challenge of motivating children to become and stay involved in productive and worthwhile activities. (Only on rare occasions are television and Nintendo classified by parents as worthwhile.) Teachers understand how much harder it is to keep 25 or more children eagerly involved in the same activity. This chapter focuses on ideas that teachers use to motivate children to become and remain involved in practice that leads to learning and understanding.

As a result of reading and understanding this chapter, the teacher will be able to

- describe and provide examples of three keys to motivating children to practice;
- explain how teaching by invitation can be used to motivate children;
- analyze the differences between teaching by invitation and intratask variation;
- describe how task sheets and learning centers can heighten the motivation of children;
- analyze the effective use of child-designed activities and videotapes as ways to involve children;
- explain why helping children to set realistic expectations may be motivating.

THREE KEYS TO MOTIVATING CHILDREN

It's common knowledge that children learn by doing. Research on teacher effectiveness also clearly supports this premise. The challenge for a teacher is to involve all of the children most of the time in activities that are appropriate for their varying skill levels.

Successful teachers motivate children. How? It seems to me that they create learning environments in which the tasks or activities are success oriented, intrinsically motivating, and developmentally appropriate.

Success Oriented

Failure, especially when we have never had much success, makes us want to quit trying. If we haven't ever succeeded, then there's no reason to believe that continuing to try and fail will eventually lead to improvement.

This rationale is quite typical of young children who have yet to make the connection between lots of practice and success. If we expect children to be motivated to practice a task, it needs to be one at which they can be successful—highly successful. The research literature as well as common sense suggest that when we're learning a new skill, success rates close to 80 percent are appropriate (Brophy & Good, 1986; Siedentop, 1991). When we can succeed most, although not all, of the time, we are willing to continue working at the task.

With experience and age, we start to make the connection between practice and expertise. For example, an adult might think, If I want to be a good skater, I will need to practice

a lot. It will probably take months or even years. In contrast a child might think, I want to be a good skater. I tried it today. I fell down a lot. I'm not a good skater.

Successful children's physical education teachers are able to create and change tasks so that children are able to succeed at high rates. They also encourage children to adjust tasks to make them easier or harder, to better match their ability. And they also make them fun, so the children enjoy doing them even though they don't realize that participating in these tasks is leading to improvement. The following three examples, taken from actual classes, show how teachers design tasks so that children are successful: self-adjusting target throwing, the slanty rope, and basketball goals.

Self-Adjusting Target Throwing

Each child in a class has his or her own bean bag and a cardboard box. The teacher challenges each child to throw the bean bag into the box but doesn't tell the child how far away from the box to stand. Watch how the children adjust the distance, based on their ability. The less skilled stand closer; the more skilled, farther from their boxes. Several successful throws may mean moving farther away; several failures mean the bean bag is thrown from a few steps closer to the box. Notice, too, that the higher skilled will be willing to tolerate a lower rate of success than the lower skilled children (Rogers, Ponish, & Sawyers, 1991).

Slanty Rope

Here's another example of ways teachers design tasks to promote success. Set up two ropes on the floor in a slanty rope design (Mosston, 1981). At one end, the ropes are close together. At the other end, the ropes are much farther

apart. The children are challenged to jump over the ropes ("the river") without landing in the "water." Observe how the children will choose the location at which they jump the ropes to match their ability to jump for distance—the less skilled will jump the river at the narrower end, the better jumpers at the wider end.

Varied Basketball Goal Heights

A third example of children wanting to be successful can be observed when several basketball goals are set at different heights on a playground. If children have a choice, many will choose to play at the lowest goal, thereby increasing their chances for success. In the past few years, equipment designers have recognized this fact and have started to design and sell adjustable basketball goals.

It's interesting to take any of these tasks and compare the involvement and interest of the children when they have no choice (i.e., when the distance or height is the same for every child). Typically, practice decreases and off-task behavior increases. The low skilled child becomes frustrated; the high skilled child, bored.

The purpose of designing and adjusting tasks so that children can be successful is so that they will continue trying. This is true in class and out of class. In math homework, for example, experts are recommending that the problems assigned to young children allow them to succeed at a 100% success rate, thereby increasing the motivation to do the homework. I wish I had had a teacher who provided math homework assignments at

which I could have succeeded. My memories are still vivid of the frustration, leading to exasperation, when I could do only 2 of the 10 math homework problems. I wonder how much that contributed to my feelings of incompetence in math today.

Obviously not every task a teacher designs can be self-adjusting and allow every child to be continually successful. The principle, however, is that success is motivating—and we want children to feel good about their physical abilities. They will have plenty of opportunities to experience failure and frustration—teachers don't need to intentionally create them for children.

How Successful Are the Children?

One way to determine the success rate of children in a class is to use a coding form to provide objective evidence (Figure 7.1). The form is relatively simply to use. In fact, some children can learn to use it quite well. It can be used effectively, however, only with skills that are easily counted. Lessons emphasizing throwing, catching, and kicking are ideal. By counting the successful and unsuccessful tries for a low and a high skilled child in a class, an observer can obtain a reasonably accurate estimate of the number of tries for each child and also the success rate (Figure 7.1).

Intrinsically Motivating

In addition to creating success-oriented environments, effective teachers also find ways to help children develop an intrinsic motivation

Analysis of practice opportunities and success rate

Teacher's name _____   Observer's name_____

Directions: Select one child (try to make it a highly skilled child) and another child (try to make it a low skilled child). Each time they attempt the skill presented in the task (kick with the instep, catch a ball, etc.) mark an "S" if the attempt is successful; mark a "U" if the attempt is unsuccessful. Switch your observation from one child to the other every other minute.

Criterion skill _____

Child #1	*Child #2*

Total successful _____   Total successful _____

Total unsuccessful _____   Total unsuccessful _____

Total attempts _____   Total attempts _____

Success rate   Success rate
  (Total successful ÷ Total attempts) _____   (Total successful ÷ Total attempts) _____

Figure 7.1 Sample form for analyzing practice opportunities and success rates.

for improving. These teachers encourage the children to practice hard so that they can gain the satisfaction of seeing their own improvement rather than improving to please the teacher or to win a contest.

They encourage children to build and sustain an intrinsic motivation by avoiding comparisons—with other children in the class or with externally validated norms. In classes taught by these teachers, for example, you

won't see contests to determine who can make the most shots, do the most sit-ups, or score the highest. Nor will you see the teacher encouraging them to compare their own performance with state or national fitness test norms.

The teachers do encourage comparisons, however, with themselves. Teachers invite the children to compare their current and past performances to recognize how they are improving and to show them that practice and hard work eventually pays off.

Perhaps the emphasis placed on intrinsic motivation can best be understood when placed in the context of a popular activity such as jogging. Most adults don't start jogging because they expect to win races or set records. They jog because they feel good about improving their personal fitness and perhaps losing weight. If they want to, they can chart their personal improvement, which occurs rather rapidly. If they were forced to run races and have their times published in the newspaper, however, I suspect many would quit jogging. From time to time, however, many choose to enter a race. The important point is that they choose to enter a race for their own reasons. They don't have to. Why shouldn't children have those same choices?

Obviously there is no way to prevent children from comparing their performances with one another. They do compare accomplishments—especially the highly skilled children. The difference, however, is that to encourage children to succeed on their own, the teacher downplays these comparisons and avoids creating situations in which children are forced to compare their accomplishments.

As with virtually any endeavor, the higher skilled children will seek extrinsic motivation by seeking out comparisons with others, typically through competition. The successful teacher makes these opportunities available but, again, only for those who choose to compete.

BAN THE SPELLING BEE

One of the most blatant violations of the idea that children should be allowed to choose whether they want to compete and have their performances compared with others is the spelling bee. For the few good spellers in a class, it's a marvelous competition. For the remainder of the class, however, who know they are not good spellers, it's not only humiliating, but it also publicly reinforces what they have been thinking all along: They just can't spell. We have had spelling bees for years, culminating in a national competition every year in Washington, DC. Has it resulted in a nation of good spellers?

Developmentally Appropriate

A third characteristic of a learning environment that is motivating to children is one that reflects age-related and physical differences in children. An environment that is *developmentally appropriate* encourages children to work hard and remain on-task.

As children develop, they are motivated by different opportunities and experiences. Primary-grade children, for example, are eager to please the teacher and are therefore motivated by teacher praise and encouragement. Observe any kindergarten class. Teachers hear "Watch me" throughout the lesson. Furthermore, if the children haven't learned to remain in one location, the teacher will continually be trailed by 5-year-olds wanting him to say "Wonderful!" after every attempt they

I'M NOT THE BEST ONE IN THE CLASS BUT I AM GETTING BETTER.

make to jump over a rope or throw a bean bag into a box.

As children grow older, the desire to please the teacher is accompanied (in some cases apparently replaced) by a desire to please their peers. The attention and respect of their friends become an important factor in understanding the motivation of intermediate-grade children. The opportunity to work in groups to design activities or solve problems is often motivating for fifth graders who are so interested in peer interaction. They are motivated by the chance to design a game, dance, or movement sequence and then show it to their classmates.

In addition to these age-related differences in children, skill level also influences the type of support that is effective. Poorly skilled children, who can be only minimally successful even when tasks are adjusted for them, need lots of praise and encouragement from the teacher to continue to work hard and to try. The highly skilled child, who receives satisfaction from succeeding at the various tasks, seems to be motivated by praise focusing on the way the task is done (sometimes the results) rather than by the fact that they are simply working hard. In fact, when a teacher continually praises a highly skilled child for succeeding at a task that is relatively easy for that child, she may inadvertently give the impression that P.E. is really for the poorly skilled child. I believe that this is true of many athletes who were not challenged in physical education classes. They received high amounts of praise for accomplishments that were much better than those of others in the class but that represented a relatively minimal effort on the athletes' part.

The Council on Physical Education for Children (COPEC) recently developed a position statement describing both developmentally appropriate and inappropriate practices in children's physical education. It can be obtained by writing to: COPEC, 1900 Association Dr., Reston, VA 22091.

SIX TECHNIQUES FOR MOTIVATING CHILDREN

There are a variety of different techniques that teachers use to motivate children in at-tempting to create a learning environment that provides for high rates of success, avoids comparisons among children, and accommodates individual differences. Included among these techniques are: teaching by invitation; intratask variation; task sheets; stations or learning centers; child-designed activities; and students' use of videotape.

Teaching by Invitation

One effective technique for children of all ages for adjusting tasks or activities to allow for individual differences is *teaching by invitation*. The teacher provides two or more tasks and allows the children to decide which task best suits their abilities. Let me provide several examples and then continue the discussion of this technique.

- "You may want to strike a balloon, a vinyl ball, or a playground ball."
- "If this is easy for you, try turning when you are in the air so that you land facing a different direction."
- "When you and your partner can catch the ball 10 times in a row, you may want to move your carpet squares farther apart."
- "Now I am going to put on some music. If you feel ready, see if you can let the music guide you in your routine."
- "I want you to do at least 25 sit-ups today. If you want to do more than that, go ahead."
- "You may want to work alone or with a partner."
- "In your game you may want to keep score or not. You decide."

When teaching by invitation, it is important that the teacher is careful not to make one alternative appear or sound better than the other. Neither is better. It's simply a way of allowing children to adjust the task so they can be successful—and challenged. As teachers begin to use this technique, they will find that children will automatically begin to adjust the tasks to better match their ability. Actually some children do it even when a teacher doesn't teach by invitation.

When a teacher uses this technique, it's always interesting to see the children decide which invitation they will accept. Some will choose to put down a balloon to work with a vinyl ball. If they realize they aren't successful, they will quickly return to the balloon; the same is true for the choice between punting a round ball or a foam football.

STRIKING WITH PADDLES— THE SELF-CHALLENGE

When I teach children to strike with paddles, I often observe them modifying the task on their own to challenge themselves. For example, if I say, "Strike the ball to yourself and stay on your carpet square," some will strike at high level, some at low level, some will strike with both sides of the paddle, and some will find it challenging to see how high they can strike the object and still remain on their carpet square.

Older children will typically choose to work with a partner or a group if they have a choice. But not always. On a number of occasions I can remember asking a child who seemed always to choose to work with a partner if he felt all right as he had chosen to work alone that day. Sometimes the child didn't feel very well; other times he just preferred to be alone. I have days like that, too.

Obviously teaching by invitation is one technique in a teacher's repertoire. There are times when safety, for example, would make it inappropriate. In other instances the teacher has a reason why all of the children need to be working on the same task at the same time.

VIDEOTAPE ANALYSIS

Watch a videotaped lesson and see if you can find instances of

1. Children changing a task on their own to make it easier or harder.
2. The teacher providing an invitation to the children to encourage them to modify the task to match their abilities.

Analyze the invitation within the context of the lesson. Was it disruptive? Did others notice? Did the children seem to make intelligent choices?

Intratask Variation

The same is true for the technique of *intratask variation*. It's a technique that is appropriate at different times and allows a teacher to modify a task based on the abilities and interests of the children. Intratask variation is different from the previous technique because the teacher makes the decision for the children (i.e., the teacher decides that a task needs to be changed for a child [or a group of children] to make it easier or harder). Probably this is a more difficult technique because the teacher is required to observe the children and then make a series of individual decisions based on his perceptions. Typically intratask variation is used to make a task easier for the

I DO BETTER WHEN I CHOOSE WHAT TO STRIKE

lower skilled—a different type of ball, landing on two feet instead of one, not turning when they jump—or harder for the higher skilled.

Another effective use of intratask variation is to provide the highly skilled children, who don't really need basic skill practice, the opportunity to play a game that they are ready for. An example from my teaching last spring is a good way to illustrate this use of intratask variation. I was teaching hand dribbling to a class of fifth graders. The majority of the children were at the stage at which they were challenged by trying to dribble and travel at the same time. A few of the children were well past this stage as they had been playing basketball on teams for several years. When I had provided the entire class with the task of dribbling slowly in general space, I called six children over who were highly skilled. My instructions were: "Go down to the other half of the playground. Get a game going that has dribbling in it. As long as you get along and don't make a lot of noise when I stop the rest of the class to talk to them, you can continue with your game." Several things happened:

- As you might imagine, the six decided to play a modified version of basketball. They played the entire time. Several times I provided them with suggestions about how to dribble more effectively.

- The remainder of the class continued to practice dribbling and traveling and dribbling and trying to keep the ball away from an opponent.

- Some asked why they couldn't be playing with the other six. I explained that they could when they were able to dribble well enough and encouraged them to practice hard—not only at school, but at home, too.

Intratask variation allowed me to better match the task to the skill levels of the children. I find this especially appropriate for the highly skilled children who always "want to play a game." The fact is that, in many cases, they are ready to benefit from playing a game. On the occasions when intratask variation is used, children become accustomed to it because they realize that it's not always the same children that are chosen to participate in the different activities. This is especially important to avoid stereotyping lower skilled children. I have also found that the lesser skilled children are delighted not to always

have the highly skilled children with them as they learn new skills.

Most of the time, intratask variation is used with individuals or small groups, and others in the class aren't even aware that a task has been changed. To use the dribbling example again, if I didn't want to set up an actual game for the higher skilled children, I might challenge them privately as I moved through the class: "Can you dribble it behind your back? Between your legs? Make a figure eight?" At the same time I might be making the task easier for the lower skilled: "Try dribbling the ball more in front of you. It's OK if you use two hands every once in awhile." The point is that in every class the range of skill level is varied. Both intratask variation and teaching by invitation acknowledge these differences by attempting to match the tasks to the child's skill level, thereby attempting to minimize the boredom or frustration that so readily occurs when all 25 children are required to do the same task.

VIDEOTAPE ANALYSIS

Focus on the children in the class. Do you see some children for whom the activity is too easy? Too hard? How might the teacher use intratask variation to better match the difficulty of the task to the ability of the children?

Task Sheets

Another approach that teachers use to provide children with higher rates of success by allowing them to progress at their own pace is *task sheets*. Task sheets are especially helpful for activities that are of a self-testing nature, for example, jump rope skills or balance activities. Typically the task sheet lists a progression from simple to complex, and the children work at their own pace on the task (see Figure 7.2). Most of the time, task sheets are composed of individual skills rather than partner or group skills.

Typically teachers devise a way to hold the children accountable for their progress. Some teachers design their task sheets so that the children can observe each other. If a task is done correctly, the child observing initials the

Striking with paddles—task sheet

Directions: This task sheet lists 15 tasks. Some will be easy. Some will be hard. When you get to a task you cannot do, that is the one to spend time practicing on. Don't worry about others in the class. Just try to practice a lot so you can improve. I will help you as you practice. When you can do a task, write your initials beside it. You will need a foam paddle for each task.

Initials	Task
	1. I can strike a balloon with a paddle 10 times in a row without the balloon hitting the floor.
	2. I can strike a balloon with a paddle 15 times and remain on my carpet square.
	3. I can spell my first and last name by saying a letter each time the ball hits the paddle—without a miss.
	4. I can strike a foam ball 20 times in a row without leaving my carpet square or the ball hitting the floor.
	5. I can dribble the ball 16 times in a row without a miss.
	6. I can strike a foam ball 18 times in a row doing "flip-flops"—one side of the paddle, then the other.
	7. I can spell the city I live in by saying one letter each time the paddle strikes the shuttlecock.
	8. I can hit a ball against a wall 13 times in a row without letting the ball bounce twice.
	9. I can hit a ball against a wall nine times in a row without letting the ball hit the floor once.
	10. I can hit a ball against a wall without letting the ball hit the floor once and not leave my carpet square.
	11. My partner and I can hit the ball back and forth nine times in a row without letting the ball bounce twice.
	12. My partner and I can hit the ball back and forth 11 times in a row without letting the ball touch the floor.
	13. I can hit a forehand, backhand, forehand, backhand, . . . against the wall 14 times without letting the ball bounce twice in a row.
	14. My partner and I can hit the shuttlecock across the net 21 times in a row without a miss.
	15. My partner and I can hit the ball to each other 25 times in a row without having the ball hit the floor. Each time I hit I have to change from a forehand to a backhand to a forehand to a . . .

Remember: This is not a race! Take your time and try to do each task well. I will be here to help you. We will use this task sheet several more times this year.

Figure 7.2 Sample task sheet for striking with paddles.

task sheet indicating that task has been accomplished. Other teachers prefer to have the children show the teacher when they are ready to be checked off on a task.

As with virtually every idea mentioned in the book, this approach works better with some classes than with others and for some teachers more than for others. Obviously the children need to be able to read and to work reasonably well on their own to effectively use task sheets. It is also difficult to focus on the quality of the movement with task sheets— the emphasis is on the results rather than on the process, which may lead to inefficient movement habits.

Task sheets are most effectively used over a period of several months so that they can be revisited from time to time, thereby encouraging the children to practice on their own because they know the task sheet will be used again later in the year. It's not very difficult for the teacher to store the task sheets in a manila folder for later use.

Another advantage of task sheets is that they represent marvelous records of a child's progress that can be shared with parents at the end of the year. Some teachers who work in schools with low turnover rates of children can use the same task sheets for several years.

Stations or Learning Centers

Another approach that motivates children is the use of *learning centers* or *stations* (see

Figures 7.3 and 7.4). The teacher designs and organizes a number of different activities in the gym or outside. The space for each activity is defined by cones or lines on the floor, a poster describing the activity is often displayed for each station, and the equipment necessary for that activity is provided. The children then rotate from one activity to another spending several minutes at each center. Obviously there are a variety of ways stations are used in children's physical education classes.

- Some teachers use centers as a review and set up five or six stations revisiting skills practiced over the past few lessons or weeks—rolling, dribbling, striking with paddles.
- At times teachers use stations as a fitness workout and set up 15 or so stations that are visited for short amounts of time because the activity at each one is so intense—bench step-ups, sit-ups, jump rope, jumping into and out of hoops.
- Teachers often find stations effective when teaching primary grades. The young children often lose interest in an activity quickly because their skill levels are low and there isn't an opportunity for much variety within the same skill. Stations provide them with an opportunity for variety even though all of the stations may require them to practice the same skill. One station may ask them to throw a ball at a square on the wall; another may ask them to throw bean bags into a box; a third might challenge them to throw tennis balls and try to knock down bowling pins.
- Stations are also helpful when equipment is limited. Waiting for a turn can be eliminated as different equipment can be used at various stations.

As with so many other topics taught in physical education, initially the children need to learn the protocol for using stations (chapter 3). Typically the protocol focuses on

1. putting equipment where it was before rotating;
2. learning where to rotate next (from Station 1 to Station 2) to avoid mass confusion; and
3. reading the poster at a station before beginning. This is especially important when the children have a choice of several activities at the same center based on their ability levels.

Directions

Station 1: Kick the ball against the wall. Try to catch it on a fly. If you catch three in a row, move your carpet square back five steps.

Station 2: One Step. Throw and catch the ball with your partner. Every time you catch the ball take one giant step backwards. If you miss, both of you move back together again.

Station 3: This is a chance to practice striking with rackets. How many times can you and your partner strike the ball back and forth? You may want to make up a game.

Station 4: Look at the chart on the wall. Each picture shows you one of the tricks we have learned this year. Practice the ones that are hardest for you.

Station 5: Dribble Keepaway. When you dribble inside the square formed by the cones, someone else can try to steal your ball. When you dribble outside the square, it is a "safe zone" and no one can try to take your ball away.

Station 6: Volley the ball back and forth with your partner. How many times can you volley it in a row? You and your partner may want to make up a game.

Figure 7.3 Example of a station or learning center format.

Child-Designed Activities

In a different vein, older children often enjoy the opportunity to work in small groups to design their own games, dances, or gymastic sequences. This is motivating because the children are working with their peers and are also encouraged to use their own creative abilities to solve the problem or meet the challenge presented by the teacher.

"Kinetic sculpturing" is a good example of a child-designed activity in which children work together to solve a problem. Groups of four to six children are challenged to create a group sculpture that moves. The sculpture can be defined as symmetrical or asymmetrical, fast or slow, interpretive (their version of an escalator, a bicycle, a volcano) or improvisational (simply an interesting movement), or any number of other characteristics. No special type of movement is required, so the low and high skilled children can work together in the same groups as integral parts of the sculpture.

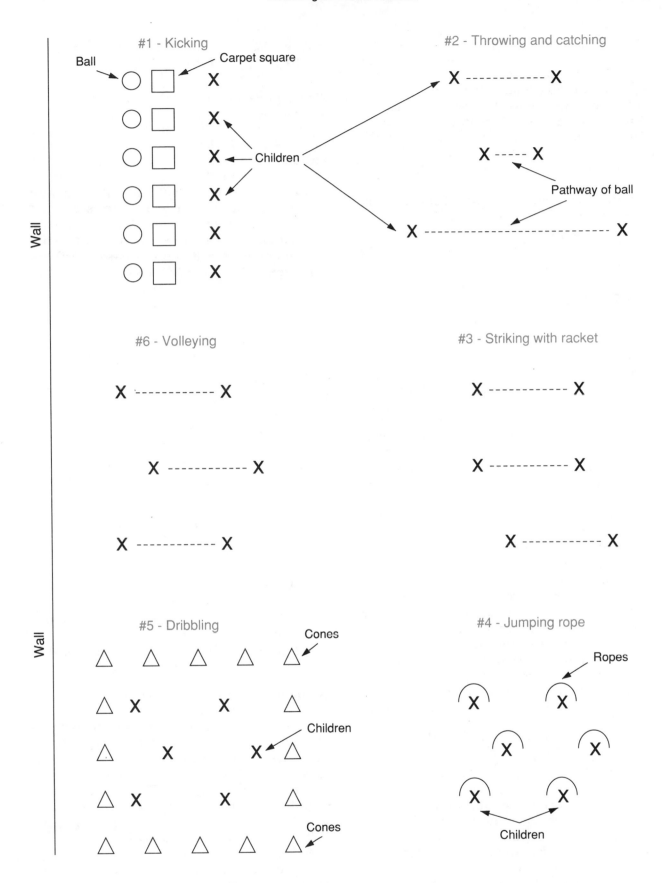

Figure 7.4 Diagram of a learning center format.

It's fascinating to assign, rather than have the children choose, groups for a challenge like this and watch the children accommodate the various ability levels within their sculpture. In a group of five, two higher skilled youngsters may be in handstands at the ends of the sculpture, supporting their legs on the two children next to them. In the middle we might find the lower skilled child on his hands, as all five sway slowly back and forth as a single unit. The feelings that emerge from an experience like this, when a solution is eventually arrived at, are often positive and motivating to the children. They can all feel good about their work together.

Videotaping

When children cooperate in groups on a project such as kinetic sculpturing, positive feelings often result, but from a teacher's perspective the movement is often lacking in quality. Children have a hard time working towards a finished product. When children are invited to show one another their creations, it's typical for children to perform a brief dance or sequence that has never been done quite that way because they never do it the same way twice. It's hard to motivate children to really refine their dances or sequences beyond simply combining a few movements.

Videotape is a valuable tool for aiding this process because the children can see their creations and begin to actually refine their work so that it achieves a certain level of quality—the slows are truly slow, the movements truly in synchrony. As children begin to see their work evolve into an interesting design, in synchrony with others, they are often motivated to continue to practice. Without this visual feedback, there is often a reluctance to work beyond the initial creation of a sequence to truly develop it into a work of art.

Videotape is also motivating when children are able to watch their performance of other skills such as batting, kicking, and rolling. It allows them to see how well they are doing and also where they can improve. No topic is more interesting to children than their own performances. Videotape allows the teacher to take advantage of this human characteristic and channel it into a motivational tool in physical education. As with any motivational device, it can be overdone, however, and needs to be used with that in mind.

HELPING CHILDREN DEVELOP REALISTIC EXPECTATIONS

The approaches to motivating children described so far have been techniques that teachers can use when teaching entire classes of children. Obviously there are numerous variations of each of these techniques that teachers use in their classes. A more long-term approach that really doesn't fit neatly into the category of a technique is helping children to create and understand *realistic expectations* about the length of time and the amount of practice it takes to learn a skill.

It seems that too often children expect to learn to throw effectively in a single 30-minute lesson, for example. The teacher provides clear and interesting instruction and a good demonstration followed by a task. The teacher neglects to tell the children, however, that the skill can't be learned in 20 minutes or after 35 throws—it takes much longer than that. When children are continually reminded that it takes a long time to learn a motor skill, they understand better that they're not failing; it takes a lot of practice to learn a skill. They also understand the need to practice beyond class.

There are things, however, that children can learn relatively quickly. For example:

- The underhand throw is used for accuracy or when you are close to a target; the overhand throw is used for distance or force.
- A wide base of support results in a more stable balance than a narrow one.
- A leap means taking off on one foot and landing on the other.
- It's harder to take a ball away from someone who is dribbling at a low level.

The idea that it takes a lot of practice and time to be successful at a motor skill is one that apparently many adults don't understand, either. Observe a foursome of golfers. If one is less skilled than the other three, watch how the skilled golfers continually provide tips to the poorer golfer. The assumption is that, if they could just provide the less skilled golfer with the right cue, instantly the poor golfer would become a good golfer.

As physical educators we know that someone doesn't suddenly become a good golfer when he is told the right cue. It may be the appropriate cue, but it takes a long time before it is incorporated into a golf swing schema that effectively integrates it into a functional motor plan.

PHYSICAL EDUCATION DROPOUTS

Sometimes I wonder if one of the contributing factors to children dropping out of physical education early isn't unrealistic expectations. Others in the class who play on teams or in the neighborhood after school have learned a variety of skills—but not in physical education. If children really expect to become as good as their classmates in relatively few lessons, it's no wonder they become frustrated and conclude early that they're no good at physical activity.

TEACHER AS CHEERLEADER

In the final section of this chapter on motivating children, it is important to comment on the idea that children can be motivated by teachers who are cheerleaders. Cheerleader teachers buzz around the gym shouting things like "Terrific! Outstanding! Out-of-sight! Marvelous!" as they encourage children to continue working and trying. It's an effective technique with some obvious limitations.

The first limitation is that some of us are not cheerleaders. Even if we wanted to be, we couldn't keep it up for 10 classes a day for 30 years. The second limitation is that, if the children come to expect this type of extrinsic motivation from a teacher, they rely on the teacher rather than on themselves for encouragement and a sense of improvement.

Fortunately, children aren't always taught by teachers who can or want to serve as the total source of motivation for children—even if they could. Given this reality, it is important for children to develop the inner satisfaction that comes from continuing to try and recognizing that, as a result of their effort, they are improving. Teachers can help children recognize that they are getting better, not as quickly as they might like, perhaps, but gradually. Teachers who motivate children this way, it seems to me, make an especially significant contribution to a child's eventual enjoyment of and satisfaction through physical activity. That's not to say that for some children, some classes, and some topics, cheerleading isn't important. It is, but children also need to experience the satisfaction that results from their own desire and motivation to continue working and trying.

SUMMARY

Obviously one of the key challenges faced by any teacher is the motivation of children so that they will want to continue learning—independently of the teacher. This chapter describes a number of the techniques that successful teachers of physical education use in attempting to motivate children. As is true of so much of teaching, one technique alone won't continually motivate children. Effective teachers create an ambiance, an environment, that makes children truly want to learn—not because of the teacher's personality but because the lessons are designed so that children succeed and feel good about their progress.

QUESTIONS FOR REFLECTION

1. Think about what motivates you to practice—success or failure? Is it different for different sports or activities? Has it changed with experience? With age?
2. Some teachers describe their classes as no-fault zones. How might this concept apply to the ideas discussed in this chapter?
3. Throughout this chapter, techniques for modifying tasks to increase success are described. Can you think of the ways you change tasks (or bend the rules) so that you can be successful?
4. Try to find youngsters (4 to 8 years old) playing together. Notice how they constantly invent and change the rules of play. Why do you think this is characteristic of the way they play? When do adults modify rules when they play together?
5. Which of the techniques described in this chapter do you feel most comfortable with as a teacher? Least comfortable? Why do you think this is so?

6. Do the children rely on you for their motivation? Do you want them to? Have you found ways to help them develop realistic expectations and intrinsic motivation? Try to understand and explain your answers to these questions.

REFERENCES

Brophy, J., & Good, T.L. (1986). Teacher behavior and student achievement. In C.M. Wittrock (Ed.), *Handbook of research on teaching* (3rd ed.) (pp. 328-375). New York: Macmillan.

Mosston, M. (1981). *Teaching physical education*. Columbus, OH: Bell & Howell.

Rogers, C.S., Ponish, K.P., & Sawyers, J.K. (1991). *Control of level of challenge: Effects in intrinsic motivation to play*. Manuscript submitted for publication.

Siedentop, D. (1991). *Developing teaching skills in physical education* (3rd ed.). Palo Alto, CA: Mayfield.

Chapter 8

Observing and Analyzing

Successful teachers provide children with plenty of developmentally appropriate practice. They rely on their ability to observe the children to determine what is appropriate (and inappropriate) for the various classes and children they are teaching. This appears straightforward. Observe the children. Analyze their movement. Make a decision about whether to change the task, provide a cue, offer a challenge, or provide individual feedback. Seems easy.

It might be easy if we were teaching only one child. The problem, however, is compounded by the numbers. Some children will stray off-task and perhaps become unsafe. It's also not the easiest skill in the world to watch someone move and instantly detect what they can do to improve their movement. We need to observe for that also. Thus another seemingly easy pedagogical skill is far more complex than it initially appears.

The purpose of this chapter is to offer some practical techniques that successful physical education teachers use to observe and analyze the movement of their children as a basis for making decisions.

As a result of reading and understanding this chapter, the teacher will be able to

- explain the difference between child-centered and subject-centered physical education;
- describe techniques for effectively observing children in physical education classes;
- explain the questions a teacher might ask to guide her observation and analysis; and
- explain the importance and difficulty of observing and analyzing movement.

CHILD-CENTERED AND SUBJECT-CENTERED DECISIONS

This chapter is one of the shortest in the book. Don't be misled by its length, however. It's also one of the most important!

Child-Centered

One of the basic premises upon which this book is written is that successful physical education teachers design their programs specifically for the children they are teaching—the programs are *child-centered*. This means that each lesson is designed for particular classes of children. Lessons aren't rigid and unchanging; they're dynamic and interactive (Hautala, 1989). There isn't, for example, one single lesson on dribbling or balancing that will be effective for every second- and third-grade class in a school. Because the abilities of the children in these classes vary, teachers also vary the way they develop the content of the lessons (chapter 9). Some classes progress more rapidly than others. Some classes are provided with different opportunities than others. In short, the program is child-centered—the selection of the tasks and activities and the time spent on them is based on the observations made by the teacher.

Subject-Centered

Subject-centered is the opposite of child-centered. In a subject-centered class, the same lesson might be taught in an identical manner to all second- and third-grade classes in a school. The assumption in a subject-centered curriculum is that all children have the same abilities and therefore are expected to learn at similar rates. In these classes teacher observation and analysis are not as important because the decisions about which activities to teach and how long to teach them are made prior to the beginning of a class and remain unchanged throughout a lesson.

Subject-Centered Dribbling for Kindergarten Children

Two examples of subject-centered activities should help make the distinction clear between child- and subject-centered physical education. Recently I observed a kindergarten class. The children were partnered up. One in each pair was given a ball. The child with the ball was asked to dribble the ball and catch the partner who was running away—but who didn't have a ball to dribble.

The task was interesting. Unfortunately, it was far too hard for virtually every child in the class. They were unable to maintain control of the ball while dribbling and standing still, let alone while running after a partner.

After attempting the task and failing, the children quickly made two adjustments so that they could succeed (chapter 7). Some of the children who were supposed to be dribbling simply tucked the ball under their arms and raced to catch their fleeing partners. Others simply abandoned the ball and chased their partners throughout the gym. If the purpose of the lesson was to help the children improve their dribbling skills, then the activity was ineffective—the children were simply not dribbling. The teacher, however, didn't seem to see (observe) the children as the activity was continued for several minutes.

Subject-Centered Volleyball

Requiring children to play by official, or adult, rules is another example of a subject-centered activity. I will use volleyball as an example. I could just as easily use basketball, soccer, softball, or flag football. Let me tell you what I often see when I observe a class of fourth or fifth graders playing by official volleyball rules. I observe

- some children who are afraid of the ball and who move quickly away from it to allow the more highly skilled children to hit it;
- some children who never hit a successful serve; and
- a lot of chasing after the ball and waiting because there are few successful rallies.

Volleyball is a great game! But only when the players have developed sufficient skills to play it. The subject-centered teacher might require a class to play volleyball (official rules) for several days or even weeks in a row. The child-centered teacher, in contrast, would observe the children, analyze their lack of ability, and then change the game to match the skill level of the children.

Fortunately, we see this happening today in many elementary schools—lowered nets, softer and lighter balls, allowing children to serve as close to the net as they want so they can get the ball over, letting the ball bounce, and opportunities to practice the skills in small groups. Teachers are designing their lessons based on the observations they make about the skill levels and characteristics of the children in their classes.

OBSERVING INDIVIDUALS

In contrast to observing an entire class to make decisions about the appropriateness of an activity, teachers also observe individual children to determine how they can help the children perform skills in a more efficient manner. In this case teachers observe individual children with the intent of helping them improve the quality of their movement and their use of the important components.

Harvey Penick, a famous golf instructor whose students include the well-known golfers Tom Kite and Ben Crenshaw, offered some fascinating insights into the difficulty of analyzing a movement as complex as the golf swing. "One of the toughest lessons I ever had to give was to Tom Kite following the 1981 season, when he was the leading money winner. He asked for a putting lesson, and after he left the shop I told one of my members that I dreaded giving Tom this lesson. The man asked why and I told him, 'There are a million things I could suggest to Tommy, and only one or two will help him. The rest could hurt, and I've got to figure out which is the right one or two' " (Wade, 1989, p. 145).

This lesson was given privately, one-on-one, to an eager student who no doubt paid diligent attention to the instructor because he was so highly motivated. The situation of teaching entire classes of children, most at beginning skill levels, and not all highly motivated, is at the opposite end of the continuum from a private golf lesson. They do have one thing in common, however—they both require an ability to analyze movement based on a thorough understanding of how the movement is acquired in developmental stages.

It's not enough simply to understand and analyze a movement, however. An instructor also make decisions about which cues and feedback the students will benefit from the most (chapters 9 and 10). Again, the thoughts of Harvey Penick are helpful for placing this chapter on observation and analysis in an appropriate perspective. "There are six different ways to make a (golf) grip weaker or stronger. You can raise or lower the hands. You can change the ball position, close or open the clubface, or adjust the hands on the club. There's no right answer for everyone" (Wade, 1989, p. 144). And once the instructor has made the decision about the content of the feedback, Mr. Penick offers the sage advice: "You have to make corrections in your game a little bit at a time. It's like medicine: A few aspirin will probably cure what ails you, but the whole bottle might just kill you" (p. 144).

As I ponder Mr. Penick's comments, I can't help but wonder what he would suggest to physical education teachers who are responsible for teaching 25 to 30 children in a single class. I don't know. Obviously, however, he would agree that analyzing movement is a difficult task even under ideal circumstances. Clearly the ability to provide feedback (chapter 10) and develop a logical progression of experiences based on observation (chapter 9) is an important one for any physical education teacher. It allows us to provide the shortcuts and the proper foundation for productive practice leading to the eventual enjoyment and satisfaction of physical activity in adulthood.

TECHNIQUES FOR OBSERVING

In a physical education class a teacher is continually required to observe 25 or more children simultaneously. There are a number of tricks that successful teachers use to effectively observe large groups of children. These tricks help them analyze the appropriateness of the tasks and activities for the children. They also help decide when and what type of feedback and cues will be most helpful. Simply knowing these observation techniques, however, is not enough. As with all of the skills described in this book, they require practice. The skills are as follows: back-to-the-wall, scanning, visitor observation, and one component at a time.

Back-to-the-Wall

One of the most obvious techniques was described in chapter 4—standing with the back to the wall or to the outside of the boundaries.

This allows a teacher to see most of what the children are doing. In contrast, when a teacher is in the middle of the action, at any given time half of the children are out of sight.

Scanning

Scanning is another technique used by successful teachers. They have developed the habit of constantly sweeping the teaching area with their eyes, even when they are providing feedback to an individual, so that they are always aware of what the children are doing. In the beginning it is a good idea for teachers to consciously scan a class. Most find it easier to scan from side to side, taking 8 or 10 seconds to find out what the children are doing. With practice this becomes automatic. Although it would be great to have the luxury of observing only one child for a number of trials, similar to the way Harvey Penick teaches his golfers, the fact is that as teachers we must constantly be vigilant, watching all of the children in a class.

Visitor Observation

Another technique that seems to be valuable is to ask as we scan, What would a visitor think if she walked into my class right now? Think of the principal of the school, one of your university professors, a member of the board of education, or a parent as you scan. This seems to help place observation in perspective and avoid the tunnel vision that sometimes mesmerizes us so that we see only one or two children and fail to see that many of the others have drifted off-task.

I am reminded of basketball dribbling lessons I have observed when the teacher focuses on a poorly skilled child, only to look up several moments later to discover that a number of children have turned the dribbling lesson into a shooting and "slam dunk" lesson. Thinking about a *visitor observation* helps some teachers keep in mind the importance of constantly being aware of every child in the class.

One Component at a Time

Observing a movement to detect errors and provide constructive suggestions is not an easy teaching skill to acquire. Some would argue that it is one of the most difficult. One technique that helps teachers become more effective observers is to select only one critical component at a time to observe. Rather than attempting to watch a child perform and pick out errors, the teacher selects an important component to observe. He then *observes only that component*. As will be explained in the next two chapters, this critical component is taught as a cue (chapter 9); then the children are provided with specific, congruent feedback (chapter 10) related to their use of that critical component.

For example, in a kicking lesson for first graders, the teacher might focus on using the instep, or "inside of the foot," rather than the toe. In a lesson focusing on striking with hockey sticks for fourth graders, the teacher

might focus on "keeping the ball close" as it is dribbled around the field. The teacher would focus only on these components during observation until she was satisfied that they had been understood and learned, and then she would move on to another critical component.

OBSERVING ONE COMPONENT AT A TIME

As I watched many beginning teachers, one of the things I realized is how difficult it is for the novice to see all that is going on in a physical education class. For this reason I began to recommend that they observe only one component at a time. It wasn't long after that I began to observe only one component at a time in my own teaching. What a difference it made—and I wasn't a novice! It's not only easier, it's also more effective, and both the teacher and the children are much clearer on exactly what is being taught in that part of the lesson.

FOUR KEY OBSERVATION QUESTIONS

As I have already said many times, teaching is so complex that it isn't possible to "do" one skill at a time—skills are constantly interwoven. Teacher observation and analysis are no different. The teacher is constantly watching the children and asking questions. The following schema for observation (Graham, Holt/Hale, & Parker, 1987) is helpful for characterizing the types of observation questions that are continually on a teacher's mind (Figure 8.1). The questions are listed in order of priority.

Are the Children Working Safely?

This is a question that must be constantly asked by a teacher. Obviously the content of some lessons (e.g., gymnastics) will require the teacher to ask this question more frequently. With so many children in a class, however, there is a constant need to observe for safety. It is a question that never leaves a teacher's mind.

Are the Children On-Task?

Teachers who spend time at the beginning of the year developing the management protocols (chapter 3) probably need to ask this question less than others. Some classes also stay on-task better than others. Nevertheless, it is a question that teachers no doubt ask a number of times during every lesson. My impression is that experienced teachers ask it subconsciously as they develop a teaching sense that lets them know something is awry almost as soon as it occurs, even when they are not directly observing the children in that area of the gym.

Is the Task Appropriate?

Another question, typically asked after the first two, relates directly to content development (chapter 9). Is the task or activity appropriate? Are the children able to work at success rates approximating 80 percent so that

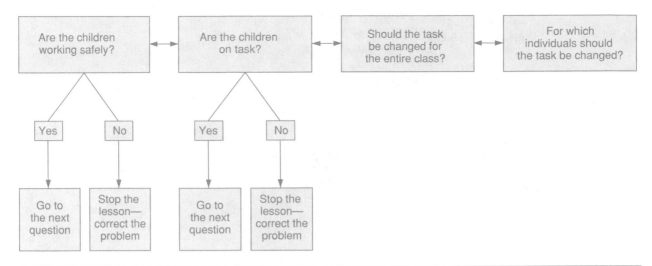

Figure 8.1 Key observation questions. (Adapted by permission from Graham, Holt/Hale, & Parker, 1987.)

they will continue to be motivated to practice (chapter 7)? Does the entire class need a cue, or can I work with children individually to provide feedback?

This is the question constantly asked by teachers in child-centered programs of physical education. Because each lesson is varied for that class of children, teachers continually observe to see whether the task is appropriate and helpful for that class (chapter 9).

How Are Individuals Using the Critical Component?

In this hypothetical observation schema (Figure 8.1), once a teacher has determined that the children are safe and on-task and that the activity is appropriate, the next question concerns the use of the critical component featured in that phase of the lesson. Initially the teacher might observe the entire class and then focus on individuals. For example, if the entire class is dribbling a ball, the teacher might look to see if they are using their finger pads rather than their palms. If they are, then the teacher would decide not to focus on that cue or critical component. The teacher might then decide to focus on another critical component such as "looking away from the ball as they dribble."

SUMMARY

The ability to see with understanding, to observe, and to analyze is a critical teaching skill for those who base their decisions on the ability of the children they are teaching (child-centered). In contrast, to a subject-centered teacher the ability to observe is far less important. As with so many of the teaching skills described in this book, in actuality there is no chronological order. Teachers are constantly analyzing children, and there are a number of techniques that help teachers observe more effectively. In addition, there are certain questions that are constantly on a teacher's mind.

QUESTIONS FOR REFLECTION

1. In some ways observing a class of children can be compared to watching a team sport—it's difficult to see everything that is happening. Describe the strategies one might use to effectively observe a team sport and then compare them to teaching physical education.
2. At times it appears as if a teacher may be teaching games without realizing the game is far too hard or easy for a number of children in the class. What do you think is going through that teacher's mind as the children play the game? What would the teacher tell you if you were able to stop the lesson and ask?

3. Observing is a teaching skill that has to be learned. Why isn't it simply automatic? What's so hard about observing?

4. Think of the sports or activities you know best and those you know least about. Do you think your observation skills might be different for these activities? How do you plan to observe in the areas with which you are unfamiliar?

5. Observing one critical component at a time seems obvious. Why do teachers tend to try to observe many components simultaneously?

REFERENCES

Graham, G., Holt/Hale, S., & Parker, M. (1987). *Children moving* (2nd ed.). Mt. View, CA: Mayfield.

Hautala, R.M. (1989). The tape recorder teacher. *Journal of Physical Education, Recreation and Dance*, **60**(2), 25-28.

Wade, D. (1989, July). An interview with Harvey Penick—Golf teacher for Tom Kite and Ben Crenshaw. *Golf Digest*, pp. 144-147.

Chapter 9

Developing the Content

The introductory activity is over. The first task has been explained and demonstrated. The children are moving. Now the teacher is faced with a barrage of questions he must answer about the tasks or activities he has outlined in his plan.

- Is this task OK?
- Should I change the activity now or wait a few minutes?
- Is there a cue that will help them do the task better?
- Is the task challenging enough?

The process of answering and implementing the answers is called *developing the content* (Rink, 1985). It is tied directly to planning (chapter 2), but it is far more than simply teaching a few activities that were planned while sitting at a desk or driving to work. It refers to the dynamic process of deciding on and implementing a developmental progression of activities so that the children will achieve the objectives decided upon by the teacher. The decisions are made as the teacher observes the children, reflects on her plan, and asks herself, What will most benefit this third-grade class that I am teaching at 10:15 on a Tuesday morning?

When a teacher truly develops the content, he is constantly observing the children (chapter 8) and asking the questions outlined previously. The purpose of this chapter is to analyze many of the decisions physical education teachers make as part of the process of developing the content.

As a result of reading and understanding this chapter, the teacher will be able to

- explain the concept of task development;
- analyze the ways tasks are made harder or easier for children;

- explain the concept of cues (refinements) and the reason they are an important feature of effective teaching;
- explain the concept of challenges (applications) and the ways they are used to heighten the children's interest in a task;
- code a teacher's task development and explain its ramifications;
- describe a task development format for planning; and
- describe the relationship between planning (chapter 2) and developing the content.

TEACHER CHOICES IN DEVELOPING THE CONTENT

As physical educators our purpose is to provide children with instruction and practice opportunities designed to provide the following:

1. Learning that is faster than trial and error
2. A developmental progression of content that gradually and sequentially leads to improvement
3. A functional understanding of the correct ways to perform skills so that they don't spend time in later years "unlearning" bad habits formed through trial and error without instruction or feedback
4. Instruction in a variety of skills rather than just a few that children might select, only to wish in later years that they had been introduced much earlier to racket sports, for example (Franck et al., 1991)

The challenge faced in virtually all programs of children's physical education is the lack of time. There are just not enough days and minutes in the school year to accomplish all that we would like. Consequently, the teacher is faced with making some very important decisions about both the content of the program and how to develop it so that it is learned quickly and efficiently. Chapter 2 discussed the planning process. This chapter focuses on developing the content by making tasks harder or easier, based on the observed abilities of the children; giving tips for quicker and more successful learning; and challenging children to remain interested in practicing activities that are important for improving.

Oversimplified, the teacher has essentially three choices during a lesson after the introductory activity (chapter 5). She can choose to

- change a task (activity) to make it easier or harder (extending);
- focus on how to do the task by providing cues that will make the children more efficient movers (refining); or
- provide a challenge to the children to give them an opportunity to test their ability and motivate them to continue working on the task (applying).

These choices are difficult when a teacher is attempting to provide *developmentally appropriate* practice opportunities for an entire class of children because classes vary widely as does the variety of ability levels within a class. It would be much easier, for example, if the teacher simply decided how long to do a task and changed by the clock rather than by the progress the children made (a subject-centered approach; see chapter 8). As one quickly learns, however, clocks are poor judges of how long children need to practice a given skill and which skill needs to be practiced next. Providing children with experiences that are developmentally appropriate requires a teacher to make decisions constantly about how to develop the content so that the progression of tasks is appropriate.

Rink (1985) and others (Gusthart, 1985; Masser, 1987) have provided us with important insights into content development in physical education. The schema that Rink developed to assist teachers in understanding, analyzing, and presenting content in physical education consists essentially of four teacher functions, which she termed informing, extending, refining, and applying.

Informing

Informing is essentially providing students in a class with information. Most often it resembles a minilecture and may focus on rules, the agenda for that day's class, how to begin a lesson, what to do in case of a fire drill, etc. Informing is the function that the lay person would consider to be "the teaching act" and is described in chapter 6. In fact, however, it is only one part of developing the content. The other three functions of developing the content have not yet been discussed in detail.

Extending (Tasks)

The term used to describe the process of making a task harder or easier to match the developmental level of the children is *extending*. It is rather easy to understand this concept. The process of changing tasks, however, so that they match the ability of the children and, as importantly, provide them with useful practice opportunities is, quite frankly, difficult. It's easy to find or invent "stuff" that the children will have fun with. Unfortunately, all too often these experiences are a dead end because they don't lead to improved motor performance. If a teacher just wants to keep children happy, "fun" activities are appropriate. Schools don't hire professionals, however, just to keep children happy.

The tasks a teacher presents to the children have a definite purpose and progression—they are designed to gradually and sequentially lead children to improved performance and/or versatility. They go somewhere! Figure 9.1 represents a rough outline of progression of tasks related to the skill theme of dribbling (Graham, Holt/Hale, & Parker, 1987).

In addition to being logically sequenced, tasks are also designed to provide children with high rates of success (approximately in the 80 percent range) (chapter 7). This is why a teacher needs to plan an entire series of tasks (chapter 2), which then allows him to extend the task, making it easier or harder, based on observations of the children in each of the classes (chapter 8).

Making Tasks Easier or Harder

It's clear that a teacher needs to have a thorough and practical understanding of the content that is being taught. This allows the teacher to sequence the tasks in a logical progression. When a teacher doesn't understand the content, however, a progression may be uneven (the difficulty from one task to the

Precontrol level

Striking a ball down and catching it.
Striking down (dribbling) continuously with both hands
Dribbling with one hand

Control level

Dribbling at different heights
Dribbling continuously while switching hands
Dribbling with the body in different positions
Dribbling in different places around the body while stationary
Dribbling and traveling

Utilization level

Dribbling and changing speed of travel
Dribbling while changing directions
Dribbling in different pathways
Dribbling around stationary obstacles
Dribbling against an opponent: one on one

Proficiency level

Starting and stopping; changing directions quickly while dribbling
Dribbling against opponents—group situations
Playing Now You've Got It, Now You Don't
Playing Dribble Tag
Dribbling and passing with a partner
Dribbling and passing in game situations
Playing Dribble/Pass Keep Away
Dribbling and throwing at a target
Playing small-group basketball
Using Harlem Globetrotters' dribbling/passing routines

Figure 9.1 Developmental progression of tasks for the skill theme of dribbling. (Reprinted by permission from Graham, Holt/Hale, & Parker, 1987.)

next is too large) or unproductive (the tasks don't truly lead to skill improvement). In general, there are several factors that are typically modified to change the difficulty of a task. Although these factors cannot be applied to every skill we teach, they do provide an overview of how tasks are made easier or harder for children.

Static to Dynamic.   One way tasks are made harder is by changing a movement from *static* (one movement done in a self-space) to *dynamic* (combining two or more movements and often changing space). It's harder to run and throw a ball than simply to throw from a standing position; it's more difficult to roll after a jump than from a standing position; it's harder to dribble a ball while traveling than while remaining in one place.

Number of Movements. The number of movements in a task also contributes to its relative difficulty. Jumping and then making a shape in the air is harder than simply making a shape on the floor. It's more difficult to jump and then catch or throw a ball. Rolling at different speeds and in varying directions increases the challenge of rolling.

Number of Children. A third factor influencing task difficulty is the number of children. When we ask children to move in relation to a partner or in a group, the task is typically harder than moving alone. This is especially true in synchronized movements, in which we challenge children to match the movement of their partners. In the upper grades the task of moving in relation to four or five others in a game or dance is complex. It takes a substantial amount of time and practice to reach a recognizable relationship with one another that can be maintained as the speed and the space change. In the same vein, games with two are typically easier to organize and implement than games with six or eight. In addition to the challenge of moving in relation to others, children also learn about cooperating with others to achieve a common goal (chapter 12).

Modification of Equipment. Equipment is clearly another way to change the difficulty of a task. In the past few years tremendous progress has been made by sporting goods companies, which have begun to design and manufacture equipment for children. Foam balls, paddles, and hockey sticks are a few examples. Smaller, lighter, more colorful balls that don't hurt when they hit you are another. Basketball goals and nets that can be easily adjusted for height are great aids to the teacher, as are plastic bats and whiffle balls. In fact, it is becoming increasingly rare to see "adult" equipment used in elementary schools. If the trend continues, wooden bats, softballs (which aren't soft), and official size and weight basketballs, volleyballs, footballs, and soccerballs may someday be as rare as inkwells in elementary schools are now.

Use of Defenders. Clearly a fifth factor influencing many game task progressions is the challenge of eluding opponents. Attempting to dribble, catch, or kick a ball when guarded is far more difficult than is attempting to do so unhindered. My sense is that this principle of progression has been violated more than any of the others by physical education teachers in the past. Youngsters were placed in game settings long before they were ready to play against an opponent. I am afraid that, as a result, the poorly skilled child quickly concluded, "I am no good" because he was unable to play a game successfully when it was necessary to elude a defender. My observation suggests that those children quickly resorted to the role of *competent bystander* (Tousignant & Siedentop, 1983). They could be found in right field and at the end of lines, allowing others to take their turns.

One of the ways teachers help the poorly skilled child to succeed is by introducing defenders into games gradually. For example, after the children become reasonably compe-

NOW FIND A PARTNER AND TRY TO KICK THE BALL SO IT GOES DIRECTLY TO YOUR PARTNER.

tent at dribbling a ball while traveling, the teacher begins by having only one or two children attempt to steal the ball from the entire class. As the children become more adept at dribbling against opposition, the number of "stealers" can be increased to four or five.

Another example of an uneven-sided game is four children trying to maneuver a ball into a goal against one defender (four vs. one). As the skill of working in this dynamic setting increases, the game might be changed to three vs. two. The advantage of uneven sides is that the child who is unaccustomed to playing in games with defenders has the chance to ease gradually into this setting without being overwhelmed by the number of defenders.

As stated at the beginning of this discussion of extending tasks, the progression of tasks the teacher uses to develop the content is crucial if the children are going to improve their skills in the limited time allotted for physical education. Children just don't learn to throw or jump or balance or move rhythmically in an hour or two—it takes a lot of practice.

HOW MANY TRIES?

One of the interesting questions I often ask is how many tries does it take an individual who is a true beginner at a skill to become proficient? Think of a major league pitcher or a professional dancer, for example. How many times did they throw a ball or leap before they became truly proficient? The number is staggering.

Refining (Cues)

In addition to the developmental progression of tasks the teacher provides, another important aspect of learning concerns the most efficient ways to perform various motor skills: the "form," "proper technique," or "strategy." This is called *refining*. The teacher refines the movement by providing cues that focus on the quality of the movement (Rink, 1985). Obviously a task can be appropriate, but that doesn't mean that the skill is performed correctly. Cues provide children with the secrets that help them learn a skill quickly and correctly and avoid the formation of bad habits.

Clearly one of the important teaching skills demonstrated by effective instructors of any sport or physical activity is their ability to provide the right cue at the right time. They are able to provide the proper "mind picture" that lets the learner pay attention to the cue that increases the efficiency of the movement and then provide practice opportunities that encourage children to focus on that cue.

A parent who has a minimal background in physical education often uses the cue "keep your eye on the ball" for many skills—catching, batting, kicking, punting, hitting a tennis ball, and so on. Occasionally this is the right cue. More often, however, it is inappropriate—the child is missing the ball but not because of where his eyes are focused. The skillful physical education teacher, in contrast to the uninformed parent, is able to provide the child with an appropriate cue that enables the child to concentrate on an aspect of the movement that will lead to an efficient motor pattern for that skill.

THE MAGIC CUE

One of the more popular misconceptions about teaching physical activity is that there is a "magic cue." If a teacher can just find that cue, the learner will instantly improve and become proficient. Golfers are notorious for trying to discover the magic cue. In reality, we know that the cue may be appropriate but that one single trial is not enough to make a cue a habit. It won't automatically help the first time it is explained and demonstrated. When I was learning to downhill ski, for example, the cue that initially helped me the most was to "keep my weight forward." The first time I heard that cue and concentrated on it, I didn't magically ski the hill without falling. Fortunately, my instructor kept repeating it and eventually I incorporated it into my motor pattern and began to fall less and less.

As with the process of extending tasks, it is important that the teacher understand the critical components of a movement and their sequence of development in children in order to know which cues to focus on and when. The cues teachers use for beginners will not be very helpful for advanced students and vice versa. Table 9.1 provides a general idea of the types of cues that might be helpful for

Table 9.1   Examples of Cues for Beginners and More Advanced Students

Beginner cues
- How to hold or grip an implement (e.g., a racket, a ball)
- Appropriate stance (e.g., knees bent, side to target)
- Movement concept (e.g., like a wheel, level, slow to fast)
- Use of body parts (e.g., arms spread, elbow leads, step with front foot)

Advanced cues
- Body parts move sequentially (e.g., hips then shoulders)
- Concentrate on how the others are moving
- To change the speed, direction, angle of the object . . .
- As you move in relation to others think about . . .

beginners and those for more advanced students. Obviously the children's physical education teacher faces the challenge of understanding many skills as she attempts to introduce the cues taught in elementary school. In contrast, the high school track coach can utilize the cues appropriate for advanced performers of a single sport.

One Cue at a Time

Because we do know skills so well and the time is so short, one of the tendencies of physical educators is to overload the children with more information than they can possibly remember or use (chapter 6). When teaching children it is wise to focus on one cue at a time (tucking the chin to the chest during a forward roll, for example). The instruction would include a brief explanation and demonstration; then the feedback (chapter 10) would focus on this single cue.

One of the questions I am often asked is, "How do you know which cue to focus on? Beginners need to concentrate on so many cues." They do. But what typically happens is that so many cues are provided that the children don't really remember any of them. The challenge of teaching is to select one cue that will help the children the most, then focus on that cue until the children know it, and then move to another one.

Thousands of adults throw and step with the same hand and foot (no opposition). Many of them were in physical education classes. They were reminded to "step with the opposite foot," but they weren't reminded often enough to have learned it. One or two lessons *focused only on this cue* will be sufficient for most children to learn the concept, assuming, of course, that it will be revisited briefly throughout the years.

Typically, the children will be able to describe the cue before they can actually do it. First they understand it. Then they begin to incorporate it into the schema of that movement. Eventually, after a lot of practice, it becomes automatic.

One way to understand the importance of cues and of teaching them one at a time is to think of learning to drive a car that had a stick, rather than an automatic, shift. When we started we understood that, in order to shift without grinding gears, we had to step on the clutch as we shifted. We understood it. We couldn't do it, however. After many attempts at shifting, the process became internalized, and we no longer had to think about stepping on the clutch as we shifted. At that point in learning to drive, however, the proper way to step on the clutch was the cue we needed. Until we learned this it didn't make much sense for our instructor to tell us how to drive in snow or enter an interstate at high speeds. We belonged in the parking lot, not on the freeway.

The same principle applies to learning other motor skills. The right cue at the right time is crucial for enhanced and enjoyable learning. When one or two cues are presented many times throughout a class while a teacher focuses on the proper techniques, it is obvious to the observer which of the cues is being emphasized—and, most importantly, it is clear to the children. During closure (chapter 13), they know the cues because they have both heard and observed them throughout the lesson.

Which Cue?

One of the difficulties faced by teachers who see their children only one or two days a week is deciding what to include in the curriculum. There just isn't time for the children to learn everything (chapter 2). Generally, however, it is agreed that the children can at least learn the basic cues for the more common skills (e.g., throwing, jumping, balancing). They may not always use them in their movements, especially when playing games, but they can verbally describe the cues so that they know the basic components for these skills.

Chapter 13 provides practical suggestions for ways that a teacher can realistically assess which cues the children know as a result of the program.

Applying (Challenging)

Cues aren't learned just because they are explained and demonstrated. They require practice. Children, however, don't necessarily see the value in repeating tasks. The connection between practicing and learning is neither understood nor valued. The dilemma faced by the teacher is how to maintain the children's interest in a task so that they can continue to focus on the cue until it is internalized. *Applying* (Rink, 1985), or providing challenges to children, is another part of the process of developing the content to maintain the children's interest.

Perhaps an example from math will illustrate how challenges are used by the teacher. When a math instructor is teaching a simple problem such as how to carry a number in long division, the successful instructor devises a variety of ways to keep the children involved with that concept until they have learned it and can apply it to other problems. The ineffective teacher covers the process, but the children don't really learn it. Consequently, they have difficulties later when they are expected to be able to carry numbers correctly in long division problems.

The same analogy is true in physical education. When children can't volley a ball thrown gently to them or strike a ball accurately with

the hand, it makes little sense for them to be required to play an official game of volleyball. The children who have yet to learn the prerequisite skills need to continue to practice those skills; those who have the necessary skills are ready to begin games using these skills (chapter 7).

TEACHER, YOU JUST LEFT ME BEHIND . . . AGAIN

One of the criticisms of education (not only physical education) is that we leave children behind who don't learn as quickly as others. Tumbling comes immediately to mind. Many teachers start, for example, with a log roll, then a forward roll, a backward roll, a cartwheel, headstand, handstand, and so forth. Many of us needed to stay at the backward roll. We hadn't learned it, but the teacher kept introducing new skills. Applications, as described in this chapter, provide a way for the teacher to challenge the children who have learned the backward roll while still working with those who are slower to grasp the cues. For example:

"Some of you may want to try two backward rolls in a row."

"Can you and your partner start and stop your backward rolling at the same time?"

"If this is easy for you, you may want to combine a forward roll and a backward roll."

Providing challenges (applications) is a technique for maintaining the interest of the children without changing the task. As with task development there are a number of ways that teachers have devised to challenge children.

Repetitions

One of the simplest ways teachers challenge children, without making the task harder, is to ask if they can repeat the task "x" times in a row. For example:

- "Can you jump over the hoop and land without falling three times in a row?"
- "How many times can you catch the ball on a fly?"
- "See if you can beat your old record."
- "Bounce the ball for each letter of your first name (the name of the school, the capital of California, the president of the United States)."

Timing

Another technique is competing against the clock. For example:

- "Can you hold the balance at least 5 seconds?"
- "Can you and your partner keep the ball going for 30 seconds?"
- "See if you can do it longer this time."

Keeping Score

Some skills lend themselves to keeping score. When fourth or fifth graders are ready to play a game with defenders, they may be challenged to figure out a way to keep score. This will motivate some to continue practicing a skill longer than if a score isn't kept. At times the scores can be cooperative (how long can one pair keep a ball going?). Although not always feasible, scoring seems to work best when the children are provided with a choice—keep score only if you want to (chapter 7).

Typically, more skillful children are interested in competing with others—they find this challenging because they have mastered the skill in static environments. These children truly enjoy and benefit from the opportunity to use their skills in competition with others.

Replays

Repetition, as a way to challenge children, is used more in a gymnastic or dance setting: "Can you repeat the movement exactly so that both tries appear identical?" This is a true challenge for children, especially if they are trying to repeat a sequence of several movements. It's even harder when the sequence is performed with a partner. Thus teachers often use repetition to heighten the challenge for children: "Imagine that I videotaped your sequence. Let's see if you can do it again exactly as I videotaped it."

Videotape

In the example above, the videotape was imaginary. When available, however, encouraging children to work on their sequence or dance to improve it to performance quality for videotaping is often highly motivating. They enjoy seeing themselves on TV. The possibility of being videotaped often provides children with an incentive to continue working on a project that might otherwise be abandoned early due to lack of interest. Obviously the teacher is attempting to motivate children to continue improving the quality of their movements.

Performing for an Audience

Another technique that is used is similar to pinpointing (chapter 6). Children are asked to show others in the class how they are doing a task. Rather than attempting to teach the children, however, this challenge is used to motivate them to continue practicing so that they can show others. It is used in several ways. For example:

- "All those on this side of the gym will do their sequences three times. After that we will switch, and that half of the class can sit down and become spectators."
- "Who would like to demonstrate their game for the rest of the class?"
- "I am looking for routines that clearly show the different speeds and levels that can be shown to the class at the end of the lesson."
- "Jon and Kathleen have found a different way to make their balance. Let's see how they have solved the problem."

Challenges for the Young Child

Young children have a limited movement vocabulary. Consequently, it is difficult to challenge them by combining two skills because they are unable to do the skills alone, let alone when skills are combined. Because of the limited vocabulary and the short attention span of these youngsters, teachers find that a minor change in a task (it is embellished more than changed) is often satisfying to the 4- or 5-year-old child. The following examples are truly minor changes, yet they interest the young child because they are developmentally appropriate for them but not for fourth or fifth graders. Young children perceive minor changes as a new challenge. For example:

- "Now find a different carpet square to balance on." (The balance may be the same, but now it is on a blue rather than a brown carpet square.)
- "After you throw five times, find a different-colored bean bag to throw." (The throw is the same except it is now done with a yellow instead of a red bean bag.)
- "Now see if you can walk on a blue line without falling off." (They are challenged

to find the color blue although they are still focusing on balancing on a line.)
- "Make a different shape with your rope. Then continue trying to jump over the rope and land without falling." (The focus is still on jumping and landing; the shape of the rope is different.)
- "Now turn and skip the other way around the hoop." (The task has been changed from a clockwise to a counter-clockwise skip, for example).

In each of these examples the challenge remains the same. The children, however, are motivated by the opportunity to try the task in, what is for them, a new setting.

CONTENT DEVELOPMENT PATTERNS

One of the fascinating aspects of teaching (developing the content) is the difficult process of deciding when to change a task, provide a cue, or offer a challenge to the class. Ideally these decisions are based on the progress made by the children, rather than arbitrary factors such as time or number of tasks to be covered in a day. Few would argue with this concept; in reality, however, it's hard to know when to change from one to another.

There are a number of content development patterns that evolve as teachers work with different classes. A brief description of these patterns might help to understand how teachers vary tasks, cues, and challenges in their teaching. These patterns can be graphed to aid understanding (Figure 9.2 on page 111). The vertical axis contains the tasks (extensions), cues (refinements), and challenges (applications). The horizontal axis simply numbers each task, cue, or challenge so that the pattern of usage can be understood. Each time the teacher stops the entire class, the observer writes down what he says and codes it later as an extension, refinement, or application. This is easily done from a videotape as well. The way the content was developed can then be interpreted by the teacher to determine the pattern he used.

All Task Pattern

When a teacher initially works with a class of children, it is not uncommon to observe changes from one task to another very quickly. This occurs as the teacher attempts to discover the skill level of the children in that class (Figure 9.3). This pattern is also observed frequently with beginning teachers who have yet to use challenges to keep the children working at the same task. Instead, they change the task when they think the children are becoming bored, rather than providing the children with a challenge.

Task-Cue-Task-Cue Pattern

Another common content development pattern is a repetition of task-cue-task-cue, etc. (Figure 9.4). In this instance the teacher may be reviewing previously taught tasks. If the lesson is not a review, however, and if the cue is different each time, then it suggests that the children are probably not learning the cues because of the limited practice time and opportunities to understand the refinement.

Task-Cue-Cue-Challenge Pattern

The pattern of starting a task, followed by instruction and demonstration of the same cue several times, and then a challenge suggests that a teacher is truly developing the content so that the children can learn it (i.e., she is emphasizing the quality of the movement and keeping the children on the same task because it is appropriate for their ability level) (Figure 9.5). This pattern is often observed in experienced teachers who are familiar with the process of content development and who strive to help their children learn the critical components of the various skills (Masser, 1987).

Interpreting Content Development Patterns

A pattern of content development can be observed and analyzed rather easily by a teacher who wants to determine the way he is developing the content in a class. The patterns, however, provide a teacher with information only about the number of tasks, cues, and challenges and their sequence. That's helpful to know.

It's at least as important, however, to make a judgment about the quality of the tasks, cues, and challenges. Just because a teacher uses a particular content development pattern doesn't necessarily mean that it was a good or poor lesson. The pattern always needs to be interpreted keeping in mind such factors as the skill level and experience of the children in the class, the number of times the skill

has been taught previously, and the progression in which the tasks were presented.

In addition, the quality of the tasks, cues, and challenges can also be judged as to their appropriateness and effectiveness. Did the pattern work with that class? Why? Why not? How might it be improved? These decisions are based on the way the children are moving as determined through observation. Let's assume the teacher videotapes a lesson and then reviews it that evening at home. She might ask herself these questions:

- Did the children understand and use the cues being emphasized during the lesson? Were they actually moving quickly to the ball (a cue for that lesson)?
- Was the cue appropriate? Was it the one they really needed at that point in their development?
- Was the progression of tasks too hard? Too easy? (She would look at the success rate of the children and also make a judgment about the children's interest in the tasks.)
- Were tasks changed unnecessarily or too quickly? (This often happens because a teacher has taught the same skill to five or six classes they day, and she is tired of it, but the children may not be.)
- Did the challenges motivate the children to practice harder? Was an application necessary?
- Were the tasks appropriate to accomplish the objective for the lesson? Did they truly provide the children with plenty of appropriate practice?

As a teacher views a videotape in the relative solitude of an office or a home, she is able to see so many more things than she can in the turmoil of teaching. This is the time when a teacher can truly evaluate the quality of her content development.

VIDEOTAPE ANALYSIS

Select a videotaped lesson and use Figure 9.2 to analyze the pattern of content development. When you have finished the analysis, the questions at the end of the preceding section will be of interest as you reflect on the way the content was developed.

Teacher's name _____   Observer _____

Class taught _____   Date _____

Lesson focus _____

Directions: Write down the statements the teacher makes to the entire class, not to groups or individuals, about motor skills—not about behavior or management. At times you may need to abbreviate but try to capture the intent of the meaning. When the lesson is over, classify each statement as extending (tasks), refining (cues), or applying (challenges). Then graph the statements in the order in which they occur. You may need to use the back of the sheet to record all of the statements.

1.

2.

3.

4.

5.

6.

7.

8.

9.

10.

(continue on back)

Figure 9.2   Assessing your pattern of content development.

Teacher's name __Ron__   Observer __Julie__

Class taught __Mrs. Speck's, 2nd Grade__   Date __Dec. 5, 1991__

Lesson focus __Dribbling with hands__

Directions: Write down the statements the teacher makes to the entire class, not to groups or individuals, about motor skills—not about behavior or management. At times you may need to abbreviate but try to capture the intent of the meaning. When the lesson is over, classify each statement as extending (tasks), refining (cues), or applying (challenges). Then graph the statements in the order in which they occur. You may need to use the back of the sheet to record all of the statements.

1. Bounce the ball with 2 hands; stay on your carpet square.

2. Bounce the ball with 1 hand; stay on your carpet square.

3. Bounce the ball at low level only; stay on your carpet square.

4. Bounce the ball with your other hand; stay on your carpet square.

5. Walk around your carpet square and dribble the ball.

6. Walk in general space and dribble the ball.

7. Walk in general space and dribble the ball at low level.

8. Jog and dribble in general space.

9. Skip and dribble in general space.

10. When the drum beats, stop traveling, but continue dribbling.

(continue on back)

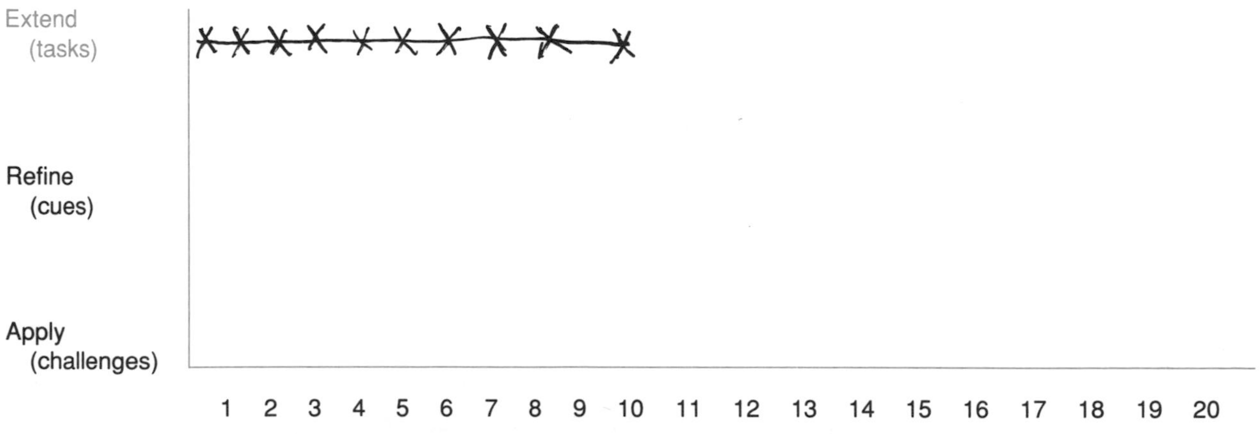

Figure 9.3   All task pattern of content development.

Teacher's name _____ *Kakki* _____   Observer _*Marilyn*_

Class taught _*Ms. Bray's 2nd Grade*_   Date _*Dec. 5, 1991*_

Lesson focus _*Dribbling with hands*_

Directions: Write down the statements the teacher makes to the entire class, not to groups or individuals, about motor skills—not about behavior or management. At times you may need to abbreviate but try to capture the intent of the meaning. When the lesson is over, classify each statement as extending (tasks), refining (cues), or applying (challenges). Then graph the statements in the order in which they occur. You may need to use the back of the sheet to record all of the statements.

1. Walk around your carpet square and dribble your ball.

2. Use your finger pads, not your palms.

3. Walk in general space and dribble the ball.

4. Look up from the ball.

5. Walk in general space and dribble at low level.

6. Look up from the ball.

7. Jog and dribble in general space.

8. Try to push the ball ahead of you.

9. Skip and dribble in general space.

10. Try to push the ball ahead of you.

(continue on back)

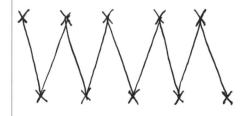

Figure 9.4 Task-cue-task-cue pattern of content development.

Teacher's name _____Steve_____   Observer _____Vickie_____

Class taught _____Ms. Sander's 2nd Grade_____   Date _Dec. 5, 1991_

Lesson focus _Dribbling with hands_

Directions: Write down the statements the teacher makes to the entire class, not to groups or individuals, about motor skills—not about behavior or management. At times you may need to abbreviate but try to capture the intent of the meaning. When the lesson is over, classify each statement as extending (tasks), refining (cues), or applying (challenges). Then graph the statements in the order in which they occur. You may need to use the back of the sheet to record all of the statements.

1. Walk in general space and dribble the ball.

2. Use your finger pads, not your palms.

3. Look over the ball.

4. When I hold up my fingers, tell me how many.

5. Jog and dribble in general space.

6. Look over the ball.

7. Try to push the ball ahead of you.

8. When you pass someone, call out their name.

9. Skip and dribble in general space.

10. Look over the ball.

(continue on back)

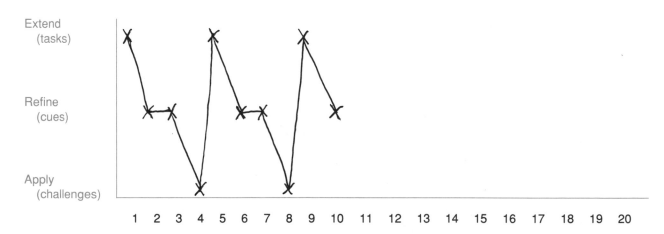

Figure 9.5   Task-cue-cue-challenge pattern of content development.

SUMMARY

Many children can learn to leap, roll, play basketball, bat a ball, and jump rope with no help from adults—if they want to. They don't learn as quickly or as efficiently as they might with instruction, however. And as with eating vegetables, they tend to choose only the skills and activities they like.

Developing the content refers to the process of helping children learn the various motor skills that are typically taught in physical education. As part of this process, teachers decide how long to ask the children to practice a task; which tasks and cues are most appropriate; and how to challenge the children so they will continue meaningful practice.

QUESTIONS FOR REFLECTION

1. In contrast to developing the content to help children truly learn, some teachers simply "teach" fun activities to children with little thought about progression or cues. Why do you think this is so?
2. Think about your background. Which skills do you know the most about? Do you know the cues that will best help children? What about the skills you know least about?
3. Again think about your background. Select a skill you know best. Can you outline a progression of tasks from simple to complex (similar to that in Figure 9.1)?
4. Throughout this chapter it has been mentioned that the teacher relies on a plan to develop the content. It has been implied, however, that the teacher doesn't follow this plan without thinking. Why is it important to base the content development on a plan but also to make changes?
5. Applications, or challenges, are an important part of the teaching process. What happens if the teacher doesn't use challenges?

REFERENCES

Franck, M., Graham, G., Lawson, H., Loughery, T., Ritson, R., Sanborn, M., & Seefeldt, V. (1991). *Physical education outcomes: A project of the National Association for Sport and Physical Education.* Reston, VA: National Association for Sport and Physical Education.

Graham, G., Holt/Hale, S., & Parker, M. (1987). *Children moving* (2nd ed.). Mt. View, CA: Mayfield.

Gusthart, J.L. (1985). Variations in direct, indirect, and noncontributing teacher behaviors. *Journal of Teaching in Physical Education,* **4**, 111-122.

Masser, L. (1987). The effect of a refinement on student achievement in a fundamental motor skill in grades K through 6. *Journal of Teaching in Physical Education,* **6**, 174-182.

Rink, J. (1985). *Teaching physical education for learning.* St. Louis: Times Mirror/Mosby.

Tousignant, M., & Siedentop, D. (1983). A qualitative analysis of task structure in required secondary physical education classes. *Journal of Teaching in Physical Education,* **3**(1), 47-57.

Chapter 10

Providing Feedback

When a teacher observes a class and makes a decision that

- the task is appropriate for the children,
- they don't need a challenge because they are practicing the task as the teacher intended, and
- the cue or critical component has been understood by the children,

then that is the time most teachers provide *feedback*—they observe children individually and apprise them of how they are moving and what they can do to improve.

The purpose of this chapter is to describe and analyze the various types and uses of feedback.

As a result of reading and understanding this chapter, the teacher will be able to

- describe the advantages and uses of feedback;
- analyze the various types of feedback; and
- explain the value of feedback for teachers of children's physical education.

TYPES OF FEEDBACK

The use of feedback by a teacher has several advantages:

- Feedback encourages the children to continue practicing because it lets them know you are watching them move.
- When teachers provide feedback, they also tend to travel around the teaching area, an effective teaching behavior (chapter 4).
- It helps the children assess their performances, which they can't really see or feel on their own.
- Finally, feedback lets the teacher assess individuals to determine how quickly (and correctly) they are learning the skill being taught.

Successful teachers provide various amounts and types of feedback to accomplish these purposes. Typically, feedback provided by successful teachers can be categorized as specific, congruent, simple, and generally positive or neutral.

Specific and General Feedback

Feedback is *specific* when it contains information that allows the children to know specifically what they need to practice or how they are moving (Claxton & Fredenburg, 1989; Mustain, 1990; Rink & Werner, 1987). Feedback is *general* when it could refer to either their movement, their behavior, or their dress, for example.

Probably the most commonly used expression of general feedback in education today is "Good!" Unfortunately, this really doesn't provide the child with the necessary information to improve—was it the outcome that was good? The movement of the arm or leg? Or was it simply a good try?

The use of expressions such as "good," "great," "terrific," "wow," and "all right" are helpful for promoting a positive and warm learning environment, especially with young children who desire teacher approval and have yet to achieve the skill level that allows them to obtain intrinsic satisfaction from being able to move in accomplished ways. Teachers often use general feedback to encourage them to continue to move and try.

As children mature, they benefit from the information the teacher provides that they can't know themselves. They know, for example, that the ball isn't going where they want it to go—they just don't know what they need to do differently. This is when specific feedback is valuable because it tells them exactly what they need to focus on to get the ball into the air or to go straight.

Here are some examples of specific feedback:

- "This time see if you can bend both your knees and your ankles."
- "Be sure to turn your side toward the target."
- "Great. That time you both started at the same time."
- "Can you make your shape even wider?"
- "This time see if you can make the slow part even slower."
- "Try to follow through so that your hand and arm go right to the target."

At times, when the children are familiar with the terminology the teacher uses, one or two reminder words (chapter 6) can provide individuals with specific feedback about how they are moving. Typically this occurs when the feedback relates to a cue or refinement recently explained by the teacher. "Side" or "wait" or "bend" might be the single word that the teacher says in these instances (Figure 6.1).

Congruent and Incongruent Feedback

When feedback focuses on the cue or refinement just explained (chapter 9) and often demonstrated to the entire class (chapter 6), this is termed *congruent* feedback (i.e., it corresponds to the idea just presented to the children that, ideally, they are thinking about as they move) (Rink & Werner, 1987). An example will help make the point.

The lesson is focused on learning to strike with a paddle. The task (extension) the fourth graders have been working on is striking the ball back and forth with a partner. The teacher stops the class and demonstrates the concept of "quick feet" (moving quickly to be in a position to hit the ball). He then asks them to continue striking with their partners and think about "quick feet"; he begins to circulate and provide feedback. If he provides congruent feedback, we will hear him tell the children how they are (are not) using "quick feet" to move to the ball.

If he provides *incongruent* feedback, we might hear him tell the children about how to hold the paddle, to watch the ball, to follow through, to extend the elbow, and other important components related to striking with paddles. These examples of incongruent feedback are often used by teachers; they are not wrong—just incongruent because they are inconsistent with what the children have been asked to think about and pay attention to as they practice.

When teachers provide congruent feedback, they attempt to limit their feedback to the information most recently provided as they explained the cue to the entire class. This doesn't mean that some children don't need feedback about other cues—often they do. Congruent feedback, however, lets the children know how their practice of the cue is going; they receive feedback about what they are thinking and practicing. This is often reinforced through pinpointing (chapter 6) when various children are asked to demonstrate the cue to the entire class.

Simple Feedback

One of the important advantages of providing congruent feedback for the teacher is that the teacher focuses on only one component at a time (chapter 8). This is referred to as *simple* feedback. This is far easier and no doubt more accurate than attempting to do a complete biomechanical analysis of all the children in the class as the teacher moves around, attempting to quickly observe and review the correct use of four, six, or even eight critical components (chapter 8).

In addition to being easier for the teacher, the children benefit because they continually hear (see) the cue being repeated as the teacher moves about providing feedback. Obviously this repetition promotes learning. It also allows the teacher to have a better idea of when to change the cue because she knows when the children are incorporating it into their movement.

Let's look at another example of simple feedback. When the most recently taught cue relates to the use of the finger pads in dribbling, this might be the feedback pattern we hear:

- "Pads, Rip."
- "Nice pads, Carol."
- "Robin, are those your finger pads?"
- "Joe, good pads."
- "Pads, Sue."
- "Use your pads, Margie."

Simple feedback can often consist of a word or two; the reminder words that are used to describe the cue during instruction (chapter 6) are repeated as feedback. When a teacher provides specific, congruent, simple feedback, it's easy to tell what is being emphasized. In fact, those teachers who say "pads" hundreds of times during their eight or more classes are sick of the word by the time the day is over. But they have the satisfaction of knowing that when the 200 to 300 children they teach in a day go home, the children can

answer the question, "What did you learn in P.E. today?" Well, realistically, many of the children will be able to answer the question.

Positive, Neutral, and Negative Feedback

Review the previous examples and you will notice that the examples of feedback are either *positive* ("nice, good") or *neutral* ("pads"). Negative feedback is just not used by many teachers. Obviously it is effective for teachers to vary the affective message of the feedback: sometimes positive, sometimes neutral, occasionally negative (Kniffen, 1988).

COACHES' FEEDBACK

My recollection of the type of feedback I received from coaches in team sports is that it was predominantly negative. If I did something right, I didn't hear much about it. But if I messed up, I sure received feedback in a hurry, and it was often negative—and loud! Why was this so? Are athletes on a team different from children in a physical education class? Does one's skill level influence the type of feedback that might be useful? Are coaches today different from the way they were 20 years ago?

While the use of negative feedback is rarely recommended, I find that teachers who provide feedback that is specific, congruent, and simple can use negative feedback occasion-

ally to let the children know that they still aren't using a cue correctly.

Although this feedback is negative, my experience suggests that it can be done in such a way that it is helpful, not damaging, to a child. A private statement such as "Mary, those are your fingertips, not your pads" is technically negative but realistically helpful to the child. An occasional use of negative feedback, interspersed with predominantly positive and neutral feedback, is an effective tool to have in one's repertoire.

Negative feedback is especially useful for the child who just doesn't understand the cue and fails to realize, after repeated feedback, that the cue still isn't being used. It's also particularly useful for the child who is an athlete and doesn't bother to listen very carefully to a teacher. The child has played on the basketball team since second grade and thinks he knows everything there is to know about the game and certainly everything about a simple skill such as dribbling. While this may sound harsh to the inexperienced teacher, the veteran will quickly recognize my characterization of the athlete who "knows it all."

PRO OR CON?

What do you think about the use of negative feedback? Should it never be used? Used sparingly? Is it damaging to a child's self-concept? How much depends on the way the teacher provides negative feedback? Can you think of an example when negative feedback will be harmful?

Brophy and Good (1986), as part of an analysis of effective teaching, have provided guidelines for praising children effectively (Table 10.1). When you review that table you will see that many of the principles described in this chapter for effective feedback—specific, simple, congruent, and generally positive—are summarized.

WHO GETS YOUR FEEDBACK?

If we're honest with ourselves, we probably tend to favor one type of child over another. Some of us prefer to teach the highly skilled; others, the lower skilled. Physical attractiveness also plays a part. Martinek (1983), for example, found that attractive children tend to get more teacher attention than unattractive children. Some teachers may provide more feedback to boys; others give more to girls.

Figure 10.1 (page 123) is a form that will help you determine which children in a class receive your feedback. It is also designed to let you know the type of feedback they receive. To use this form, list the names of all the children in a class in the left-hand column. Videotape yourself teaching the class (if possible using a wireless microphone so you can hear your individual interactions with the children). It is also possible to use an audiotape to assess your feedback by wearing a small tape recorder on your belt. (The problem with an audiotape recorder is that you don't know who you are talking to unless you remember

Table 10.1 Guidelines for Effective Praise

Effective praise	Ineffective praise
1. Is delivered contingently	1. Is delivered randomly or unsystematically
2. Specifies the particulars of the accomplishment	2. Is restricted to global positive reactions
3. Shows spontaneity, variety, and other signs of credibility; suggests clear attention to the student's accomplishment	3. Shows a bland uniformity that suggests a conditioned response made with minimal attention
4. Rewards attainment of specified performance criteria (which can include effort criteria, however)	4. Rewards mere participation, without consideration of performance processes or outcomes
5. Provides information to students about their competence or the value of their accomplishments	5. Provides no information at all nor gives students information about their status
6. Orients students toward better appreciation of their own task-related behavior and thinking about problem solving	6. Orients students toward comparing themselves with others and thinking about competing
7. Uses students' own prior accomplishments as the context for describing present accomplishments	7. Uses the accomplishments of peers as the context for describing students' present accomplishments
8. Is given in recognition of noteworthy effort or success at difficult (for *this* student) tasks	8. Is given without regard to the effort expended or the meaning of the accomplishment
9. Attributes success to effort and ability, implying that similar successes can be expected in the future	9. Attributes success to ability alone or to external factors such as luck or low task difficulty
10. Fosters endogenous attributions (students believe that they expend effort on the task because they enjoy the task and/or want to develop task-relevant skills)	10. Fosters exogenous attributions (students believe that they expend effort on the task for external reasons—to please the teacher, win a competition or reward, etc.)
11. Focuses students' attention on their own task-relevant behavior	11. Focuses students' attention on the teacher as an external authority figure who is manipulating them
12. Fosters appreciation of, and desirable attributions about, task-relevant behavior after the process is completed	12. Intrudes into the ongoing process, distracting attention from task-relevant behavior

Note. Reprinted by permission from Brophy & Good, 1986.

to call each child by name.) When the lesson is finished, you can use the form to tally and analyze the feedback statements made to the students. Some of the questions you can answer will be:

- Which (if any) children did not receive feedback from you?
- Did you tend to favor any particular group—the highly skilled, the more personable children?
- Do you tend to use specific or general feedback?
- Was your feedback congruent with your cues?
- Are you satisfied with the ratio of positive to neutral to negative?
- Did you vary your use of positive terms? Or did "good" or "all right" predominate?

Obviously there are a number of other questions you could also ask about your feedback. This type of analysis from time to time helps you better understand and analyze your teaching.

RESEARCH ON PHYSICAL EDUCATION TEACHER FEEDBACK

Historically, physical education teachers have been taught that teacher feedback is an important technique to help students learn motor skills. No doubt this is true. In fact, however, feedback may be overrated in terms of its value as a teaching skill.

Essentially, the value of feedback has been documented in laboratories by motor learning researchers. In these labs they are able to create settings where a subject receives absolutely no feedback whatsoever. The subject presses a button, for example, and has no idea if she pressed it too soon or too late. The researcher can then provide the subject with any type of feedback that is being tested. In studies of this type, feedback is virtually always superior to no feedback.

In contrast, when students are learning a motor skill on the playground, they always receive some type of internal feedback—they know, for example, where the ball went, how far it went, how high, and so on. If they were rolling or jumping, they have some sense of how it felt and where they ended up. Although different from feedback provided by a teacher or researcher, the students' internal feedback sense lets them know how they are moving.

The feedback studies that have been done in gyms and on playgrounds have also suggested that feedback is valuable. Unfortunately, however, researchers have failed to control for the amount of practice the students received. Obviously, when teachers are providing feedback, students are practicing. Thus students who received higher amounts of feedback sometimes learned more—or better. They also practiced more, however, making it difficult for the researcher to know whether their improvement was due to

Feedback analysis form

Date __11/20__   Class __Ms. Browne__   Grade __4ᵗʰ__

Topic of lesson __Gymnastic sequences – smooth rolls into balances__

Names	General feedback	Specific feedback							
		Behavior			Skill			Cong	
(May not want to list entire class)	(No specific referent)	+	0	−	+	0	−	Yes	No
1. Jacob	I				I	I		I	I
2. Kathy	I			II					II
3. Nathan					II	I		I	II
4. John			I			I	I	II	I
5. Lois					I	II		III	
6. Jim	I			I			I	I	I
7. Peggy					III			III	
8.									
9.									
10.									
11.									
12.									
13									
14.									
15.									
16.									
17.									
18.									
19.									
20.									
21.									
22.									
23.									
24.									
25.									
26.									
27.									
28.									
29.									
30.									

Figure 10.1   Feedback analysis form.

teacher feedback or simply more practice. As researchers begin to control the amount of practice so it is equal for all students (Goldberger, Gerney, & Chamberlin, 1982) and to set their studies in the real world of physical education, we will gain an increased understanding of teacher feedback and its contribution to student learning.

Today we think that teacher feedback is important, especially when it is specific, congruent, simple, and mostly positive and neutral. We know, however, that lots of practice at high rates of success contributes to student learning and obvious feelings of satisfaction and enjoyment. Keeping this in mind, the successful teacher first makes sure that all of the students are practicing appropriately. Only then does he begin to provide individual feed-back. When a teacher spends time with individuals, and many of the class drift off-task, then the provision of individual feedback is probably counterproductive.

SUMMARY

Feedback is important to children. They want and need to know how they are doing. Ideally children receive reasonable amounts of feedback from a teacher—they are not neglected. Feedback that is specific (rather than general), congruent (rather than incongruent), simple (rather than complex), and positive or neutral (rather than negative) is most effective with children.

QUESTIONS FOR REFLECTION

1. Why is feedback an important teaching skill? What happens when a teacher provides no feedback at all to children?
2. Can you think of some instances when general feedback may be useful to children? Try to provide several specific examples.
3. Think of your physical education experiences as a student. Was feedback important to you? Can you remember the types of feedback you received? If you were an athlete, it might be interesting to compare the feedback you received from a coach as compared to that from a teacher.
4. Why is congruent, simple feedback so rare in physical activity lessons? Why do instructors tend to overload students?
5. Can you think of several examples when a lot of feedback might not necessarily be beneficial to a lesson? To children?

REFERENCES

Brophy, J., & Good, T.L. (1986). Teacher behavior and student achievement. In C.M. Wittrock (Ed.), *Handbook of research on teaching* (3rd ed.) (pp. 328-375). New York: Macmillan.

Claxton, D., & Fredenburg, K. (1989). Coaching young athletes: Strategies for success. *Strategies*, **3**(2), 5-8, 19.

Goldberger, M., Gerney, P., & Chamberlin, J. (1982). The effects of three styles of teaching on the psychomotor performance and social skill development of fifth grade children. *Research Quarterly for Exercise and Sport*, **53**, 116-124.

Kniffen, M. (1988). Instructional skills for student teachers. *Strategies*, **6**, 5-8.

Martinek, T. (1983). Creating Golem and Goleta effects during physical education instruction: A social psychological perspective. In T. Templin & J. Olson (Eds.), *Teaching in physical education* (pp. 59-70). Champaign, IL: Human Kinetics.

Mustain, W. (1990). Are you the best teacher you can be? *Journal of Physical Education, Recreation and Dance*, **61**(2), 69-73.

Rink, J., & Werner, P. (1987). Student responses as a measure of teacher effectiveness. In G.T. Barrette, R.S. Feingold, C.R. Rees, & M. Pieron (Eds.), *Myths, models and methods in sport pedagogy* (pp. 199-206). Champaign, IL: Human Kinetics.

Chapter 11

Questioning and Problem Solving

It's time to switch gears. The first ten chapters have assumed that the teacher is using a *direct* style of teaching: the teacher tells the students what to do and when to do it, and the students comply. My sense is that the majority of teachers use this style for the majority of their lessons. Some lessons, however, may be taught using a more *indirect* style of teaching, involving the children in problem solving as they respond to questions posed by the teacher (Mosston, 1981). In these lessons we want children to explore, discover, create, and generally experiment with a variety of ways of moving—both for enjoyment and as a way to stimulate their cognitive involvement in physical education (Franck et al., 1991). In fact, physical activity is an excellent medium for involving children in higher level thinking opportunities.

The purpose of this chapter is to describe and analyze the teaching skills of questioning and setting problems as alternatives to more direct styles of teaching.

After reading and understanding this chapter, the teacher will be able to

- explain the value of problem-solving activities in physical education for children;
- describe the differences between convergent and divergent problem solving; and
- analyze the teaching skills and characteristics of teachers who are effective at teaching problem-solving lessons.

VALUE FOR THE CHILDREN

Problem-solving lessons use movement as a catalyst to stimulate the higher order thinking skills of children as they are challenged to explore and create solutions to the movement problems posed by the teacher. When children grow accustomed to this type of lesson, it is fascinating to observe their concentration and interaction as they work through various responses. It is especially interesting and rewarding when the children are able to work cooperatively in these types of lessons.

As any teacher who uses a questioning/ problem-solving approach will attest, it takes time and practice to learn to use this style of teaching successfully. Used adeptly it provides children with an intellectually challenging learning environment. Used ineptly it often results in puzzlement which leads to bewilderment and eventually off-task behavior by the children. Successful teachers are able to ask questions and pose problems that are productive, thought provoking, and conducive to a worthwhile experience understood and enjoyed by the children.

This chapter discusses both convergent and divergent problem solving, including specific teaching behaviors used in each approach. In addition, the teaching skills of asking questions and setting problems are discussed, along with some recent thinking about verbal, rather than movement, problem solving.

CHILDREN WITH NO BODIES

From time to time I become involved in a discussion about the value of physical education in schools—especially when budgets are being cut. One argument I use to support the importance of physical education is that schools are responsible for educating the whole child, not just their heads. If this weren't the case—I argue facetiously when I am losing the discussion—just think of the money that could be saved in busing and classroom space if parents just sent their children's heads to school and kept their bodies at home.

This same argument can be turned around to make the point that when children come to physical education, both their bodies and their heads are present. Clearly our unique responsibility as physical educators is to focus primarily on the physical but certainly not to neglect the cognitive and affective development of the child. While it may take more time to use a questioning/problem-solving approach, it is certainly a valuable approach in the repertoire of master teachers for use at appropriate times throughout the year.

CONVERGENT PROBLEM SOLVING

In a *convergent* problem-solving lesson, the teacher guides the children to discover one or more solutions to a problem. There is a right answer, sometimes several. But rather than simply telling the children the answer, the teacher leads the children to discover the so-

lution gradually. For this reason convergent problem solving is also referred to as guided discovery (Mosston, 1981).

My favorite example of convergent problem solving is Mosston's (1981) now classic "slanty rope" lesson. (This concept was also discussed in chapter 7 as a way to design tasks to accommodate different skill levels.) Imagine a class of children organized into small groups. Each group has two ropes placed parallel on the ground about 12 inches apart. The children are challenged to jump the imaginary river formed by the two ropes without getting wet or being swallowed by the alligators. They all succeed. Now they are asked to widen the river so that it is 24 inches apart and see if they can still jump it. Gradually they continue to widen the river, and some children are unable to jump the river successfully. Now the groups are ready to hear the problem: "Is there a way you can set up the ropes so that everybody in your group will be able to jump the river successfully?"

There are at least two solutions to this problem. One solution is to arrange the ropes so that at one end they are close together and at the other end farther apart (refer to slanty rope cartoon in chapter 7). The other solution is to keep one rope straight and curve the other so that the river is narrower in the middle and wider at the ends.

This is one example of a convergent problem-solving lesson. Other approaches suitable for this type of lesson include:

- "What are the five basic ways we can take off and land when we jump?"
- "What are the most balanced and least balanced positions you can make?" (Later there will be an example of how this might be developed.)
- "How do you land from a jump so that the landing is very soft and quiet?"
- "What is the quickest way to mount the bench (box, table, beam, bars)?"
- "How can you stand so that you are ready to move quickly?"
- "In your game you can pass the ball to your partner using only two hands at middle level." (After playing for some time, the children are guided to understand the need for developing the ability to pass the ball at a variety of levels, using both one and two hands.)

FINDING MOVEMENT PROBLEMS FOR CHILDREN TO SOLVE

A good resource for developing problem-solving lessons is the series *Basic Stuff in Action*. One book is written for grades K through 3; the other, for grades 4 through 8. These books are available from the American Alliance for Health, Physical Education, Recreation and Dance, 1900 Association Dr., Reston, VA 22091. Each book contains chapters on motor skills, personal fitness, and joy, pleasure, and satisfaction.

In the final section of this chapter, a number of teacher characteristics or behaviors are described that we employ when developing successful convergent as well as divergent lessons. There are several guidelines, however, that are specific to convergent lessons.

Never Tell the Answer

The most obvious guideline is that the teacher never tells the answer. If the teacher does tell the answer, then the children will become less willing to truly explore the solutions, knowing that the teacher will eventually provide the answer. In fact, it's not at all unproductive to finish a lesson that the children still haven't discovered an answer to. Wonder and curiosity are valuable mental processes that can be readily stimulated through physical activity. And, after all, what's so bad about children leaving a class and still not knowing the answer the teacher had in mind?

Responding to Incorrect Solutions

In convergent problem solving there is at least one correct answer—sometimes more. When the children reach a conclusion that is incorrect, rather than simply telling them it is wrong, many teachers will ask, "Do you need more time?" or "Have you checked your answer?" or "Can you explain your answer to me?" This preserves the atmosphere of discovery and problem solving in contrast to the lessons in which the teacher is providing the answers.

Convergent problem solving is probably easier with young children who have little or no prior knowledge or habits related to the problem posed by the teacher. They are eager to explore movement. Older children, unfortunately, have had some of their curiosity dampened and often are more interested in right answers. Typically they will respond quickly by recalling prior experiences if the problem posed by the teacher is not unique to their background. This is not to say that convergent problem solving cannot be used with older children—just that it is more challenging for the teacher to develop truly interesting lessons using this approach.

LOOK AT IT THIS WAY

My experience is that children have a much more creative and mirthful way of interpreting our questions. Two examples come to mind. I remember asking one class to make a narrow shape with their bodies. As I looked at one child, she definitely had a wide shape: arms and feet spread wide apart. When I queried her about her "narrow" shape, she said, "You're looking at it the wrong way. Look at it from the side." She was right! Viewed from the side, her shape was narrow.

Asking children to balance with "X" number of body parts touching the floor is also fascinating. Some children, for example, view a foot as one part; others count each toe, so a one-foot balance, for them, is interpreted as five parts. Some count their rear end as one part, others as two.

Discussing Solutions

During closure (chapter 13), many teachers discuss the responses with the children. Some do not. It depends on the teachers and the importance they place on children discussing the concept(s) taught during the lesson. Some teachers, for example, want the children to be able to verbalize their movement responses (to be able to describe a stable or unstable balance); others are satisfied if the children are able to provide movement answers (to be able to demonstrate stable and unstable balances).

DIVERGENT PROBLEM SOLVING

In contrast to convergent, *divergent* problem solving asks children to explore alternatives and discover many different ways to solve a problem. Convergent problem solving has one or more correct answers; divergent has an infinite number of responses. There is no limit to the diversity and range of possible answers. While convergent problem solving leads children to focus on the depth of an answer, divergent problem solving emphasizes a breadth of responses. The exciting part of this approach is the variety of unique solutions children create as they explore answers to the questions posed by the teacher.

Examples of topics that might be developed in divergent problem-solving lessons include

- different ways to travel in general space;
- different ways to balance on the floor or on apparatus;
- the number of different, *safe* ways one might mount/dismount a bench, table, or vaulting box;
- ways to outmaneuver opponents in a game;
- alternative ways to "shoot" a ball when guarded by an opponent;
- sequences of gymnastic or dance-like movements;
- ways of passing a ball from Player A to Player B; and
- ways of creating a game.

Asking the Divergent Question

There are many ways of asking questions leading to divergent movement. Some are better than others. Mosston (1981) suggests that two frequently used questions may be counterproductive:

- The question "Can you . . . ?" may result in the response "No, I can't."
- The question "How many ways . . . ?" may lead some children to respond with only one movement or to become intimidated because they can hardly think of one response, let alone several.

He recommends that divergent questions take the following form:

- "What are three possible ways to . . . ?" When (if) children discover three ways, then the teacher can ask for three more ways. This format of questioning allows the children to be successful at finding three solutions.

The way the question is asked is more important when a teacher is first beginning to teach using a divergent problem-solving approach. In time, when the children become accustomed to problem solving in the gym, the form used to ask the question (not the content) will become less crucial. The children will enjoy the uncertainty of exploring and discovering movement alternatives. They also realize that the teacher can be trusted to present interesting, fun problems to solve.

Learning Atmosphere

The atmosphere for divergent problem solving to be effective also needs to be supportive. Most of the feedback statements are neutral (chapter 10) as the teacher encourages the children to continue exploring alternatives. For example, the teacher might say to the child who has found two ways to move at low level, "That's two different ways. Can you find a third?"

When a response simply does not address the question, it is most effective to explain to the child or the group why the response is inappropriate so that they are clear on the problem that they are to solve.

Pinpointing

At times pinpointing (chapters 2 and 6) is helpful for showing children the diversity of responses that you encourage. In the beginning children are often looking for the right answer and fail to understand that there is no single answer that the teacher is looking for. In these instances the teacher can pinpoint several children who are making appropriate responses so that the others can see the type of diversity that the teacher encourages.

If the teacher had asked for different ways to travel in general space, for example, many of the children might be traveling on their feet. The teacher might pinpoint children traveling at low level on their hands and knees or those transferring weight (as in a cartwheel) to encourage children to explore the alternatives. In this instance, however, it is important that the teacher explain that she is looking for ways to move other than those that were just pinpointed. If this is not clear to the children, they will instantly mimic the movement(s) previously pinpointed—the opposite of what you are searching for in divergent problem solving.

VERBAL PROBLEM SOLVING

Up to this point, this chapter has assumed that the responses of the children will be movement rather than verbal responses. Clearly, however, there are times when the teacher asks for verbal responses to questions. There are two guidelines we have devised based on classroom research about verbal responses to questions. One relates to children calling out answers; the other relates to waiting for an answer from the children.

Callouts

One clear finding is that callouts (situations in which the children respond immediately and

simultaneously) are not as effective as calling on children who have their hands raised. We have all asked questions to a class of children, only to have eight children answer at the same time. Children in another class at the same school—when asked the same question—might respond by raising their hands but remaining silent. Clearly the way they respond is based on the protocol that the classroom teacher established at the beginning of the year (chapter 3).

Generally it is thought that asking children to respond by raising their hands to be recognized by the teacher is more effective than simply allowing children to call out. The exception to this generalization is for those truly unmotivated classes that seem to respond better in a rapid-fire question-and-answer setting—the type that is often depicted in the movies.

Wait Time

One of the reasons children are taught to raise their hands is so the teacher can pause for several seconds (three is suggested) before calling on a child to respond. This allows every child to think about the answer without knowing who will be called upon. It seems that once a teacher names a child, the others tend to relax and discontinue thinking about the answer. The three seconds or so also allows the children to formulate better responses. We have all observed kindergarten and first-grade classes in which all of the children raise their hands to respond to every question asked by the teacher. When no time is allowed for thought (and even sometimes when it is), it is common to call on a child only to realize that she didn't really have an answer but just wanted to see if she could be the one called upon.

The concept of wait time (pausing 3 seconds or more) before calling on a child is an interesting teacher behavior to begin to use. It's interesting because initially 3 seconds seems like an eternity. Over a series of lessons, however, both the children and the teacher become accustomed to wait time, and the children benefit more from this type of questioning than when they are called on immediately. It's obviously even less productive when a child is named to answer the question even before the question is asked.

EFFECTIVE QUESTIONING AND PROBLEM SETTING

As with any aspect of pedagogy, there are a variety of related teacher behaviors and characteristics that blend together to compose an effective method or technique. Asking questions and setting problems is no different. Teachers who challenge and motivate children to think about movement in creative and intellectually challenging ways have patience, a good knowledge of the content and developmental level of the children, and are positive and accepting.

Patience

Teaches who successfully develop lessons using a problem-solving approach have patience. Problem solving takes time; it's a much slower process than simply telling children the answers. This may be why we see problem solving less often than we see other types of lessons—the process takes longer and most programs are severely limited in time.

Initially, it takes time just for the children to learn to effectively explore solutions to a problem. Children aren't instantly terrific problem solvers. Naturally this depends on what they are accustomed to in the classroom. If problem solving is used in the classroom, then it is reasonable to expect that class to be adept at the process. In contrast, a class that is taught using only a direct approach will take much longer to learn to problem solve effectively.

Once a class of children has learned the process, it still takes much longer for them to discover a solution or explore various alternatives on their own than it would if the teacher simply told or showed them an answer. Obviously, however, certain content we teach lends itself to problem solving, and this is the reason many teachers use this approach. It may take longer, but the children benefit from the process.

One indicator I have always used to determine how well children are adapting to the problem-solving approach is the amount of time they remain involved in a problem. Initially children are satisfied with a sequence or game created in just a few minutes. As they have more experience with the process, however, it seems that they always need more time. As children expand their movement repertoires and understand what is meant by the quality of a sequence, they want (and need) more time to refine the sequence or game so that it is truly satisfying to them. The fifth-grade class who initially had their sequence finished in 5 minutes may need two or three class periods once they understand all that is involved in creating and polishing a routine or game so that it is interesting and satisfying.

Content Knowledge

In addition to patience, another skill needed by a teacher to successfully pose questions and set problems is a thorough knowledge of the content that is the topic for that lesson. Ideally this is true for every lesson we teach, but it seems that it is even more so in this approach because the teacher is gradually leading the children to one or more solutions. An example of teaching the concept of balance to a class of young children will help illustrate:

"What does the word balance *mean?"*

"Right. It means that you are not falling down and that you are able to remain steady."

"Show me one way to balance with your body."

"Now let's see how you can make that balance even steadier."

"Is this your most balanced position?"

(In time, under the guidance of the teacher, the children will realize that the lower and wider the position, the more stable the balance. A few children may actually lie flat on the floor.)

"Now let's see how you can change your balance to make it less steady."

"Even less steady?"

"Show me your least balanced position" (Mosston, 1981, p. 176).

During closure (chapter 13), the teacher can discuss the ways the children changed from most to least balanced (i.e., the characteristics of balance). This basic concept is one example of content that lends itself well to problem solving because the children easily and accurately grasp the essence of balance through this process.

In the next example, the teacher uses problem solving with content (the overhand throw) that leads to a possible misunderstanding by the children. This lesson used problem solving to attempt to help children understand the concept of using the opposite foot when forcefully throwing overhand:

"Using an overhand throw, throw the ball hard against the wall."

After a number of tries, the teacher might ask, "Which foot do you step with? The one on the same side as the throwing hand? Or the one on the opposite side?"

"Try some throws now and use the other foot—the one you haven't been stepping with. Does the ball travel faster when you step with one foot or the other?"

This process might continue for some time as the teacher continues to ask the children to change feet, sometimes using opposition, sometimes an ipsilateral step. During closure the teacher might then ask, "Which foot do you step with to make the ball go faster—the one on the same side as the throwing arm or the one on the opposite side?"

My experience and my observation of other teachers suggest that this teacher would probably receive a mixed response. Some students would argue for opposition. Others would not.

Compared with the concept of balance, opposition is typically not a good topic to use in a guided discovery lesson (the teacher attempting to gradually lead the children to discover that it is better to use opposition than a unilateral stepping pattern). The reason it is not a very effective lesson is that the child who does not use opposition when he throws is not quickly comfortable. He is also not convinced that opposition improves his throwing ability. Because it is a new and awkward feeling for the child, the ball doesn't necessarily go farther or harder. So the child concludes that a unilateral stepping pattern results in better throws for him. The teacher is then faced with a dilemma: whether to tell the child he has drawn the wrong conclusion, causing him to distrust his ability to discover, or to allow that solution to stand until a lesson later in the year (Ainsworth & Fox, 1989).

Obviously there may be ways of guiding children to discover the effectiveness of opposition that are not counterproductive. Over the years, however, I have observed this lesson taught by enough different teachers to conclude that some content lends itself well to problem solving, whereas other content is harder to teach using this approach. The important point is that, in addition to patience, a teacher needs to know the content well to design and implement an effective problem-solving lesson.

Children's Developmental Level

Along with the content being developed, it is important for the teacher to be familiar with the age and developmental level of the child. This is rather an obvious statement, especially as it relates to the content, but I have included it as a separate characteristic because it is not enough simply to know the content well. The teacher also needs to know what type of question or problem will be interesting and provocative at various grade levels. The two examples related to balance and opposition are appropriate for primary-grade children. With intermediate-grade children, however, they won't be of much interest. If the children don't already understand these concepts, they probably aren't interested in spending a whole lot of time exploring the solutions.

They are often interested, however, in working in small groups to design and synchronize a series of movements (as in a gymnastics or dance routine) or to design a game. Identifying strategies used in escaping from a defender is another problem which fascinates many older children. The following examples are often interesting to children in grades four through six:

- With a partner, design a sequence that has at least one roll, one balance, one weight transfer, and a beginning and ending shape. Repeat it three times, each time varying the speed of the sequence.
- In a group of four to six, make up a game. The game must have kicking (a ball) in it. Use cones to clearly define your boundaries.
- In groups of three or four, see if you can find at least three ways to form a counterbalance. Everyone must keep at least one foot on the floor.

THE HIGHLY SKILLED CHILD AS A PROBLEM SOLVER

My experience has been that the highly skilled child often finds it harder to problem solve in physical education than the lower skilled child. This may be true because highly skilled children already have a movement repertoire that has been polished and refined through practice. They have a series of responses to the questions posed by the teacher and therefore see no need to search for alternatives. I am particularly reminded of children who are excellent gymnasts. My experience has been that many of them, when asked to create a sequence, will rely totally on their predesigned stunts so that their sequence appears very similar to an Olympic gymnastics routine. Personally I find these routines far less interesting than those of the children who are less skilled and yet able to discover creative solutions to the movement problem. As I work with highly skilled children who rely solely on traditional rolls, balances, and weight transfers, I want to tell them that they can't use any of these movements in their sequences. I remind myself, however, that that's my need—and try to remain patient and accepting of their efforts.

Positive and Accepting

In addition to being patient and having a good knowledge of the content and the developmental level of the children, teachers also need to create an environment in which children feel comfortable trying out new ideas and solutions without fear of failure. Teachers typically create this environment by being positive and accepting with the children.

As children offer solutions, either verbally or in movement, they naturally explore some ideas that are recognized by the teacher as counterproductive—silly or uninventive or lacking in much effort. What is important to remember, however, is that the teacher is a more sophisticated problem solver who typically knows many of the solutions. The children do not. Thus part of the process is encouraging the children to continue to work and try even though they may appear to be a long way from the solution.

When a teacher isn't positive and accepting, the children may sense it and become unwilling to genuinely participate in the process. This is especially true when the teacher makes the children feel as if their responses are not worthwhile or appropriate. The challenge for the teacher, of course, is to distinguish between the child who is off-task and just goofing around and the child who is creatively working at solving the problem. The off-task child needs to be refocused; the creative child, reinforced for her efforts.

SHOULD I USE A DIRECT OR AN INDIRECT APPROACH?

Successful teachers are always searching for better ways to help and motivate children to learn. The teaching approach they select for various lessons is one decision they continually face: Would a direct or an indirect approach be better with this lesson?

Some of the questions to consider relate to the role of the teacher and the children. Ainsworth and Fox (1989) have developed a helpful analysis comparing what they term a traditional (direct) and a cognitive process (indirect) approach to learning in physical education (Figure 11.1). Although the analysis doesn't fit exactly with the approaches discussed in this chapter, it is a helpful summary for teachers as they decide which approach to use in their classes.

SUMMARY

A master teacher is one who is adept at different styles of teaching—both direct and indirect. Questioning and problem solving represent an indirect style of teaching. Convergent problem solving (discovering answers to a problem) and divergent problem solving (searching for a variety of alternatives

rather than one or more answers) are two of the ways teachers can involve children in higher level thinking skills in physical education. To do so effectively, however, there are certain teaching skills and characteristics that are used by successful teachers. Obviously teachers must know and understand children, the content, and their own characteristics as a teacher if they are going to effectively lead children in problem-solving activities.

Traditional (behavioral) approach	Cognitive (processes) approach
Subject centered	Learner centered
Teacher tells	Learner explores
Ignores learners' rich repertoire of movement memories	Utilizes learners' rich repertoire of movement memories
Learner plays relatively passive role in the process	Learner assumes a major responsibility for his/her own learning
Teacher identifies errors and prescribes corrections	Learner identifies errors and makes adjustments
May be less time-consuming in early stages	May be more time-consuming in early stages

Figure 11.1 Comparison of traditional behavioral (direct) and cognitive processes (indirect) approach. (Reprinted by permission from Ainsworth & Fox, 1989.)

QUESTIONS FOR REFLECTION

1. List several concepts or skills typically taught in physical education. Which of them might be taught using a divergent problem-solving approach and which a convergent problem-solving approach?
2. Do you think problem solving is widespread or barely used in physical education classes today? Explain the reasons for your answer and why this might be the case.
3. Problem solving requires more time than a direct teaching approach. Why is this so?
4. When you think of your characteristics as a teacher, are you more or less apt to use a problem-solving approach? Can you understand the reasons for your answer?

5. It seems that teachers in the classroom are reluctant to use problem-solving lessons that involve children in movement. How would you go about convincing a classroom teacher that higher order thinking skills can be developed in the gym as well as they can when children sit at a desk?

REFERENCES

Ainsworth, J., & Fox, C. (1989). Learning to learn: A cognitive process approach to movement skill acquisition. *Strategies*, **3**(1), 20-22.

Franck, M., Graham, G., Lawson, H., Loughery, T., Ritson, R., Sanborn, M., & Seefeldt, V. (1991). *Physical education outcomes: A project of the National Association for Sport and Physical Education*. Reston, VA: National Association for Sport and Physical Education.

Mosston, M. (1981). *Teaching physical education*. Columbus, OH: Bell & Howell.

Chapter 12

Building Positive Feelings

As I begin this chapter, Funky Winkerbean, the cartoon character created by Tom Batiuk, is hanging from a climbing rope. He can't get down. He's been stuck on the rope all day. Now everyone is gone except the janitor, who's sweeping the gym floor. I will have to wait until tomorrow to discover how Funky solves his dilemma.

Last week the cartoon focused on the overweight, sweatshirted, bewhistled coach and how he only showed movies when he taught in the classroom. One day the principal was commenting on the coach and how he had already burned out three movie projectors this year. Another day the students were discussing why the windows in the coach's classroom had been painted black—they concluded it was because the coach did nothing but show films.

These are funny scenarios—to some. For me, however, they hurt more than amuse. That's my profession and those are my colleagues he is mocking. Obviously Tom Batiuk, the creator of the Funky Winkerbean cartoon, had some unpleasant experiences in physical education. Unfortunately, he's not the only one. All too many adults share his feelings about physical education classes.

This chapter focuses on those feelings and their development related to physical activity:

- Feelings about one's self
- Feelings about others
- Feelings of joy
- Feelings of satisfaction
- Feelings of pleasure
- Feelings of self-accomplishment

The list could continue. All of these feelings fall into the category of the affective domain: how children feel about themselves and about physical activity. There's a lot we don't know or understand about feelings. We do know, however, that participation in physical activity has the potential to create powerful and lasting impressions—both painful and joyous.

Obviously our goal as physical educators is to create environments that are pleasant, warm, and caring—and result in children developing positive attitudes. Perhaps if Tom Batiuk had been in such classes, Funky Winkerbean might find physical education more enjoyable—and the coach would be depicted as a caring, sensitive, and respected teacher.

This chapter focuses on the ways physical education teachers can help to create the types of environments that lead to the development of desirable attitudes towards physical activity and one's involvement in it. It is designed to focus on the everyday things we do as teachers and how they influence children's feelings.

As a result of reading and understanding this chapter, the teacher will be able to

- describe the feelings of children that are related to experiences in physical education;
- analyze the intentional and unintentional actions of teachers that contribute to how children feel about themselves and physical activity;
- analyze various games and activities taught in physical education and how they influence children's feelings;
- explain how games can be modified to de-emphasize competition;
- describe some of the ways teachers have found to avoid making children feel bad about testing and test results in physical education classes; and
- describe how teachers can help children get in touch with and understand their feelings about their involvement in physical activity.

INTENTIONAL AND EVER-PRESENT

Teachers who help children create positive attitudes seem to do two things:

1. They make a special effort to create these positive attitudes—it's not simply an accident.
2. Their effort is ever-present, not just for a few games or activities that they do from time to time.

There are a number of texts (e.g., Flugelman, 1976; Orlick, 1978a, 1978b; Turner & Turner, 1984) that describe games and activities that promote cooperation and cooperative experiences. It seems, however, that developing positive attitudes is more than simply playing "Hug Tug," "Frozen Beanbag," "Lap Sit," "Cooperative Musical Chairs," or "Long, Long Jump." It's an environment created by the teacher that says, "You're OK; I'm glad you are here even if you aren't very skilled or very fit. This class is to help you improve and enjoy physical activity, not to make you feel bad because you are unable to do something." To create such an environment, teachers do a variety of things. Some of these actions are more subtle than others, but together they say to the children, "You belong here, and my goal is to help you feel good about yourself as you participate in physical activities."

TEACHER ACTIONS

There are a number of ways that teachers have developed to help every child, not only the highly skilled, to enjoy physical activity.

They include providing alternatives, analyzing their interactions, audiotaping, creating an environment that says, "It's OK to make mistakes in this class," and helping children to understand that motor skills aren't learned as quickly as we would like.

Provide Alternatives

Poor Funky Winkerbean! His teacher provided no choice but for him to attempt to climb to the top of the rope. And so he got stuck. A caring teacher would have provided Funky with several choices so that he would avoid the embarrassment of being asked to do something that he probably knew he couldn't do—but was required to do anyway (chapter 7).

When children are asked to play in a game that singles them out (e.g., batting in a softball-type game, dribbling in a basketball-type game, being the only one who is "it" in a tag game), any feelings of inadequacy and incompetence are reinforced in a hurry if they fail by striking out, losing the ball, or being unable to catch anyone else. They fail in front of the entire class.

Caring teachers create environments in which children are not singled out in front of the class and embarrassed by their awkwardness. Activities are designed and taught so that children can avoid these embarrassing situations (e.g., every child has a ball to dribble; there are three or four batters in several minigames; or there are three or four "its" in a tag game). Teaching by invitation and intratask variation are also used to avoid placing children in uncomfortable situations (chapter 7). Funky Winkerbean, for example, might have been invited to climb only halfway up the rope if he wasn't comfortable climbing to the top.

Interaction Analysis

Another way teachers avoid contributing to the development of negative attitudes towards physical education is to become aware of who they interact with and how. If teachers interact differently with the skilled or attractive child as compared with the unskilled or unattractive child, then this subtle message comes through to the children, reinforcing

any tendency toward feelings of incompetence. The teacher may not be aware of her interaction patterns, but the children are! When teachers meet several hundred children a day, it's hard to make the hundreds, perhaps thousands, of interactions all ideal. We hope that a single embarrassing or unfortunate incident won't instantly create a negative attitude. But several years of negative interactions and experiences will clearly contribute to feelings of inadequacy and incompetence. Figure 10.1, the feedback analysis form, provides some insights about which children we are interacting with. It can easily be modified to answer different questions about who we are interacting with and how.

Audiotaping

Another technique that a teacher can use to ascertain the type of environment he is creating is to audiotape a class. Strap a small tape recorder on your belt, attach the microphone to your shirt, and then audiotape a lesson. When you listen to the tape, try to hear what you communicate to the children about what is important to you. For example:

- Do you care more about trying hard to improve or about skillful performances?
- Do you sound too demanding or too critical?
- Is there a tone of warmth and caring communicated to the children?
- Do you sound supportive? Encouraging? Understanding?

When you listen to the audiotape you will have to determine how you sound in relation to how you want to sound (i.e., the decision is yours). At times you may want to ask someone you trust to listen to part of the tape so they can help you interpret the affective messages you are communicating. Be careful not to be too hard on yourself. Remember that teaching is a complex and difficult job.

Mistakes-OK-Here Zone

Another way teachers help children feel good about themselves is to help them realize that learning inevitably involves mistakes. That's how we learn! We try not to make them, but they happen—and that's OK.

One of the ways teachers do this is to declare the playground or gym a "mistakes-OK-here zone." It's expected that everyone, including the teacher, will make mistakes from time to time. It's normal—an important part of learning. And when a mistake does occur, there's no reason to laugh at or ridicule or single anyone out: We try to accept it and understand.

Obviously the mistakes-OK-here zone can be described. But that's not enough. When a child does make a mistake and is ridiculed or laughed at, the teacher immediately stops the class and focuses on the idea of a mistakes-OK-here zone—to let the children know that she will not accept criticism or sarcasm when a mistake is made.

The mistakes-OK-here zone is also created when the children see the teacher making mistakes when he tries to learn something he has yet to master. Obviously, how and when this is done will depend on the teacher, the class, and so forth, but it is an important way of communicating the idea that learning involves trial and error. Children learn a lot from watching someone they respect try to learn something. They begin to realize that skills are learned, not inherited, and that mistakes are part of the learning process, not something to become upset about.

P.E. TEACHERS ARE SUPERHEROES

Many children, especially the youngest, regard their P.E. teachers as superheroes. They can do everything! The children don't realize that our adeptness came from lots of practice and hard work. I am sure they just assume we were born that way. We reinforce this perception when we demonstrate only the skills we can do well. Would it be beneficial to the children if we also let them know that there are some skills we don't do so well? Or do we want to preserve our superhero image?

The "Yet" Intervention

Agnes Stillman (1989) described one of the ways she helps students feel positive about physical education. She has humorously titled it, "The Stillman Two-Part 'Yet' Intervention."

Part 1. When a student forgets and says, "I can't," Stillman adds "yet" on the end of the comment. She concluded after 21 years that the phrase "I can't" will never be totally eliminated from the vocabulary of students.

Part 2. She makes a deal with the student. She asks the student to try the skill 37 times and if it still can't be done, then she will accept that the student can't do it.

A SCENARIO DEPICTING THE "YET" INTERVENTION

"I can't!"

Hearing Ralph's voice attached to that, I turn to him and say (with my finger up), "Ralph, what did I hear you say?"

"I can't . . . yet."

"Thank you. Now, how many tries have you made?"

"Eleven."

"So, how many more tries do you have?" (We can integrate math skills!)

"Twenty-six."

I give him some encouragement and then move on to Sarah and Sam. Sure enough, I look over at Ralph in time to see him execute the skill well enough that he is actually smiling about it. I've got him now.

I eventually get back around to Ralph.

"Well, what are we up to now?"

We both know he lost count. He creates a number—33. He could have said 37, but he's an honest kid. By saying 33, he knows he has only four more tries to close our deal. By now, however, he's not trying to prove me wrong. He has had some success, although he hates to admit it.

I ask if I may watch his last four tries, which I point out should be his best efforts. And, of course, they're successful enough to bring praise, pats on the back, and high fives. Ralph heads for the locker room with a feeling of accomplishment and I say a quiet "thank you" and prepare for the next Ralph's to arrive.

Note. From "The 'Yet' Intervention" by A. Stillman, 1989, *Strategies,* **2**(4), pp. 17, 28.

Obviously the number 37 is arbitrary. Her point, however, is that she wants children to try—and try hard. But if they truly try and still can't do it, she accepts that and suggests something else for the student to try.

SELECTION OF ACTIVITIES

In addition to the actions of the teacher, the activities we select to teach and the way we group children also have an impact on how children feel. Obviously we can select activities that will mean public failure (or success) for children. Picking teams, elimination games, and relays typically contribute to undesirable feelings for some of the children in a class—typically the poorly skilled children who stand to benefit the most from physical education.

Captains Picking Teams

This section is probably unnecessary today—at least I hope it is. We now realize that asking children to form teams by selecting two captains and having them pick the children one at a time is excruciatingly painful to children and creates lasting, haunting impressions as adults. It should be banned from schools—against the law! It simply hurts too much to stand and wait, only to be picked last or next to last. Sadly, children don't understand that they are being picked last because they are unskilled; rather, they think that they are picked last because they are unpopular, or bad, or ugly, or any number of self-imposed, harmful perceptions.

FORMING TEAMS IN PHYSICAL EDUCATION

Ideally the formation of teams whereby one half of the class competes against the other half is a rare occurrence in children's physical education classes. There may be instances, however, when it is developmentally appropriate to divide the children into two teams. There are several ways to do so that are relatively quick and do not damage a child's self-esteem.

One of the easiest ways is to ask the children to find a partner (but don't tell them you are about to organize them into teams). Ask one partner to stand on the blue line and face her partner who is standing on the red line. All of the children will be standing on two lines, facing one another. The children on the blue line compose one team, the ones on the red line the other team. Interestingly this is one of the quickest and easiest ways to form teams of equal ability, as so often in physical education classes children will pick partners of similar ability.

Another quick way to form teams is by asking the children to "count off." The ones are on one team; the twos are on the other. Or you can ask the children to "count off in fours"—ones and threes, for example, on one team, twos and fours on the other.

Another way to form teams is to ask the children with birthdays in the first 6 months of the year (January through June) to stand on one line; those with birthdays in July through December stand on the other line. This should come out reasonably close in numbers.

Elimination Games

Another vestige from the past that I wish were gone forever are games where children are eliminated. Who is eliminated first? The child who needs the most practice, of course. This is simply a prehistoric practice that needs to be stopped in schools—not only in physical education.

Relays

A third type of activity that promotes feelings of inferiority in some children is relays. Inevitably the poorly skilled, overweight children end up at the back of the relay lines. They are the ones still lumbering along when the race has already been decided and, invariably, the last thing that happens in a game is remembered as the most important part. Thus the child who comes in last becomes the target of ridicule and is often blamed for the loss—even though the other team members were also slow. Again this presents a lasting, harmful feeling about physical activity, clearly resulting in painful and unpleasant memories of physical education. How can it possibly result in feelings of eagerness and enthusiasm toward participation in physical activity?

Relays, picking teams, and elimination games are simply unnecessary. They are potentially damaging to a child's self-concept, and we long ago developed superior approaches to selecting teams and motivating children to participate in physical activity.

DECISION MAKING BY THE LOUDEST

Have you ever watched a class of children respond to the question, "What game do you want to play today?" Invariably a few children respond quickly and loudly—"kickball" or "dodgeball" or "killerball." Especially to beginning teachers, it sounds as if the whole class is in agreement. In fact, the loud response is made by a few children—often the highly skilled. But they are forceful. Needless to say, those who really don't want to play those games keep quiet.

COMPETITION FOR CHILDREN

If a teacher isn't careful, competitive games can also be damaging to a child's self-esteem. Obviously, at various times in physical education classes, there will be opportunities for

children to participate in competitive games. Score will be kept, winners determined. Competitive games put pressure on children, especially the poorly skilled. There are several alternatives that allow a teacher to avoid putting the pressure (and potential damage to self-concept) on those children who do not enjoy competition. They include allowing children to choose the type of game they want to play, alternative scoring systems, and child-designed games.

Choice of Games

One alternative is simply to provide children with a choice: "We are going to play two games. In this game we are going to keep score; this game is just for fun—no score will be kept." While some might think it difficult to have two games going on simultaneously, the fact is that it's becoming increasingly common in physical education classes to see many games played at once.

Alternative Scoring Systems

A second alternative is to change the scoring system to encourage a spirit of cooperation and support, thus avoiding the critical comments and harshness that often are observed in competitive games. For example, points can be awarded for instances of good sportsmanship. A positive comment made to an opponent, a gesture of sportsmanship such as helping an opponent up after she falls, or an offer to show someone a trick to help them improve might all earn a point. Clearly the scoring system needs to be developed with the students so that they understand why it is necessary and will feel a sense of ownership.

Alternative scoring systems are especially instructive to highly skilled, competitive children who become so intensely involved in games in which a score is kept that they totally lose a sense of perspective, especially when they become frustrated with their poorly skilled classmates. My experience is that these children find it difficult to adjust initially to these alternative scoring systems; nevertheless, these are often the children who need to develop a perspective on their behavior in competitive situations.

Child-Designed Activities

Asking children to design their own games, dances, or gymnastics sequences also encourages children to invent activities that match their own ability (chapter 11). While the activity the children design will often be different from a teacher-designed activity, there is a certain degree of satisfaction and enjoyment derived from creating a new activity. This seems especially true for children who may not be highly skilled but are terrific at inventing enjoyable sequences, games, and dances.

COMPETITION FOR CHILDREN: CONVINCING THE SKEPTICS

Occasionally I encounter the view that competition for children is good for them. "They need to learn how to lose!" is the battle cry often emitted by the frustrated ex-athlete or "wannabe superstar." While there may be a grain of truth to the need for learning to lose gracefully and with understanding, I remain convinced that learning to cooperate with others is a far more important skill than learning how to lose. An occasional loss may not be harmful to children. Losing every day, however, is certainly unpleasant—if not harmful. And if we're not careful and sensitive, some children can easily be placed in situations where physical education class is a series of losses.

When individuals confront me on my views of competition for children, I refer them to Tutko and Brun's book, *Winning Is Everything: And Other American Myths*, and Rainer Martens' book, *Joy and Sadness in Children's Sports*. I don't know if they read them, but I hope they do because these books create a very powerful and sensitive portrayal of the damage an overemphasis on competition can do to a child's emerging self-concept.

Once again, the teacher will need to decide when it is appropriate to include child-designed activities. Obviously the children need a background before they can begin to design successful activities; they can't design out of thin air.

Although it might appear limiting, children seem to do better when the invention is delimited by the teacher. For example:

- Make up a game with your partner. It needs to have kicking in it. You may use one or two foam soccer balls. There are also hoops and cones if you need them.
- Your game can be played with three or four people. The equipment is limited to a maximum of three cones, one ball, one hoop, and three carpet squares.

TESTING

In addition to competitive games, another way we can make a child feel inferior and physically inept is in testing situations. In the classroom, tests are relatively private affairs—only the teacher and the child know if mistakes are being made on a math test. In physical education, however, the results are public. All of the children know who came in last in the mile or who can't catch a ball. As physical education teachers, we need to be sensitive to this fact and be careful to minimize any harmful effects that might influence the feelings of children. Fortunately, we have developed some ways to avoid placing children in uncomfortable situations, including ways to help children understand test results and set their own goals.

Interpreting Test Results

At various times teachers will choose to share test scores with children. How this is done is very important. Posting scores on a wall for everyone to see can quickly lead to ridicule and magnify feelings of incompetence for the unskilled child. Certainly we ask children not to discuss others' scores, but that's naive on our part. Children do compare scores.

It also seems that standardized norms and criterion scores are harmful to those children who know they are less skilled than many others in the class. What good does it do to reinforce feelings of inadequacy?

The most humane and sensitive approach to reporting test scores to children is to enable them to compare their current scores with their past scores. Is the child improving? That's the truly important score—and the one the child has the most control over. Probably the only advantage of being poorly skilled is that practice can rather quickly result in drastic improvements on sensitive tests (i.e., it's easier for the poorly skilled child to show improvement than it is for the highly skilled child). With the advent of the computer, it is becoming increasingly easy and time efficient to provide children with individual reports of their test results and to show them how they have improved since the last test.

Setting Own Goals

Another way teachers help children feel good about themselves is by helping them set their own goals. This works better with older children who can begin to understand that improvement takes time and practice. No matter how old the children are, at the beginning they will need help in setting realistic goals that can be accomplished in a relatively short period of time. Increasing the number of times they are able to jump a rope or dribble a ball or do sit-ups in 30 seconds is readily achievable. If we're not careful, however, children will set unreasonable goals that are simply unreachable, even in a year. For example, making 9 of 10 free throws or running a mile in under 6 minutes are goals that are difficult to attain—even for the highly skilled or fit child.

In time, the goals can become harder as the children realize what is required to achieve various goals. Having decided to ask children to set their own goals, the teachers must devote time to explaining the whole process of goal setting. Teachers must also explain the meanings of success and failure as well as the idea that the goals are for themselves, not to impress the teacher or a friend.

UNDERSTANDING FEELINGS

One of the advantages of aging is that we are better able to understand our feelings. Children, however, have a difficult time separating their feelings from their own self-worth. "I can only do a few push-ups and I miss the ball a lot when I am batting; therefore, I must not be a very good person" is the way some children think. In time, however, mature adults realize that athletic prowess has no relationship to self-worth. We can help children understand this fact in physical education by asking them to keep student logs and by implementing discussion circles.

Student Logs and Journals

Asking children to write about the feelings that arise from participating in physical education is another way that a teacher can get better in touch with children's feelings. With the increased emphasis in elementary schools on "writing across the curriculum," more classroom teachers are willing to devote 5 minutes or so to allow the children to write in their logs immediately after they return from physical education class.

A question such as "How do you feel about dance?" can often be answered better in a paragraph than a single word. The log allows a teacher to gain deeper insights about children that may otherwise go undetected. Wentzell (1989) has suggested a number of ideas for stimulating children to write about physical education. Many of the ideas could be adapted for children in grades four through six (Figure 12.1).

It seems to work best if only one or two classes at a time keep physical education logs and then only for a period of several weeks. When we teach 400 or more children, it is simply overwhelming (and unenjoyable) to spend an entire weekend reading logs. The purpose of the logs is to allow the children to get in touch with their feelings and for you to better understand how children feel about your teaching and your program. This can be accomplished by reading the logs of a few children—not all 400. This also allows the teacher to make comments in the logs if she thinks it is appropriate and would be valued by the children.

- I felt prepared/unprepared for the lesson because. . . .
- I was/wasn't motivated to participate in the lesson because . . . .
- The most important thing that I learned today was. . ., because. . . .
- The lesson was well organized/needed more organization because. . . .
- Too much time/not enough time in the lesson was devoted to . . . (explain).
- I most enjoyed/disliked . . ., because. . . .
- Next class I would/wouldn't like to review . . ., practice . . ., experience. . . .
- Physical education is/is not/should be. . . .
- The two activities/sports in physical education that I feel most confident in are . . ., because. . . . I feel most awkward in . . ., because. . . .
- I feel that students my age do/don't obtain enough exercise . . ., I suggest that. . . .
- If I were the teacher of physical education this year, I would remove/add/make the following changes in the way the class is conducted. . . .
- I believe that personal health/wellness is. . . . My present health status is. . . .
- If I desire to maintain/change my present state of health/wellness, I must. . . . Personal health/wellness is/is not important to me because. . . .
- Competition is good/not good because. . . . Cooperation is good/not good because. . . . I prefer competition/cooperation because. . . .

Figure 12.1 Ideas for writing about P.E. (Reprinted by permission from Wentzell, 1989.)

Discussion Circles

Another way to get in touch with the children's feelings is a discussion circle. Again this can be done occasionally with a class or two. The purpose is to determine how children are feeling about physical education.

The children and you sit in a circle and talk about how things are going in class. Specific questions seem to work best. For example:

- "How do you feel about coming into the gym and getting started immediately?"
- "How do you feel about the way I ask you to find partners or form groups?"
- "Do you feel tired when you leave P.E. class?"

- "Is there some activity that you wish I would teach from time to time?"
- "This week we have been striking with rackets. Have you practiced that skill after school? Why or why not?"

For teachers who have never used a discussion circle, there are several techniques that are important. For a discussion circle to be productive, the teacher needs to plan carefully any questions that will be asked and then be certain that the children don't wander too far off in the discussion. It also helps to set a time limit at the beginning so the children understand how long is going to be spent in the discussion.

Second, the children need to be encouraged to say what they feel. If the teacher becomes defensive or even angry, the discussion circle will not succeed.

Third, these are children, and they will say what they think. If a teacher wants to hear only good things about the program, then it is probably not a good idea to use a discussion circle. Teachers who successfully lead discussion circles are able to remain objective about what the children say and help them express their feelings about the program.

CONCLUDING THOUGHT

Much of what has been described in this chapter doesn't require a new curriculum. What we teach doesn't necessarily have to be changed although the way we teach certain activities may be altered.

The important message of this chapter is that we need to be sensitive to all the children in our classes so that they are comfortable and feel our support. When children come to physical education class, we want them to feel secure while they are with us and trust that we will try not to embarrass them or put them in uncomfortable situations. We want our classes to be a special place where children feel good about themselves—and about physical activity.

Funky Winkerbean got down from the rope with the help of the custodian. He was embarrassed, but he made it. The coach is still showing movies to his classes. In some schools physical education is still being taught the way it was 30 years ago, but it's changing. I hope that this chapter will contribute to these changes so that the Funky Winkerbeans of the future will no longer be placed in embarrassing situations that lead to a dislike of physical activity and the development of a poor self-image.

SUMMARY

Physical activity has a powerful influence on how children feel about themselves. Consequently, it is imperative that physical education teachers do everything they can to be sensitive to how children feel and help them build positive feelings about their involvement in physical activity. Teachers who help children build positive attitudes are constantly aware of children's feelings and consciously modify and select activities that are considerate of both the highly and the poorly skilled, the enthusiastic and the reluctant, and the physically fit and the unfit children. They understand that competition may cause

some children to "turn off" to physical activity and find ways to provide alternatives to games that emphasize winning and score keeping. They also try to make any testing they do positive for children and make specific attempts to understand the feelings of children.

QUESTIONS FOR REFLECTION

1. Think back to your experiences in physical education classes. Recall the things that your teachers may have done that were probably unpleasant or even harmful to the poorly skilled or unfit children in your classes. Why do you think the teachers weren't sensitive to these children?

2. Reflect on your own teaching. Do you tend to favor any certain group of children—high or low skilled? Attractive or unattractive children? Boys or girls? What do you do, as you teach, to be sensitive to your tendency to favor a certain group?

3. As physical education teachers we tend to have many friends who are also highly skilled. Think about your friends or acquaintances who have been turned off to physical activity. Do you know why this is so? Why do they find it so hard to exercise regularly? Can any of these feelings be traced back to their experiences in physical education classes?

4. When testing in physical education, it is difficult to make it a very private affair. Describe some of the ways that teachers might test in physical education to help ensure the relative privacy of the test. Do you think children can test one another? Why or why not?

5. Children and adults do not have the same feelings or understandings. Recall several examples of these differences and explain the implications for teaching physical education.

REFERENCES

Flugelman, A. (Ed.) (1976). *The new games book*. Garden City, NY: Doubleday.

Franck, M., Graham, G., Lawson, H., Loughery, T., Ritson, R., Sanborn, M., & Seefeldt, V. (1991). *Physical education outcomes: A project of the National Association for Sport and Physical Education*. Reston, VA: National Association for Sport and Physical Education.

Martens, R. (Ed.) (1978). *Joy and sadness in children's sports*. Champaign, IL: Human Kinetics.

Orlick, T. (1978a). *Cooperative sports and games books*. New York: Pantheon.

Orlick, T. (1978b). *Winning through cooperation*. Washington, DC: Acropolis Books.

Stillman, A. (1989). The "yet" intervention. *Strategies*, **2**(4), 17, 28.

Turner, L.F., & Turner, S.L. (1984). *Alternative sports and games for the new physical educator*. Palo Alto, CA: Peek.

Tutko, T., & Bruns, W. (1976). *Winning is everything: And other American myths*. New York: Macmillan.

Wentzell, S.R. (1989). Beyond the physical—expressive writing in physical education. *Journal of Physical Education, Recreation and Dance*, **60**(9), 18-20.

Chapter 13

Assessing
Children's Progress

Since chapter 2 (Planning), each of the chapters has discussed active teaching skills—the skills that teachers use when they are actually with the children. This chapter focuses on another aspect of teaching that is decided upon primarily in one's office or at home. Essentially, it attempts to answer the question, "How can I realistically determine whether the children are learning what I want them to learn as a result of my teaching?"

As a result of reading and understanding this chapter, the teacher will be able to

- explain why testing is an important part of a quality program of physical education;
- describe realistic approaches to assessing children's improvement and understanding related to physical fitness;
- describe realistic approaches to testing children's improvement and understanding related to motor skills;
- describe practical ways of assessing children's cognitive understanding related to various physical education concepts;
- describe practical ways to assess children's attitudes and feelings related to various aspects of physical education; and
- explain how grading can be used in conjunction with assessment in physical education.

WHY TEST CHILDREN?

No one disagrees with the idea of assessing or testing children to determine their progress and their needs. It's logical; it makes sense, but it's rarely done in elementary school physical education aside from the annual physical fitness tests (Safrit, 1990). Why?

There are some very good reasons why teachers don't spend much time testing children in physical education classes. The most obvious reason is numbers—the typical specialist probably teaches 400 to 600 children a week. That's a lot of children to test, even if the teacher does nothing but test all day long.

In addition to the numbers, another reason teachers rarely test is time. The average number of times a teacher sees his children is two days a week. That amounts to less than 60 minutes in most schools. Many test batteries take much longer than one hour to administer to a class of 30, assuming, of course, that the tests can be done with only one teacher.

At this point it might appear that I am leading up to recommending that we simply not test children. I'm not. I do think we need to assess children, but I think we need to discover ways to test that are realistic, given the large numbers of children we teach in the limited amount of time we have. I am going to suggest some of these techniques later in the chapter, but first I want to respond to the question, "Why do we need to assess children?" There are at least four reasons.

One reason is that it forces us to look carefully at every child in a class—at least for a few moments. This allows us to briefly reflect on that child and how well he is able to do on that particular test item. Most of the time we are reasonably accurate about our subjective assessments of the ability of our children. There are surprises, however, and testing helps to uncover them.

Another advantage is that testing that is done in fifth or sixth grade provides us with an overall assessment of our program. Testing allows us to gain important insights about what our children have and haven't learned in 5 or 6 years, assuming we have been at that school for the entire time. In this sense testing provides us with an assessment of the effectiveness of our program.

Testing also increases our credibility as professionals (Arbogast & Griffin, 1989). Parents and administrators expect us to be able to assess the progress of children. When we have a testing program in place with some recorded evidence about the progress our students are making, it allows us to make more informed, sounder decisions about the individual children in our program. This is in contrast, for example, to the teacher who is asked about a child by a parent and has no recorded evidence except what she can (or cannot) remember about the child.

A fourth reason is that testing, as described in this chapter, becomes a self-imposed accountability measure. I suspect that every teacher has been surprised at one time or another by what their students didn't know—when the teacher thought it had been taught so well and so clearly that no one could possibly have not learned it. When teachers test the things they have taught, not the things someone else thinks they ought to test, it can be a real eye opener.

These are four reasons it makes sense for teachers to assess the progress of their children. The next important question is how to test realistically in an elementary school setting to determine

1. the individual progress the children are making, and
2. the influence of our program on the children when they are in fifth or sixth grade.

REALISTIC TESTING PROCEDURES

One of the ways I considered writing this chapter was to include the published tests that I thought would be most useful to teachers of children's physical education. I decided not to do this, however, because they are already published in tests and measurement texts, and most physical education teachers have taken a course in tests and measurement. The challenge, as I see it for the teacher of physical education, is not so much to find tests that are valid and reliable but rather to find the time to test. For this reason I chose to focus this chapter on some of the ways teachers have found to realistically assess children in elementary school physical education settings.

Typically, in physical education our curriculum can be divided into several domains

(Franck et al., 1991): physical fitness, motor skills, cognitive understanding, and feelings about one's self and about physical activity. In the remainder of this chapter I want to suggest a number of modifications teachers might make to assess children in these domains within the context of teaching 8 to 12 classes a day, typically 400 to 600 children per week.

PHYSICAL FITNESS TESTS

The most common test we use in physical education is a fitness test. Today there are several versions that a teacher might use. Typically they include a distance run and a measure of flexibility and upper-body and abdominal strength. Regardless of the version a teacher uses, there are ways to save time administering the tests and also to make them more valuable for the children.

Self- and Partner Testing

One way to save time is to teach the upper-grade children to test themselves or one another. Obviously some time will need to be spent teaching the children the proper way to administer and perform the tests. Will this work with every class in every school? No. Will it succeed with many classes? Yes, depending on the children and how well they are taught the process of self-testing.

Ultimately the most important part of any test is to let the children know how they are improving in relation to their past performances—their progress. Children can be taught to measure their own progress, and, for this reason, it is important to emphasize recording honest scores. This works especially well if there is no pressure to compare scores with other students in the class (chapter 12). It also allows teachers to test various items throughout the year, rather than only once a year in the spring, for example.

Many teachers use predesigned forms (see Figure 13.1) or design their own (Figure 13.2) (Petray, 1989). These forms allow children and their parents to easily see their progress and, we hope, their improvement.

During the year a teacher may need to turn in an official set of scores. These scores may need to be administered by the teacher or at least be more closely supervised than some of the more informal tests done by the children.

Another advantage of teaching the children to test themselves is that they can do it on those days when the classroom teacher is responsible for physical education. This allows more time for instruction and practice during the days scheduled with the specialist (Parker & Pemberton, 1989). When the fitness sheets are kept in the classroom, it also makes less bookkeeping for the P.E. teacher.

Broad Categories

In reality when we fitness test we are interested in broad categories rather than actual scores. For example, whether a child runs a mile in 9:15 or 9:25 is important to the child, but not very important in assessing a child's cardiovascular fitness (based on the assumption that the mile run is a valid measure of that component of fitness). Categories of

REPORT CARD

_____
Name

_____
Age

_____
Grade

Fitness component	Test Item		Score Date _____	My goal	Score after training Date _____
Aerobic endurance	Distance run (check one) Mile _____ 1/2 Mile _____ Other _____				
Body composition	Skin folds (check those used)	1. Subscapular			
		2. Triceps			
		3. Calf			
		Sum of 2 & 3			
	OR BMI				
Flexibility	Sit and reach				
Abdominal strength/endurance	Sit-ups				
Upper body strength/endurance	(check one) Pull-ups _____ **OR** Modified pull-ups _____				

Figure 13.1 "Physical Best" report card. (Reprinted by permission from American Alliance for Health, Physical Education, Recreation & Dance, 1988.)

Personal physical fitness record

Name _____ Age _____ Grade _____

	Pretest	Self-test	Self-test	Posttest
Date	_____	_____	_____	_____
One-mile run/walk	_____ : _____	_____ : _____	_____ : _____	_____ : _____
Sum of skinfolds	_____ mm	_____ mm	_____ mm	_____ mm
Triceps	_____ mm	_____ mm	_____ mm	_____ mm
Calf	_____ mm	_____ mm	_____ mm	_____ mm
Sit and reach	_____ cm	_____ cm	_____ cm	_____ cm
Modified sit-ups	_____	_____	_____	_____
Pull-ups	_____	_____	_____	_____
Modified pull-ups	_____	_____	_____	_____

Figure 13.2 Example of a teacher-designed physical fitness report card. (Reprinted by permission from Petray, 1989.)

fitness require a lot less bookkeeping and provide for a much quicker assessment. For example, as the children complete a mile run, their times can be placed in three categories: under 7:30; between 7:31 and 9:30; and 9:31 and over. Sit-up scores might be recorded as under 10, 11 to 40, and over 40.

When a teacher is trying to assess the overall value of the program, this is one quick way to learn whether children are improving. The scores I listed are arbitrary, but they illustrate how to use categories as a barometer of any fitness progress without having to take the time to record individual scores and then average them to see if a class has improved.

Outside Help

A third idea to save time in fitness testing is not a new one, but it is effective. Recruit parents, classroom teachers, high school or university students, or retired volunteers to help with the testing (East, Frazier, & Matney, 1989). Once the volunteers are contacted and trained, you can save a lot of time on the days the tests are administered.

Any one of these ideas will save time and probably be more effective than when a teacher attempts to administer an entire fitness test battery by himself with no help. This also allows the teacher more time to use other types of assessment. Currently the emphasis

in our profession seems to be primarily on physical fitness testing. Most programs, however, do more than simply try to enhance fitness performance scores; many teachers and children want to know about the progress they are making in other areas also.

A FRIGHTENING THOUGHT

Increasingly, schools are being held accountable for what children are or are not learning. I am frightened that—if we don't design our own ways of assessing children—a test battery will be handed to us, similar to the standardized tests used in the classroom, and we will have to administer those tests to every child. In some districts this has already happened with the physical fitness tests. While fitness is an important part of what we teach in physical education, good programs certainly do more than just attempt to improve fitness (Franck et al., 1991). We need to begin to discover ways of assessing our children in all of the domains, not only fitness; otherwise, the success of our programs will be measured only by how many pull-ups children can do or how fast they run a mile. Is that the truly important measure of a physical education program? Do we really want this to be the only measure of our effectiveness as teachers?

MOTOR-SKILL TESTS

Improvement in motor skills is a goal of many children's physical education programs. Motor-skill testing is far less prevalent than physical fitness testing, however. There are a number of ways to test motor skills (Safrit, 1990; Ulrich, 1985). Unfortunately, many of these tests require a rather elaborate set-up and also are difficult to administer to groups of children—probably the reason they are used infrequently. It's possible to test for motor skills, however, without devoting substantial amounts of class time to the process.

Permanent Markings

One way to save time is to permanently mark the test dimensions on walls, the gym floor, or the pavement so that time need not be spent remeasuring the test every time the teacher wants to give it.

In one research project, for example, two of the tests required a 10-foot-high, 20-foot-long rectangle (Graham, Metzler, & Webster, 1991). Each time we had to draw the rectangle with masking tape. If we had been at the same school, it would have been much easier to paint (tape) the rectangle on a wall so that we didn't have to spend 10 or 15 minutes measuring the rectangle each time. Obviously this means that some time needs to be spent selecting an appropriate test and trying it out before it is permanently marked. The advantage, of course, is that once it is permanent, time is saved and the children can self-test at recess or after school if they want to. Permanent markings also allow a teacher to include a test as a station when the class is organized into learning centers (chapter 7).

Assessing Critical Components

Typically, motor skill tests provide a quantitative score: the number of times a target was hit or a ball was caught. In recent years there seems to be an increasing interest in assessing how children are using the qualitative components of a skill. Many teachers are dissatisfied with knowing only that a child, for example, can throw a ball and hit a target. They also want to know how well they throw a ball—whether their movements are biomechanically correct (Ulrich, 1985).

Unfortunately, qualitative assessment can take a lot of time. Probably the most accurate way to assess children's use of the various qualitative components is to videotape them and then use the stop action feature of the videotape recorder to analyze the various critical components. Few teachers have the time to do this. There are alternatives, however.

Observing One Cue at a Time

One alternative is to provide a task for the children and then observe only one critical component (cue, refinement) at a time (chapters 8 and 9). For example, the task might be to see how many times the children are able to strike a ball against a wall using a racket. Once the children begin, the teacher can then observe to see if the children are turning the appropriate side to the wall (forehand or backhand) as they strike. A general estimate can be obtained in 5 minutes or less and recorded on a class list (Figure 13.3).

Some qualitative components are more easily assessed than others using live observation. For example, it is relatively easy to observe whether, when catching, children use their hands appropriately (thumbs together for a catch at high level; little fingers together for a low level catch). Other critical components, such as sequential hip and shoulder rotation, are very difficult to observe in a live setting unless the teacher has had a substantial amount of practice in live observation.

For this reason it is a good idea to spend some time with a teacher at another school discussing the various critical components and what might or might not be observed. I find it helpful to have a videotape of children doing the skill being discussed so that you can spend time actually looking at various children to be certain that you are in agreement. This tends to sharpen observation skills and results in more reliable observation.

Videotaping

Another use of videotape technology is to analyze the progress children are making in a less formal way by simply videotaping a class every once in a while as they do various activities, not necessarily test items. This provides a teacher with an interesting way to assess how children are doing with skills and with behavior. The camera can be placed in one corner of the gym or playground and focused on various children in the class throughout the lesson. Later the teacher can view the videotape and assess the children's use of the

Critical components

Names of children	Quick feet	Side to target	Level swing	Follow through to target
1.				
2.				
3.				
4.				
5.				
6.				
7.				
8.				
9.				
10.				
11.				
12.				
13.				
14.				
15.				
16.				
17.				

Figure 13.3 Checklist for striking with racket.

critical components. This is especially interesting when the children are playing games, as there is a tendency to forget some of the critical components when youngsters become excited about their game.

Obviously there are innumerable motor skills that might be tested. As with the physical fitness tests, it makes sense to choose several skills that are emphasized in the program and assess those throughout the program rather than attempting to assess 15 or 20 motor skills. Skills such as throwing, catching, kicking, and striking with rackets or paddles are ones that seem to be emphasized in many programs.

COGNITIVE TESTS

The same is true for any type of cognitive testing that a teacher might decide to use. There's no dearth of cognitive information that a teacher might assess (Franck et al., 1991). Realistically, a teacher needs to make several decisions about what, when, and how to test the children's understanding of various cognitive concepts.

First, the test items need to reflect what is taught in the program. Second, the test needs to be manageable. As with the fitness and motor skill tests, there are several ways to save time and still gather valuable information.

Tests in the Classroom

The most obvious way is to ask the classroom teacher to administer short paper-and-pencil tests (provided by the physical education teacher) in the classroom during the time allotted for physical education. Rainy and cold days, when the children will remain in the classroom anyway, are the logical times to ask the classroom teachers to help you out.

Clearly, we are not talking about spending more than a few minutes a year devoted to this type of testing, so it won't drastically reduce the time the children have for physical activity. This assumes, of course, that the classroom teachers are actually organizing physical education lessons.

In most schools, however, there are some classroom teachers who are conscientious and really teach physical education to the children. These teachers can also be immensely helpful in designing the test items for that age child's ability to read and comprehend any test items you might develop.

It seems to me that the most effective questions are those designed by the physical education teacher for assessing what she is trying to teach in her program. Good questions take time to write and need to be revised based on the children's understanding and responses. In time, however, a teacher can develop a battery of questions to use at different times to measure what the children are (or are not) learning in her physical education programs.

When a few questions are asked at a time, the physical education teacher can realistically assess the program without overburdening the classroom teacher or the children. For example, it may make a lot more sense to ask 10 questions three times a year than to administer a predesigned test consisting of 30 questions once a year. Also, because the teacher is doing this for her own information, there is no need to test all grades at the same time. The testing and grading can be done in manageable blocks of time, rather than attempting to correct several hundred tests in a single weekend. Figures 13.4 and 13.5 provide examples of the types of test items a teacher might want to ask the children to see how well they are understanding the concepts taught in the program.

The Quick Written Test in the Gym

Obviously the standard paper-and-pencil test comes to mind when we think of assessing children's cognitive understanding. The process, however, need not take a long time (Griffin & Oslin, 1990). One technique for children that is easily done on a cafeteria floor or blacktop playground is to ask the children to "Help your friend, Murgatroid. . . ." Here's how it works.

Before one or two classes (not necessarily every class taught that day), set out paper and pencils for each child in the class in an area away from the actual activity. Sometimes 5 × 8 cards work better if you are outside. At some point in the lesson, ask the children to go to this area and respond to a question such as "Your friend Murgatroid doesn't know how to dribble a ball. List up to five things (cues) that you would tell her so that she could become a good dribbler." As soon as the children are finished, they can resume activity. This takes less than 5 minutes and provides some valuable information about what the children

1. To throw a ball farther, you should
   a. keep your back very straight as you throw.
   b. turn your body to the side before you throw.
   c. jump off the ground with both feet as you throw.
   d. I don't know.

2. You should do warm-up exercises before physical activities so that
   a. you will not get cold during the activities.
   b. you will be less likely to get sore muscles.
   c. your bones will not get tired as quickly.
   d. I don't know.

3. If you are trying to jump over a bench, what should you do to help you jump higher?
   a. Keep your legs straight before you jump.
   b. Stand on your toes before you jump.
   c. Bend your knees before you jump.
   d. I don't know.

4. To lift a heavy object from the floor safely, you should
   a. bend your knees.
   b. bend your back.
   c. keep your legs straight.
   d. I don't know.

5. To catch a ball correctly you should
   a. bend your elbows.
   b. keep your arms straight.
   c. turn your head to the side.
   d. I don't know.

Figure 13.4 Examples of questions teachers might develop to assess children's cognitive understanding.

1. When performing stretching exercises, the stretch should be done as quickly as possible.

   Yes   No

2. In general, we should do strenuous exercise about three times per week.

   Yes   No

3. "Crunches" help prevent low back pain.

   Yes   No

Figure 13.5 Sample questions that can be asked in written or survey form at the end of a class.

have learned. The example provided (Figure 13.6) was given to a group of fourth-grade children several days after they had finished a sequence of lessons on dribbling with their hands. It provided the teacher with a measure of how effective he had been teaching the children the refinements (chapter 9) of dribbling.

1. To use the finger pads of your hand not the palm

2. Not to **hit** the ball down Push it so you will stay in control

3. Don't have your wrist like a peice of metel but don't have it so loose you can't keep control of it

4. Keep your eyes looking in front of you to make sure you don't run into anything

5. Don't bash the thing so hard it go's above your head keep it at your waist

Figure 13.6 Your friend Murgatroid doesn't know how to dribble a ball with her hands. List five things that would help her become a good dribbler.

Checking for Understanding

Another quick way to learn how well children understand a concept is to use the technique of *checking for understanding*. When used at the end, or closure, of a lesson, this is also termed *closure assessment* (Marks, 1988). Ask the children to show you their understanding of a particular cue (critical component) or concept you have taught. For example, when the children are assembled around you, and you ask them to

- "Show me how your hands should look when you are trying to catch a ball at high level";
- "Show me one good way to stretch your lower back muscles"; or
- "Show me how your knees should look after you land from a jump."

A quick visual survey will rapidly let you know how well the children have understood that concept. Of course, simply because they can show you they understand doesn't mean that they will always do it, but it is a necessary first step. This also serves as an excellent way to conclude the lesson and review the one or two cues (reminder words) (chapters 6, 9, and 10) that were emphasized throughout the lesson.

Poker Chip Survey

Another technique that some teachers use is to survey the children at the end of a class to determine how well they have understood a

cognitive concept. For example, a teacher might demonstrate a stretch incorrectly (bouncing rather than stretching statically). As the children leave the class, they are asked to put a red poker chip in the box if the stretch was done correctly or a blue poker chip if the stretch was done incorrectly. A quick survey of the color of the chips will tell the teacher how well the children have understood the concept. Obviously the teacher can make his own "chips" by laminating colored paper, which works just as well as poker chips. For non-poker-playing teachers, checkers work just as well.

Some cognitive concepts can be assessed this way; others can't. These ideas, however, represent several ways that teachers can assess the cognitive understanding of the children.

ATTITUDE "TESTS"

In addition to assessing cognitive understanding, there are also several ways teachers can begin to understand the attitudes of their children toward physical activity and toward themselves. Many of us feel that the attitudes of children are very important barometers for determining their proclivities for developing active, healthy lifestyles that endure into adulthood.

Smiley-Face Exit Poll

One simple, albeit rather imprecise, way to learn how children feel is similar to the poker chip survey. This time, however, the teacher can laminate a number of faces: smiley, neu-

tral, and frowny. As the children leave the gym, they are asked to pick a face that best represents their feelings about their ability, their enjoyment, or the lesson from one of the three shoe boxes by the door (one contains the smiles; one, the neutrals; and one, the frowns) and deposit it in the ballot box. These are some sample questions:

- "How do you feel about your ability to strike a ball with a bat?"
- "How do you feel about doing sit-ups over the weekend?"
- "How do you feel about continuing to work on designing your own dances next class?"
- "How do you feel about today's lesson?"

Paper-and-Pencil Surveys

As with the questions assessing cognitive understanding, the attitude questions can also be asked effectively as part of paper-and-pencil tests. They can also be very revealing.

For example, in one of our studies, we asked the children to indicate how they felt about a variety of different activities (Graham, Metzler, & Webster, 1991). Consistently they circled smiley faces until they came to the question on their feelings about dance and gymnastics. Then many circled neutral or frowny faces. This suggested that the dance and gymnastics programs needed to be re-evaluated because, apparently, they were turning children off, rather than on, to these activities. Unfortunately, boys tended to circle frowny faces on the questions related to dance. A number of sample questions are provided in Figure 13.7 to suggest ways that teachers might assess the feelings and attitudes of their children.

1. I would rather exercise or play sports than watch TV.

   Yes   No

2. People who exercise regularly seem to have a lot of fun doing it.

   Yes   No

3. In school I look forward to attending physical education class.

   Yes   No

4. During physical education class at school I usually work up a sweat.

   Yes   No

5. When I grow up I will probably be too busy to stay physically fit.

   Yes   No

6. How do you feel about your ability to strike a ball with a racket?

7. How do you feel about your ability to kick a ball hard and hit a target?

8. How do you feel about your ability to run a long distance without stopping?

9. How do you feel about your ability to play many different games and sports?

10. How do you feel about your ability to participate in gymnastics?

11. How do you feel about your ability to participate in dance?

Figure 13.7 Sample questions designed to understand children's feelings and attitudes toward physical activity.

Logs, journals, and discussion circles also provide valuable insights about how and what children are (and aren't) learning in physical education classes (chapter 12).

GRADING

Any chapter on assessment and testing would be incomplete without a section on grading. I have purposely avoided the "g" word up to now because assessment and grading have very different purposes. Assessment tells the teacher and the children how they are improving or what they need to work on. Grading attempts to communicate, primarily to parents, all that we do in our programs in a single letter or number.

My impression is that most school districts include a place on the standardized report card for a physical education grade. Some districts use letter grades; others use a variation of the Satisfactory/Unsatisfactory format. In either event, condensing a program into a single grade is a difficult process, even for those who teach only 25 to 30 children. For the physical education specialist who teaches 400 to 600 children, grading is even more challenging.

Many elementary school physical education teachers seem to use the standardized grade report form to let parents know whether their child is doing very poorly or very well in physical education. No doubt it is also used as a way to let parents know their child is misbehaving.

Realistically, however, a grade of Satisfactory in physical education doesn't let parents know a great deal about the progress being made by their child. A fifth-grade child, for example, who can't catch, hit, or throw a ball but who does above average on the fitness tests and behaves in class might be graded "S."

Some teachers prefer to let parents know more about the progress their child is making by devising physical education progress reports that are sent home periodically. Obviously, progress reports can be more comprehensive and include information about the child's progress in the various aspects of the physical education program that are emphasized for that particular grade level. Depending upon the number of children taught by the teacher and the time commitments, a teacher may be able to send home physical education progress reports one or more times a year.

Portman (1989) developed a program for parents of children who were at a low (precontrol) skill level to help them improve their basic motor skills, such as throwing and catching. Instead of simply reporting to parents that their child was doing poorly, she actually provided realistic, practical drills that parents could do with their children at home. Figure 13.8 provides an example of the

Your child is catching a ball as shown in the top illustrations. In order to move your child to the next stage (bottom illustrations), please practice the following drill.

Stand ten feet away from your child and toss the ball to arrive chest high. Ask your child to catch the ball with the hands. Practice the drill 20-25 times, three days a week. When your child is successful catching the ball with the hands 15 out of 20 times over two consecutive days, have the child see me for a new drill.

Figure 13.8   Example of a drill for a parent to help a low skilled child improve catching ability. (Reprinted by permission from Graham, Holt/Hale, McEwen, & Parker, 1980.)

information that parents would be provided for their child who needed more practice to improve his catching ability.

SUMMARY

The examples provided in this chapter are more than any teacher would use in a year. Some will never be used. Others will be used occasionally; some will be used frequently. The point is that, as teachers, we need to be smart about assessment. If it is overwhelming, then it becomes a burden. We need to fig-

ure out ways to determine how our children are progressing but not allow it to become so time consuming that we abandon the entire process. What seems to work best is to test or assess different classes at various times. Some classes will do well with some aspects of assessment, but others won't. Some classes are terrific in discussion circles, for example, whereas others do a poor job at self-testing. The program is voluntary (it is for your information), so there is no need to test every child in every grade. Sample the classes intelligently—based on their characteristics and your time.

There's an expression people use when they are overburdened with work: "My plate is full." Many of the children's physical educators I work with have plates that are overflowing. Developing, administering, and scoring tests for their children will just add to the overflow. That's why I have tried to stress throughout this chapter that any assessment—physical fitness, motor skills, cognitive or attitudes—needs to be time efficient and intelligently sampled.

A well-thought-out and planned assessment program has two advantages. The first is that it provides us with some valuable insights about our children that we wouldn't know otherwise.

Second, in this era of increasing school accountability, an assessment program allows us to share some relatively objective information about what children are learning and thinking as a result of our programs. Without assessment it is much harder to defend our programs when they are questioned as they so often are today because of budget constraints. Our assessment programs may not be ornate or comprehensive, but they are important ways that we can demonstrate the value our programs have for children.

QUESTIONS FOR REFLECTION

1. It is generally agreed that elementary school physical education teachers do not typically test their children to any great extent. In this era of accountability, why do you think this is true? Do you have any evidence that this is changing?

2. Children can learn to test themselves on various fitness and motor skills. Discuss the pros and cons of this process and the circumstances under which it would (and wouldn't) work.

3. Typically we have relied on a few standardized items to test physical fitness. Describe several other ways we might assess physical fitness beyond the current test items used.

4. Is it important to assess the critical components of motor skills? Why or why not?

5. This chapter describes a variety of ways that a teacher might realistically assess the progress children are making in physical education. Of all the ways, which ones do you think you are most likely to use? Which ones are you least likely to use?

6. What do you think are the potential consequences of simply not testing children?

REFERENCES

Arbogast, G.W., & Griffin, L. (1989). Accountability—Is it within reach of the professions? *Journal of Physical Education, Recreation and Dance*, **60**(6), 72-75.

East, W.E., Frazier, J.M., & Matney, L.E. (1989). Assessing the physical fitness of elementary school children—Using community resources. *Journal of Physical Education, Recreation and Dance*, **60**(6), 54-56.

Franck, M., Graham, G., Lawson, H., Loughrey, T., Ritson, R., Sanborn, M., & Seefeldt, V. (1991). *Physical education outcomes: A project of the National Association for Sport and Physical Education*. Reston, VA: National Association for Sport and Physical Education.

Graham, G., Metzler, M., & Webster, G. (1991). Specialist and classroom teacher effectiveness in children's physical education [Monograph]. *Journal of Teaching in Physical Education*, **10**(4), 321-426.

Griffin, L., & Oslin, J. (1990). Got a minute? A quick and easy strategy for knowledge testing in physical education. *Strategies*, **4**(2), 6-8.

Marks, M. (1988). A ticket out the door. *Strategies*, **2**(2), 17, 27.

Parker, M., & Pemberton, C. (1989). Elementary classroom teachers—Untapped resources for fitness assessment. *Journal of Physical Education, Recreation and Dance*, **60**(6), 61-63.

Petray, C.K. (1989). Organizing physical fitness assessment (grades K-2): Strategies for the elementary physical education specialist. *Journal of Physical Education, Recreation and Dance*, **60**(6), 57-60.

Portman, P.A. (1989). Parent intervention program. *Strategies*, **3**(2), 13-19.

Safrit, J. (1990). *Introduction to measurement in physical education and exercise science* (2nd ed.). St. Louis: Mosby.

Ulrich, D.A. (1985). *Test of gross motor development*. Austin, TX: Pro-Ed.

Chapter 14

Continuing to Develop as a Teacher

"Those who can, do. Those who can't, teach. Those who can't teach, teach physical education."

—WOODY ALLEN

This book began with the same quote by Woody Allen. I hope that, by now, you have been stimulated to think about many of the ways that teachers have found to avoid turning kids like Woody Allen off to physical activity—and on to learning and enjoying physical activity.

I hope, too, that you have recognized many of the skills and approaches you already use as a teacher and that you have been stimulated to expand your pedagogical repertoire with some of the skills that were new to you. Teaching, as described in the last 13 chapters, isn't easy. It's darned hard work! The purpose of this final chapter is to describe some of the ways that teachers have found to maintain their enthusiasm for teaching and continue to develop as professionals.

We need to find ways to continue our enthusiasm and development so that we avoid the stagnation and fatigue that eventually come to any professional who settles into a comfortable routine that remains unchanged year after year.

As a result of reading and understanding this chapter, the teacher will be able to

- describe the three stages of a teaching career and their influence on the way we teach;
- analyze the various ways teachers continue to improve and learn throughout a career; and
- explain why it is important that teachers continually strive to remain current and improve their teaching ability.

STAGES OF TEACHING

As teachers of children it is important that we know and understand how children develop. This knowledge allows us to comprehend why children are able (or unable) to learn various skills or movements at various ages and stages. It also is helpful in designing and implementing experiences that are developmentally appropriate for children.

It is also helpful to understand how teachers develop so we can better understand our own feelings, attitudes, and professional growth. It makes sense for us to know and understand the developmental stages of teaching.

- Why is the first year of teaching typically the most difficult?
- How do experienced teachers seem to know so much about children and how they move and learn?
- Why do beginning teachers seem to have more discipline problems than veterans?
- How do teachers improve and develop?
- What are ways teachers can retain their freshness and eagerness throughout a career?
- Are there actually stages in a teaching career?

This chapter is the only one in the book that is not directly about teaching children. It is a very significant chapter, however, because it addresses those of us who do the teaching.

Feiman-Nemser (1983) suggests three stages of teacher development. Her analysis will provide a starting point to discuss the types of things teachers do to remain current and enthusiastic about their teaching and to improve throughout their careers.

In a rather simplified overview, Feiman-Nemser (1983) suggests that teachers pass through two stages on the way to mastery, the third stage in her developmental analysis. The initial stage is induction, and the second stage she characterizes as a period of consolidation.

Induction Stage

Undergraduate practicum experiences in schools, student teaching, and the first year of teaching are all included within the category of induction. For many of us the first year is the most challenging year of teaching for three reasons:

- In most instances we are alone with little or no collegial support.
- So much of what we do is brand new: discipline, unknown children, unfamiliar school and colleagues, new boss (principal), and content that must be developed for an entire year rather than a few weeks.
- The day-to-day schedule is demanding of time and energy.

One challenge of the induction year is simply to learn how to talk to various ages of children so they will listen and understand. We quickly learn, for example, that telling a class of kindergarten children to form a circle out-

side on the grass is futile—for both the teacher and the children. So too is a direction such as "Stand with your right side facing the wall" or "Read the directions written on the board." As we watch their perplexed faces and disorganized responses to our statements that they are not yet ready for, we learn a lot about teaching.

During the induction year we also begin to learn which content is appropriate for which grade level, how long to spend at various tasks, what to do when one child refuses to be a partner to another child, effective ways to deal with tattling, ways to quickly organize children to avoid pushing and shoving, and techniques for explaining the qualities of various movements and skills. For these reasons and numerous others, the first year of teaching is often referred to as a "survival year."

Throughout induction, especially toward the beginning, two questions that were addressed in chapters 3 and 4 seem to dominate our thoughts about teaching:

1. "Do the children like me?"
2. "How can I find better ways to control the children?"

Consolidation Stage

During the next phase of teaching, the consolidation stage, these questions become less dominant and are replaced by concerns related to learning how to accommodate the varying skill levels of the children in a single class and also concerns about the lack of time available to really enhance children's learning. This is especially true for those teachers who see their children only once or twice a week.

It is during this stage that teachers' pedagogical content knowledge truly begins to develop. For example:

- We begin to understand how a 5-year-old is different from an 8-year-old who is different from an 11-year-old child. Consequently, our lessons become more developmentally appropriate.
- We begin to know the tasks that will succeed with third graders and those that won't, and we no longer have to rely on the first one or two lessons of the day to adjust the lesson (chapter 9) (Graham, Hopple, Manross, & Sitzman, in press).
- The "functional fixedness" of the induction phase dwindles, and we become

comfortable exploring different ways to use the equipment and facilities (Housner & Griffey, 1985). For example, we are no longer devastated when we discover, 5 minutes before a class is scheduled to begin, that the indoor facility is in use for the Christmas play rehearsal.
- We learn that children will still like and respect us even when we are firm and demanding (chapters 3 and 4).
- Our observational skills become much sharper (chapter 8), and we are able to quickly scan a class and analyze what is (or isn't) going on (Housner & Griffey, 1985).
- As we know the content better because of the lessons we have taught, we change tasks less and focus more on a horizontal, rather than vertical, progression (Graham, Hopple, Manross, & Sitzman, in press).

As a result of our experience and hard work, the satisfying feeling that we are doing a good job comes more frequently. We know when an unsuccessful lesson was a result of poor teaching and when it was a result of external circumstances (a substitute teacher, Halloween, dogs or bees on the playground). We realize that we still have a lot to learn, but we also understand how much we have learned since the induction stage.

Mastery Stage

Feiman-Nemser (1983) suggests that after several years some teachers begin to approach mastery. They are able to effectively orchestrate many of the teaching skills described in the previous 13 chapters.

Master teachers have learned through experience and hard work to develop lessons that are enjoyable and beneficial for children. Their lessons also have definite and obvious purposes that mesh with the long-term goals of their programs (chapter 2). Whether they're teaching dance, games, gymnastics, or fitness concepts, they have mastered the process of presenting the content (chapters 6 and 9) so that the children are interested, challenged, and successful (chapters 5, 7, and 11). Master teachers are able to observe and understand the children as they move (chapter 8) and to improvise appropriately based on their vast storehouses of knowledge and information that have been accumulated in earlier years of teaching (Borko & Livingston, 1989).

Discipline problems are minimal, and when they do occur they are dealt with effectively and humanely (chapters 3 and 4). Feedback is both useful and pervasive (chapter 10). Children view physical education class as a warm and supportive experience that they enjoy and look forward to (chapter 12).

In contrast to the consolidation stage teacher, the majority of the lessons taught by a master teacher are both effective and satisfying to the teacher and to the children. There are surprises, but their past experience and hard work help them to deal with many of the problems that every teacher encounters—and to deal with them in ways that are beneficial to the children and personally fulfilling to the teacher.

People aren't simply born master teachers. While they may have many of the characteristics that allow one to succeed at teaching, it is only through experience and a continuing effort that they are able to truly become masters of teaching. One prevalent characteristic of highly successful teachers is their inquisitiveness and ability to analyze and reflect on their own teaching (Schon, 1990). When they might be satisfied, it seems that they are constantly trying to improve their teaching and their programs. This point is poignantly made by David Hawkins, observing a veteran teacher of 35 years and a student teacher:

> The veteran teacher commented that what held her to teaching after all these years was that there was still so much to be learned. The student teacher re-

sponded in amazement that she thought it could be learned in two or three years. (Feiman-Nemser, 1983, p. 150)

Teaching is a dynamic, ongoing journey that never ends. While it's possible to teach the same content, using the same process, essentially repeating the first year 30 times, most of us desire more from our careers. We want to improve, to learn, to develop, to change, to explore new ideas and approaches—to become better teachers than we were the year before. How do children's physical education teachers do this?

TECHNIQUES FOR CONTINUING TO IMPROVE AS A TEACHER

They work at it! They purposely search for ways to remain refreshed and excited about their teaching year after year. In this section I want to briefly describe some of the more common techniques teachers use to remain current in and energized about their profession.

Reading

Reading is one way to remain current. Some teachers purchase one new elementary school physical education textbook every year and read it as a way of remaining current. Some prefer to read journals such as *Strategies* or *Journal of Physical Education,*

Recreation and Dance (*JOPERD*) or newsletters such as *Teaching Elementary Physical Education* (*TEPE*). Others locate books on physical activity in mall bookstores and remain current that way. In recent years videotapes have allowed teachers to learn the various techniques and strategies used in different sports and to use this information to upgrade their teaching of those skills or activities.

It saddens me when I meet teachers who haven't remained current. They just aren't abreast of recent developments. They know it. Their older children know it. And, unfortunately, their principal and parents know it. Needless to say, that hurts our profession because it reflects on our image as physical educators. Comedians like Woody Allen and cartoonists like Tom Batiuk are living testimony to these teachers' ineffectiveness and the harmful effects of being in their classes.

Conferences and Workshops

Attending conferences and workshops is another way teachers gain new ideas. They are harder to schedule and more expensive than reading, but some find the interaction with colleagues is a way to replenish their supply of teaching energy. Increasingly, throughout the United States, we are seeing an emergence of conferences focused solely on children's physical education. These seem to be more valued by specialists than are the more generic state and regional conferences.

Veteran teachers report that the most advantageous part of attending conferences is the opportunity to meet with others and share ideas and concerns. They may not go to many sessions, but they learn a lot from these discussions.

Support Groups

The need to share ideas and concerns with other teachers seems especially important for elementary school P.E. teachers because they are so alone and isolated in their schools. Second-grade classroom teachers have chances throughout the day to vent their emotions, celebrate their small victories, and generally be sociable with teachers in similar situations. For many P.E. specialists, however, the majority of their adult interactions during a school day are with the cooks in the cafeteria or the custodian.

Because this is so, some teachers form support groups with other specialists. They meet monthly, sometimes weekly, in person or over the phone, to share ideas and provide emotional support for one another. In recent years I have become increasingly convinced that these opportunities to gain and give support are vital if a teacher is going to reach her potential. The support may come from a spouse or a friend, but, given the challenges

of teaching children's physical education, teachers who remain enthusiastic about teaching seem to find ways to obtain support.

Teachers Visiting Teachers

Another renewal technique is to visit other teachers. Many teachers find this more valuable than attending conferences or reading. These visits typically reinforce some of what a teacher already does while also stimulating new ideas. Unfortunately, many school administrators have yet to see the value of teachers visiting teachers, so release time may be hard to obtain.

Sharing Videotapes

Sharing videotapes of lessons is another way teachers gain fresh approaches to teaching. A videotaped lesson on dance, task sheets, or intratask variation is traded with another teacher. The advantage of this approach, of course, is that teachers don't need to be close by—the discussions and questions can occur over the telephone.

If a teacher has viewed several videotapes and has developed a support group, he may be willing to take a risk and explore a new way of teaching. Many veteran teachers, for example, find it difficult to use a scattered formation where every child has a ball and is moving at the same time. The transition from lines to scattered formations is not an easy one. When a teacher has watched a videotape, for example, and developed a relationship of trust with a colleague, he may be more willing to experiment with a scattered formation.

We often read about an idea or hear it described at a conference but are still unwilling to try it. When we see it on a videotape, however, and know that we can call a friend and ask, we are often more willing to try that new idea.

Committee Work

Believe it or not, some teachers remain current by serving on physical education committees within a district or at the state level. Occasionally the committee work itself is stimulating; more often it seems that the interaction with other teachers is the valuable part of committee work. The value, of course, is that it allows teachers to see other viewpoints and ideas. For most teachers a little committee work goes a long way, but it can be helpful for opening new horizons. Interestingly, it's not hard to be on a committee—volunteers for committee work are about as rare as winning lottery tickets.

Supervising Student Teachers

Opportunities to supervise student teachers or serve as mentors for beginning teachers are other ways to gain new ideas and insights by working with someone fresh out of college. Invariably, when a supervisor is conscientious as she works with her student teacher, she reflects on how she teaches, what she teaches, and why she has done it that way over the years—a learning experience in itself. Good supervision is time consuming; it's also professionally stimulating.

Making Presentations

Making presentations is stimulating for some teachers. Others hate even thinking about it.

IT HELPS ME TO HEAR THAT YOU ALL HAVE SCHEDULING CONCERNS—I'M NOT ALONE

It's nerve wracking and time consuming, but an occasional presentation about an idea or activity that has been successful is also a stimulant for personal growth. I have been told countless times by teachers that they have nothing of value to share. After some prodding and encouragement, they realize that they have an idea or two that others might benefit from. When teachers make slides or a videotape of their kids, the time flies by—and the audience benefits.

Graduate School

The degree of stimulation teachers find in graduate courses seems to depend on the content of the course, the professor, and the personal motivation of the teacher taking the course. It seems that teachers who have been instructing for several years derive more benefits from returning to school than do those who have just finished their degree. They seem to know the questions they want to ask and also appreciate being back in school. And if they are able to explore ways to apply the course work to their teaching, they often notice an improvement.

Recertification

Increasingly, states are providing alternatives to graduate courses for teachers who wish to obtain recertification. This provides teachers with some interesting ways of recharging batteries (e.g., some states give recertification credit for attending conferences, writing an article, or participating on state committees). The temptation, of course, is to take the easy way out and simply do what's quickest and requires the least amount of work. While this is understandable, it certainly doesn't lead to improvement in one's career.

WHAT TYPE OF TEACHER WILL YOU BECOME?

Realistically, teachers who do the hard work necessary to develop and improve their careers participate in some of the activities described previously to enhance their teaching; no doubt they find other ways to improve, also. Obviously, not all of these suggestions are worthwhile for every teacher.

In our profession, as with most others, it is essentially up to the individual to remain current and continue to develop. There are easy ways to satisfy professional growth requirements imposed by a state accrediting agency, but they may be of virtually no worth to professional growth as a teacher. The same is true for physicians, attorneys, and accountants.

It seems, however, that if a teacher wants to be truly successful, he will continue to study and learn and try new ideas throughout his career—not because he has to but because he wants to. When this doesn't happen, the teacher may decline in effectiveness or perhaps simply never become very adept at teaching.

PARTING THOUGHT

Good teaching is hard work. Part of the hard work is continuing to grow and develop as a

IT'S SO IMPORTANT TO HELP CHILDREN GET STARTED IN THE RIGHT DIRECTION.

teacher. There are times when we all ask the questions, "Is it worth it?" "Why am I working so hard when others don't seem to care?"

When I ask these questions, there are two quotes that help me continue to work hard and do the best job I can for my students. One quote is from President John F. Kennedy: "Children are our most important natural resource and our best hope for the future." That statement reminds me of the importance of my job—and what I have dedicated my life to professionally. In fact, when I reflect on his statement, I realize that no job, no matter how much it pays or what status it carries, is more important than teaching.

The other statement that I reflect on from time to time is framed on my wall. It helps me realize that I am not the only one who is tempted to say, "What the heck. Why work so hard?" Bobby Kennedy wrote:

Sometimes it seems to me that it doesn't matter what I do, that it is enough to exist, to sit somewhere, in a garden, for example, watching whatever is to be seen there, the small events.

At other times, I'm aware that other people, possibly a great number of other people, could be affected by what I do or fail to do, that I have a responsibility, as we all have, to make the best possible use of whatever talents I've been given, for the common good.

It is not enough to sit in that garden, however restful or pleasurable it might be.

The world is full of unsolved problems, situations that demand careful, reasoned, and intelligent action.

As children's physical education teachers, we influence hundreds of children a year. When we're successful and work hard, we do our part to make the world a little bit better place for children to grow up in. I hope that by writing this text I have helped you to become a better teacher.

QUESTIONS FOR REFLECTION

1. Why is it important for a teacher to continue to work at improving throughout a career? What are the consequences of not remaining current and enthusiastic?

2. This chapter describes three stages of teaching—induction, consolidation, and mastery. Do you agree with these stages? Why or why not? How might they be expanded to include five or six stages?

3. The cartoon on page 167 depicts a hypothetical teacher expressing her views on how things change in physical education. What would you say to that individual?

4. A variety of techniques for remaining current and enthusiastic about teaching are included in this chapter. Which ones appeal to you most? Least? Why is this the case? Do you think your view might change over a career?

5. In the final section of this chapter, I shared two quotes that are personally motivating to me. Do you have any quotes that you find encouraging? How might you share them with other teachers?

REFERENCES

Borko, H., & Livingston, C. (1989). Cognition and improvisation: Differences in mathematics instruction by expert and novice teachers. *American Educational Research Journal*, **26**(4), 473-498.

Feiman-Nemser, S. (1983). Learning to teach. In L. Shulman & P. Sykes (Eds.), *Handbook of teaching and policy* (pp. 150-170). New York: Longman.

Graham, G., Hopple, C., Manross, M., & Sitzman, T. (in press). Novice and expert children's physical education teachers: Insights into their situational decision-making. *Journal of Teaching in Physical Education*.

Housner, L.D., & Griffey, D.C. (1985). Teacher cognition: Differences in planning and interactive decision-making between experienced and inexperienced teachers. *Research Quarterly for Exercise and Sport*, **56**(1), 45-53.

Schon, D. (1990). *Educating the reflective practitioner*. San Francisco: Jossey-Bass.

Credits

FIGURES

Figure 1.2 From *Physical Education Outcomes: A Project of the National Association for Sport and Physical Education* by M. Franck, G. Graham, H. Lawson, T. Loughrey, R. Ritson, M. Sanborn, and V. Seefeldt (The Outcomes Committee of NASPE), 1991. Reprinted by permission of the National Association for Sport and Physical Education, Reston, VA.

Figure 2.1 From "Curriculum Design Model" by L.E. Kelly. This figure is reprinted with permission from the *Journal of Physical Education, Recreation & Dance*, August, 1988, p. 29. The *Journal* is a publication of the American Alliance for Health, Physical Education, Recreation and Dance, 1900 Association Drive, Reston, VA 22091.

Figure 4.1 From "Class Management Skills" by A.N. Sander. This figure is reprinted with permission from *Strategies: A Journal for Sport and Physical Education*, **2**(3), p. 15. Copyright 1989 by the American Alliance for Health, Physical Education, Recreation and Dance, 1900 Association Drive, Reston, VA 22091.

Figure 4.3 From "Teaching for Affective Learning in Elementary Physical Education" by L.S. Masser. This figure is reprinted with permission from the *Journal of Physical Education, Recreation & Dance*, September, 1990, p. 19. The *Journal* is a publication of the American Alliance for Health, Physical Education, Recreation and Dance, 1900 Association Drive, Reston, VA 22091.

Figure 6.1 From "Thinking and Moving" by D.S. Melville. This figure is reprinted with permission from *Strategies: A Journal for Sport and Physical Education*, **2**(1), p. 19. Copyright 1988 by the American Alliance for Health, Physical Education, Recreation and Dance, 1900 Association Drive, Reston, VA 22091.

Figure 8.1 From *Children Moving* (2nd ed.) (p. 121) by G. Graham, S. Holt/Hale, and M. Parker, 1987, Mountain View, CA: Mayfield. Copyright 1987 by Mayfield. Adapted by permission.

Figure 9.1 From *Children Moving* (2nd ed.) (p. 524) by G. Graham, S. Holt/Hale, and M. Parker, 1987, Mountain View, CA: Mayfield. Copyright 1987 by Mayfield. Reprinted by permission.

Figure 11.1 From "Learning to Learn" by J. Ainsworth and C. Fox. This figure is reprinted with permission from *Strategies: A Journal for Sport and Physical Education*, **3**(1), p. 21. Copyright 1989 by the American Alliance for Health, Physical Education, Recreation and Dance, 1900 Association Drive, Reston, VA 22091.

Figure 12.1 From "Beyond the Physical— Expressive Writing in Physical Education" by S.R. Wentzell. This figure is reprinted with permission from the *Journal of Physical Education, Recreation & Dance*, November/December, 1989, p. 19. The *Journal* is a publication of the American Alliance for Health, Physical Education, Recreation and Dance, 1900 Association Drive, Reston, VA 22091.

Figure 13.1 Used with permission: American Alliance for Health, Physical Education, Recreation and Dance, 1988.

Figure 13.2 From "Organizing Physical Fitness Assessment (Grades K-12)" by C.K. Petray. This figure is reprinted with permission from the *Journal of Physical Education, Recreation & Dance*, August, 1989, p. 59. The *Journal* is a publication of the American Alliance for Health, Physical Education, Recreation and Dance, 1900 Association Drive, Reston, VA 22091.

Figure 13.8 From *Children Moving* (pp. 379-380) by G. Graham, S.A. Holt/Hale, T. McEwen, and M. Parker, 1980, Mountain View, CA: Mayfield. Copyright 1980 by Mayfield. Reprinted by permission.

TABLES

Table 2.1 From "Instructional Time" by L.E. Kelly. This table is reprinted with permission from the *Journal of Physical Education, Recreation & Dance*, August, 1989, p. 32. The *Journal* is a publication of the American Alliance for Health, Physical Education, Recreation and Dance, 1900 Association Drive, Reston, VA 22091.

Table 2.2 From "Instructional Time" by L.E. Kelly. This table is reprinted with permission from the *Journal of Physical Education, Recreation & Dance*, August, 1989, p. 32. The *Journal* is a publication of the American Alliance for Health, Physical Education, Recreation and Dance, 1900 Association Drive, Reston, VA 22091.

Table 2.3 From "Instructional Time" by L.E. Kelly. This table is reprinted with permission from the *Journal of Physical Edu-cation, Recreation & Dance*, August, 1989, p. 30. The *Journal* is a publication of the American Alliance for Health, Physical Education, Recreation and Dance, 1900 Association Drive, Reston, VA 22091.

Table 3.1 From "Shuffling the Deck" by D. Lambdin. This table is reprinted with permission from the *Journal of Physical Education, Recreation & Dance*, March, 1989, p. 26. The *Journal* is a publication of the American Alliance for Health, Physical Education, Recreation and Dance, 1900 Association Drive, Reston, VA 22091.

Table 10.1 From "Teacher Behavior and Student Achievement" by J. Brophy and T.L. Good. In *Handbook of Research on Teaching* (3rd ed.) (pp. 5-32) by C.M. Wittrock (Ed.), 1986, New York: Macmillan. Copyright 1986 by the American Educational Research Association. Reprinted by permission of the publisher.

Index

About the Author

George Graham has a theoretical as well as a practical knowledge base in children's physical education. A professor in the Division of Health and Physical Education at Virginia Tech, he routinely teaches children physical education at Margaret Beeks Elementary School in Blacksburg, VA.

Since receiving his doctoral degree from the University of Oregon in 1973, Dr. Graham has been a consultant on children's physical education curriculum and teacher effectiveness to over 60 school districts throughout the United States. He has also provided consultation on teacher education to six universities and serves as a consultant on teaching children for the United States Tennis Association and the Professional Golf Association. In 1990, he was selected Outstanding Teacher of the Year at Virginia Tech and was inducted into the Virginia Tech Academy of Teaching Excellence.

During 1991-92, Dr. Graham chaired the executive committee of the Council on Physical Education for Children (COPEC), an organization of over 9,000 professionals interested in children's physical education. He has served on the editorial boards of *Teaching Elementary Physical Education*, *Journal of Teaching in Physical Education*, and the *VAHPERD Journal*. He has also been a reviewer for *American Educational Research Journal*, *Journal of Research in Childhood Education*, *Journal of Physical Education, Recreation and Dance*, and *Quest*.

179

N